MODERN PHILOSOPHY

Modern Philosophy

N Subba Rao

MD Publications Pvt Ltd
New Delhi
www.mdppl.com

Published by :

MD Publications Pvt Ltd
"MD House", 11, Darya Ganj,
New Delhi - 110 002
Phone : +91-11- 45355555
E-mail : contact@mdppl.com
Website: www.mdppl.com

ISBN : 978-81-7533-337-6

Published and Printed by Mr. Pranav Gupta on behalf of **MD Publications Pvt Ltd** at Repro India Limited.

Preface

The major figures in philosophy of mind, epistemology, and metaphysics during the seventeenth and eighteenth centuries are roughly divided into two main groups. The "Rationalists," mostly in France and Germany, assumed that all knowledge must begin from certain "innate ideas" in the mind. Major rationalists were Descartes, Baruch Spinoza, Gottfried Leibniz, and Nicolas Malebranche. The "Empiricists," by contrast, held that knowledge must begin with sensory experience. Major figures in this line of thought are John Locke, George Berkeley, and David Hume. Ethics and political philosophy are usually not subsumed under these categories, though all these philosophers worked in ethics, in their own distinctive styles. Other important figures in political philosophy include Thomas Hobbes and Jean-Jacques Rousseau.

In the late eighteenth century Immanuel Kant set forth a groundbreaking philosophical system which claimed to bring unity to rationalism and empiricism. Whether or not he was right, he did not entirely succeed in ending philosophical dispute. Kant sparked a storm of philosophical work in Germany in the early nineteenth century, beginning with German idealism. The characteristic theme of idealism was that the world and the mind equally must be understood according to the same categories; it culminated in the work of Georg Wilhelm Friedrich Hegel, who among many other things said that "The real is rational; the rational is real."

Hegel's work was carried in many directions by his followers and critics. Karl Marx appropriated both Hegel's philosophy of history and the empirical ethics dominant in Britain, transforming Hegel's ideas into a strictly materialist form, setting the grounds for the development of a science of society. Soren Kierkegaard dismissed all systematic philosophy as an inadequate guide to life and meaning. For Kierkegaard, life is meant to be lived, not a mystery to be solved. Arthur Schopenhauer took idealism to the conclusion that the world was nothing but the futile endless interplay of images and desires, and advocated atheism and pessimism. Schopenhauer's ideas were taken up and transformed by Nietzsche, who seized upon their various dismissals of the world to proclaim "God is dead" and to reject all systematic philosophy and all striving for a fixed truth transcending the individual. Nietzsche found in this not grounds for pessimism, but the possibility of a new kind of freedom.

The 19th-century British philosophy came increasingly to be dominated by strands of neo-Hegelian thought, and as a reaction against this, figures such as Bertrand Russell and George Edward Moore began moving the direction of analytic philosophy, which was essentially an updating of traditional empiricism to accommodate the new developments in logic of the German mathematician Gottlob Frege.

Modern philosophy traditionally begins with Rene Descartes and his dictum "I think, therefore I am." In the early seventeenth century the bulk of philosophy was dominated by Scholasticism: written by theologians and drawing upon Plato, Aristotle, and early Church writings. Descartes argued that many predominant Scholastic metaphysical doctrines were meaningless or false. In short, he proposed to begin philosophy from scratch. In his most important work, Meditations on First Philosophy, he attempts just this, over six brief essays. He tries to set aside as much as he possibly can of all his beliefs, to determine what if anything he knows for certain. He finds that he can doubt nearly everything: the reality of physical objects, God, his memories, history, science, even mathematics, but he cannot doubt that he is, in fact, doubting. He knows what he is thinking about, even if it is not true, and he knows that he is there thinking about it. From this basis he builds his knowledge back up again. He finds that some of the ideas he has could not have originated from him alone, but only from God; he proves that God exists. He then demonstrates that God would not allow him to be systematically deceived about everything; in essence, he vindicates ordinary methods of science and reasoning, as fallible but not false. This book is useful for philosophy students, researchers and for all those associated with philosophy. In bringing out this book I am thankful for my parents, friends and colleagues for their support and encouragement.

I am very grateful to Mr. Pranav Gupta, Director of MD Publications Pvt Ltd, New Delhi, for his kind cooperation and support for this book.

N Subba Rao

CONTENTS

Preface — *v*
1. Rise of Modern Philosophy and its Traditions — 1
2. Natural Rights in Modern Philosophy — 15
3. Rise of Modern Science and Philosophy — 33
4. Logic and Critical Thinking in Philosophy — 49
5. Libertarian Challenge for Modern Philosophy — 83
6. Anarchists and Socialists in Modern Philosophy — 99
7. Cartesian Revolution in Philosophy — 117
8. Libertarian Challenge in Philosophy — 127
9. Political Philosophy from Hobbes to Hegel — 149
10. Hegel and its Influence in Philosophy — 167
11. Deeper Sense of Politics and Philosophy — 185
12. Political Philosophy and its Global Trends — 207
13. Phenomenology and Existentialism in Philosophy — 227
14. Techniques and Dialectic Method in Philosophy — 245

Bibliography — 271
Index — 277

1

Rise of Modern Philosophy and its Traditions

Introduction

The spirit of Plato, and that of his pupil and critic Aristotle, have haunted philosophy throughout its history, and it is to them that almost all medieval controversies in the subject can ultimately be traced. They each bequeathed to the world arguments and conceptions of superlative intellectual and dramatic power, and it is not surprising that, wherever they were read, their influence was felt. Each of the important Mediterranean religions Judaism, Christianity and Islam attempted either to assimilate their doctrines or to present some alternative that would be equally persuasive and equally compatible with our intuitive sense of the nature of the world and of our place within it.

From Plato and the neo-Platonic tradition the medievals inherited a cosmology which both justified the belief in a supersensible reality, and at the same time presented an elevated picture of our ability to gain access to it. Plato had argued that the truth of the world is not revealed to ordinary sense-perception, but to reason alone; that truths of reason are necessary, eternal and (as we would now say) *a priori*; that through the cultivation of reason man can come to understand himself, God and the world as these things are in themselves, freed from the shadowy overcast of experience. The neo-Platonists developed the cosmology of Plato's *Timaeus* into a theory of creation, according to which the entire world emanates from the intellectual light of God's self-contemplation. Reason, being the part of man which participates in the intellectual light, knows things not as they seem but as they are. This theory initially metaphysical seemed to imply a corresponding 'natural philosophy' (a natural philosophy which had both Platonic and Aristotelian variants). According to this natural philosophy the earth and earthly things reside at the centre of the turning spheres, each representing successive orders of intellection, and each subordinate to the ultimate sphere of immutability, where God resides in the company of the blessed. Reason is the aspiration towards that ultimate sphere, and man's mortality is the occasion of his ascent towards it. This ascent is conditional upon his turning away from preoccupation with the ephemeral and the sensory towards the contemplation of eternal truth. This 'natural philosophy', persuasively expounded by Boethius (c. 480–524 AD) in his *Consolation of Philosophy* (one of the most popular works of philosophy ever to have been written), influenced his predecessor St Augustine (354–430 AD) who nevertheless retained a sceptical stance towards much of Plato's metaphysics—and reappears in one or another variant, described, upheld and celebrated in countless works of medieval and early Renaissance literature, from popular lyrics to such masterpieces of high art as Chaucer's *Knight's Tale,* Dante's *Divine Comedy* and Spenser's *Faerie Queene.*

The consoling vision of neo-Platonic physics was accompanied, however, by no prescription against metaphysical uncertainty. At every point in the neo-Platonic system problems of seemingly insuperable difficulty were presented to the enquiring mind. What, for example, is this 'reason' upon which our knowledge of ultimate truth depends, and what are the laws of its operation? In what sense does it generate eternal, as opposed to transient, insights, and how do we learn to distinguish between the two? What is the nature of God, and how do we know of his existence? What are the laws which govern the movement and generation of sublunary things, and how is the Platonic hypothesis that man's residence among them is temporary, and that the end of his being lies elsewhere compatible with his subjection to those laws? At every point the neo-Platonic cosmology raises problems of a philosophical kind. These problems seem not to be amenable to scientific resolution. On the contrary, they are posed precisely by the suggestion that sensory perception, which is the principal vehicle of scientific thought, leads us not to truth but to systematic (if sometimes persuasive) illusion.

As the theories of Aristotle began to become known among European thinkers filtered through the writings of Arab philosophers and theologians who had gained them, as it were, by right of conquest they were avidly studied as the source of new answers to these metaphysical queries. Some of the Aristotelian arguments were familiar to the early Christians. In particular, these arguments had been used in giving philosophical formulation to the doctrine of the Trinity. It was thanks to the philosophers of Alexandria, in particular to Clement (c. 150–215) and Origen (c. 185–254), both of whom had seen the inadequacies inherent in the neo-Platonism of their day, that all the resources of Greek philosophy were used together in the attempt to achieve a coherent statement of Christian dogma. And with the victory over Arianism, and the consequent acceptance of the doctrine of the Trinity, one of the most important of all Aristotelian concepts, the concept of substance, took a central place in the formulation of the credo of the Christian Church. Thus already, by the time that the Council of Nicaea (325) declared the Son to be consubstantial with the Father, a dependence of theology upon Aristotelian metaphysics had arisen. Boethius, in his writing on the Trinity and his surviving translations of Aristotle, did much to reinforce this dependence. But it was only later, at the end of the 'dark ages', that the full content of Aristotelian metaphysics began to enter into the philosophical speculations upon which the Christian world-view sought to found itself; and by then the Aristotelian theories had been systematised and adapted by such thinkers as Al-Farabi (875–950), Avicenna (890–1037) and Averroës (c. 1125 to c. 1198), all of them Moslems, and Moses Maimonides (1135–1204), a Jew well versed in the philosophical speculations by which the doctrines of the Koran were currently supported. Aristotelian doctrine therefore entered the arena of theology already bearing the stamp of a monotheism which had found it congenial.

The final conversion of Christian theologians to Aristotelian ways of thinking occurred during the eleventh and twelfth centuries, and led, with the founding of universities at such important centres as Paris and Padua, to the rise of that philosophical movement now known as 'scholasticism'. The greatest luminary of this movement was St Thomas Aquinas (1225–1274), whose *Summa Theologica* purported to give a complete description of the relation between man and God, relying only on philosophical reasoning, and without recourse to mystical assertion or unsupported faith. His master at every point was Aristotle, and the subsequent synthesis of Christian doctrine and Aristotelian metaphysics known after its creator as Thomism has remained to this day the most persuasive of the foundations offered for Christian theology.

In order to understand subsequent developments in the history of philosophy it is necessary to grasp some of the conceptions, disputes and theories that emerged from the attempt to set neo-Platonic and Aristotelian doctrine into a framework of monotheistic religion, and in the course of doing so to reconcile classical science and morality with the dogmas of faith. Contrary to the opinion of their successors, the medieval philosophers were not merely slaves of authority, nor were they easily deterred from speculations which led them into conflict with Church or State. As the scholastics themselves were given to saying, 'authority has a nose of wax', meaning that if you can get hold of it you can bend it as you will. Nevertheless it is undeniable that, looked at as a whole, their philosophy has a conciliatory aspect, upholding through reason doctrines that either coincide with or leave room for the articles of faith. Consequently, if we are to see what is distinctive in the speculations of this period, we must look behind the doctrines to the logical and metaphysical arguments that were used to support them.

The Concept of Substance

The Aristotelian logic, expounded in the works known as the *Organon,* was preserved in part by Boethius, and later delivered up in full by the scholars of Islam. Fundamental to this logic is the distinction between subject and predicate. Every proposition, it was thought, must consist at least of these two parts, and, corresponding to these parts, reality itself must divide into substance and attribute, the latter being 'predicated of' or 'inherent in' the former. The distinction has its origins in logic, and in the Aristotelian attempt to classify all the valid 'syllogisms' within a single scheme. But it has clear metaphysical implications. Since substances can change in respect of their attributes, they must endure through change. Moreover, if we can refer to substances it must be possible to separate them, at least in thought, from the attributes with which they might at some particular moment be encumbered. Hence we should distinguish the 'essence' of a substance that without which it could not be the particular thing that it is from its 'accidents', the properties in respect of which it might change without ceasing to exist altogether. Finally, it is substances, in the Aristotelian view, which are the ultimate constituents of reality, and our knowledge of the world consists in our various attempts to classify them into genera and species.

One of the problems that the medievals bequeathed to their seventeenth century successors was that of whether, and how far, it makes sense to say of a substance that it can cease to exist, or be created. We find that there is an innate tendency in the Aristotelian metaphysic to regard all change as a change in the attributes of a substance. Hence the coming to be or passing away of a substance demands a very special indeed metaphysical—explanation. For many philosophers influenced by Aristotle, these 'existence changes' *have* no explanation. Later philosophers such as Leibniz went further, arguing that a substance must contain within itself the explanation of all its predicates. In which case it becomes hard to envisage how one substance might create or destroy another, except by a miracle which, in the nature of things, it lies beyond the capacity of human intellect to understand. A further problem arose from the inability of the traditional logic fully to distinguish individual and species terms from quantitative (or 'mass') terms. For example, 'man'—which can denote both an individual and the class which subsumes him—refers to individual substances. It also expresses a predicate which generally describes them. But what about 'snow' or 'water' ? There are not individual 'snows' or 'waters', except in an attenuated sense which would seem to obliterate a distinction fundamental to scientific thought. This is the distinction between 'stuff' and 'thing', between what can be measured and what can be counted. The difficulty of forcing the idea of 'stuff' into the conceptual frame of 'substance' is responsible for much of the rejection of Aristotelian science during the seventeenth century, and for this reason, if for no other, the concept of substance became the focus of philosophical enquiry.

The Nature of Universals

Any philosophy which asks itself serious questions as to the nature of substances, must also examine the nature of the 'attributes' or 'properties' that inhere in them. The neo-Platonic cosmology had transformed the original Platonic realm of Ideas the realm where the 'forms' reside, unchanged, unchanging and known to reason alone into the blessed sphere of immutability. But the old metaphysical dispute between Aristotle and Plato as to the nature of universals remained central to medieval thought. This was because the dispute bore on what is perhaps the single most important issue in the theory of knowledge, the issue of how far the world is knowable to reason. Using as their basic text a passage from Porphyry's *Isagoge,* transmitted and commented upon by Boethius, philosophers enquired whether genera and species exist only in the mind or in reality; and, if the latter, whether they exist in individual substances or in separation from them. In answer to this question some philosophers reaffirmed the original Platonic position, upholding the independent existence of universals, in the realm of 'Ideas'; others went to the opposite extreme, the extreme of nominalism, holding that universals are mere names, and that only individuals exist. There is no independent reality to the idea of 'blue': the only fact of the matter here is that we classify things under that label.

One of the most important thinkers to defend a version of the nominalist theory—William of Ockham (*floret* 1300–1349) also combined it with a doctrine which seems to be its natural associate. This is the doctrine of empiricism, according to which reason, far from being the sole authority in determining how things are, is subordinate to and dependent upon the senses (upon empirical enquiry). Such empiricism was by no means unusual in medieval thought; it is foreshadowed in Aristotle, and to some extent approved by Aquinas, who lent support to the scholastic tag '*nihil in intellectus quod nisi prius in sensu*' ('there is nothing in the understanding that is not first in the senses'), a saying which, under one interpretation at least, implies a thoroughgoing scepticism as to the powers of reason. Ockham was prepared to develop that scepticism to the full, and to combine it, as later empiricists combined it, with a theory of the nature and function of language which would remove the basis from much of the traditional claims made on reason's behalf. In the course of developing this theory, Ockham was to anticipate many of the major conceptions of later philosophers, including Hume's theory of causality, Leibniz's theory of relations, and the attack on absolute space and time. Followed in his scepticism by the vigorous Nicolas d'Autrecourt (c. 1300-after 1350), he provided a powerful challenge to many of the dogmas of the Church, arguing that these must be founded not in reason, which could never stretch so far as to comprehend them, but in faith. In this way, the ancient dispute about the nature of universals served as a focus for the growing disagreement between empiricism and rationalism (as they came to be known). Moreover, it became increasingly apparent, during the course of these disputes, that much in philosophy, perhaps the very possibility of philosophy, depends upon the truth about language. It was consequently in the scholastic age that philosophy began to incorporate the theory of meaning and the study of usage as a central focus of its arguments. Out of this study there emerged important specific theories—such as that of abstract ideas (adopted by Peter Abelard (1079–1142) and bequeathed to Locke and British empiricism) and the doctrine that entities should not be multiplied beyond necessity. This last doctrine, known as Ockham's razor (though not in fact found in Ockham's writings), provided the inspiration to much later scientific thought. There also emerged at this time a sense of the centrality of logic to philosophy, and of the need for fine distinctions in the discussion of all philosophical problems.

The Ontological Argument

Not surprisingly, the rationalist, Platonic tradition of speculative thought lent itself more readily to the support of theological dogma than the empiricist scepticism which took so much inspiration from Aristotle's attack on Plato's theory of Ideas. Nevertheless it was an argument that was Aristotelian both in content and in form which was to have the decisive influence upon medieval theology. This argument is known as the ontological proof (adopting a term of Kant's) for the existence of God. The discovery of this proof is normally credited to St Anselm, Archbishop of Canterbury (1033–1109), but it is not too great a distortion to find glimpses of it in certain passages of Aristotle's *Metaphysics* and in the commentaries of Al-Farabi and Avicenna. It was rejected by Aquinas in his systematic exposition of the basis of Christian doctrine, but nevertheless belongs to a class of arguments others of which he was inclined to accept, and all of which derive their proof for the existence of God by way of the concept of a necessary being a being whose essence involves existence.

Put very simply, St Anselm's argument is as follows. By 'God' I mean an entity than which no greater can be thought.

Suppose that God, so defined, does not exist; I can nevertheless *think* that he exists. But an entity is greater if it does exist than if it does not. Hence it is possible to think of something greater than God namely an entity which is not only greater than any that can be thought, but which also exists. But this is contrary to the definition. Hence the hypothesis that God does not exist must be false.

If valid, the argument establishes not merely that God exists, but that he exists by necessity, since it follows from his nature (his essence) that he exists. Later versions (such as that endorsed by Descartes) rely on the idea that existence is a perfection and therefore a property of whatever possesses it. It is not clear that St Anselm's argument relies on this assumption; indeed, to this day it is not clear that the argument makes any questionable assumptions at all. Some philosophers think that it is valid, although only when stated in a refined and novel way; others think it was decisively refuted by Kant, with his attempted proof that 'existence is not a true predicate'. In any case, despite its sophistical appearance, the argument had a peculiar philosophical tenacity, being accepted in one or another version by all three of the major rationalist thinkers of the seventeenth century.

There is a special reason for the argument's popularity with medieval theologians, which is that it gives credibility to the idea of God as a 'necessary being'. Many writers had tried to show that there must be something which exists of necessity (or which is *causa sui,* cause of itself) if anything is to exist contingently. The ontological argument provides a description of this necessarily existing being, and therefore an answer to the fundamental question of metaphysics, the question why (for what reason) *is* there anything? Or (to put it more tendentiously) why should Being be? We see here too the origin of that dark dispute, which still appears to live in the obscure pages of existentialist philosophers, as to the relation of existence and essence. If there is no being for whom existence and essence coincide, then what of the remainder? Do contingent objects (among which we must place ourselves) partake of an essence that precedes their existence, or is it the case that, for them, existence must take priority over essence? When we come to discuss this, as yet scarcely intelligible, question, it will be important to bear in mind its relation to those medieval discussions of the nature of God and of universals, which many modern thinkers might unreflectingly suppose to be of merely academic interest.

Free Will and Human Nature

The acceptance of the ontological argument and the resultant conception of a 'necessary being', endowed with omnipotence and omniscience, leads almost inevitably to a rigid determinism. If all that is contingent depends ultimately upon the divine nature, and if that nature is governed by necessity, then the world too must follow its course in accordance with the laws which express God's nature. How then is human freedom possible? This problem arises in slightly different form for those philosophers who adopt the more Platonic conception of the divine nature. Hence it had already been discussed by the Fathers of the Church, and in particular by St Augustine. With the acceptance of the Aristotelian metaphysics it acquired a new dimension, and some of the greatest achievements of modern philosophy result from the continued attempt to describe human freedom, following arguments that had already been surveyed and as often as not abandoned by the scholastics, in their endeavour to fit a plausible account of human nature and human morality into the theological absolutism which reason seemed to demand.

The greatest of these attempts to describe the relation between God and man and to fit the full complexity of human nature into a coherent theology, is undoubtedly the *Summa Theologica* of St Thomas Aquinas. This work contains what is perhaps the most subtle and complete philosophical account of the nature of human emotion that has ever been produced. As well as incorporating into his work what he considered to be the totality of what was true and well argued in the classical sources available to him, Aquinas attempted to bring to completion the picture of human nature and human virtue presented by Aristotle in his *Nicomachean*

Ethics, and to show its compatibility with the doctrines of revealed religion. While many of Aquinas's assumptions were soon to be subjected to the scepticism of Ockham and his followers, there is no doubt that he succeeded in convincing his contemporaries that philosophy could not only generate the truth about human nature but also sustain the doctrines of the Christian faith, in such a way as to leave little room for doubt about the major questions of morality and religion which all of us must at some stage in our thinking lives encounter.

Aquinas's philosophy leaned heavily upon the Aristotelian doctrine of substance and upon the achievements of medieval logic. But, despite its frequent digressions towards empiricism, it was assiduous in the support that it offered to the doctrine of the power and autonomy of human reason. In particular Aquinas did much to revive interest (an interest already exhibited by Abelard) in the Aristotelian theory of 'practical reason', as definitive of the active nature of man. The theory of practical reason was held to provide an account of human freedom, together with a description of the 'good life for man' that would recommend itself on the basis of reason alone. Aquinas thus handed on to later philosophers a concept without which the study of ethics is either empty or non-existent.

The Rejection of Scholasticism

The triumph of Thomism was, however, short-lived. Its first serious enemy was the humanism of the early Renaissance. This was accompanied by revolutions in the practice of education which tended to take intellectual authority from ecclesiastics and vest it in the hands of courtiers and literary men; and also by the gradual ascendancy of a spirit of scientific enquiry hostile to the ready reception of theological dogma. During the fourteenth and fifteenth centuries there was therefore increasing criticism of the influence of the schools, and increasing awareness of the lacunae in the systems which they propagated. The intellectual history of this period is complex, and the transition from medieval to modern approaches in education and intellectual life was far less abrupt than our modern taste for clear transitions represents it to be. As late as 1685 William of Ockham's textbook on logic was standardly used in the University of Oxford, while as early as the *Metalogicon* of John of Salisbury, Bishop of Chartres (1120–1180), the seeds of Renaissance humanism had been sown and the medieval theories of education thrown in doubt. Nevertheless, it is clear that between these two periods a change took place in the intellectual climate of Europe that could not but have the profoundest repercussions on the history of philosophy. And two philosophers in particular stand out both as embodying the new spirit of criticism and as laying down the intellectual presuppositions of that style of philosophy which we choose to call modern: Francis Bacon and René Descartes. These two are united by their rejection of traditional authority and their radical search for method. But in the case of Bacon neither motive led him in the direction of those philosophical enquiries which we, with hindsight, see as proper to the modern age, so that, for all his brilliance and learning, it is difficult to see him as the founder of the modern, rather than a destroyer of the medieval, modes of thought. Nevertheless it is fitting to conclude this brief summary with a few remarks about Bacon's distinctive contribution to modern philosophy.

Sir Francis Bacon (subsequently Viscount St Albans and Lord Chancellor of England) was born in about 1561 and died, dismissed from courtly offices, in 1626. He was a polymath and scholar of the highest order, and even had he never engaged in philosophical or scientific speculation, he would be known through his *Essays* as one of the great stylists of the English language. But his distinguished place in intellectual history lies in his exploration of the fundamental principles of scientific thought, summarised in the *Novum Organum* (1620). In this work Bacon sets out to show the inadequacies of Aristotelian science and of the barren *a priorism* which he associated with the traditional Aristotelian logic of the *Organon.* He argued that the Aristotelian logic, being purely deductive in character, provides no method for the discovery of new facts, but only a means of arriving at the logical consequences of what is already known. The resulting science must therefore have a purely classificatory character, contenting itself with a division of the known contents of the world into 'species' and 'genera', without understanding the true causality which leads objects to manifest the similarities whereby we could so classify them in the first place. Instead of Aristotelian science he proposed his method of 'induction' the postulation of universal laws on the basis of observed instances and thereby hoped to promote the 'true and lawful marriage between the empirical and the rational faculty'. While Bacon's development of this method was of necessity speculative and incomplete, he did in the course of it make various striking criticisms of the Aristotelian tradition, and at the same time introduce conceptions which were later to prove fundamental to scientific thought. He criticised the theory of 'final causes' (the theory that the cause of an event might be found in its purpose), and with it many of the rationalist preconceptions about causation that we shall encounter in later chapters. In place of these ideas he put forward the notion of causality as the generation of one thing from another, in accordance with underlying 'laws of nature'. He argued that science must always aim at greater and greater universality and abstraction, so ascending 'the ladder of the intellect'. This could be achieved by a theory whose fundamental laws were expressed not in qualitative but in quantitative terms, since 'of all natural forms. Quantity is the most abstracted and separable from matter'. It was this conception of science, as the formulation of quantitative laws, that was shortly to gain intellectual ascendancy in the wake of the discoveries of Galileo and Harvey. Bacon also attacked what he saw as the arbitrary and conventional element in the Aristotelian science, and in the course of doing so introduced his doctrine of 'Forms', which foreshadowed another, entertained by Locke, that science should treat of the real and not of the nominal essences of things.

But before Bacon's influence could be widely felt, philosophy had undergone a radical convulsion. This was induced by Descartes' declaration that all of philosophy's results were without foundation until its premises could be agreed, together with a method whereby to advance from them. Only in the wake of Cartesianism was the nature of Bacon's thought fully to be appreciated, and by then the disputes of scholasticism seemed irrevocably distant.

2

Natural Rights in Modern Philosophy

Introduction

The British force resumed its march to Concord. There the British entered the town without resistance and destroyed the few military supplies that had not been removed. After a brief exchange of fire between British and American forces at North Bridge, on the edge of Concord, with light casualties on both sides, Colonel Smith, considering his mission accomplished, ordered British troops to begin the march back to Boston. By now, however, enraged colonials from nearby towns and farms had taken up positions behind the trees and stone walls that lined the road. From these protected positions they fired at the red-coated British troops marching along the road. By dusk, when the British troops reached the safety of Charleston, more than 70 soldiers had been killed and 175 had been wounded.

What could possibly lead peaceful farmers and tradesmen to inflict deadly fire on a line of marching soldiers? To be sure, the killing of Americans at Lexington and Concord must have provoked great anger. But why did the Americans resist in the first place? Why were arms stored at Concord? Why did the local militia take up arms and line up across the green at Lexington?

The Lexington militia did not act in haste. Warned that the British were coming, they met in a tavern near the village green for several hours before the British arrived, where they discussed what to do. Clearly the minutemen of Lexington believed that resistance to the British was right and that the issues involved were sufficiently important to kill or be killed for their sake.

In fact, the town of Lexington had been discussing these matters for some time. In 1765, when the British government passed the Stamp Act to raise revenues in the colonies, the town of Lexington voted to instruct its representative in the General Court of the colony to protest the act. The actual instruction sent by the town, setting out reasons why the act was unjust, was written by Jonas Clarke, a clergyman and prominent leader in Lexington. It was at Clarke's home where the colonial leaders Samuel Adams and John Hancock were staying on the night of the British expeditionary force's move against Lexington and Concord.

In the instruction that he had written for the people of Lexington, Clarke advanced a number of different reasons for thinking the Stamp Act was unjust. He claimed that it violated the ancient right of British subjects to be taxed only with their own consent. He also maintained that the act violated the agreement between British kings and their subjects enshrined in the Magna Carta. Finally, Clarke also held that the Stamp Act violated the rights and liberties of men who were "beings naturally free." Clarke's appeal to the ancient rights of British subjects and his appeal to the Magna Carta justified resistance to the Stamp Act on historical and legal grounds. These reasons appealed to rights belonging to British subjects in virtue of their being British. Neither the ancient rights of British subjects nor the Magna Carta had anything to say about the rights of human beings who were not British subjects. By contrast,

Clarke's third argument left behind the particular claims to rights that belonged to the American colonists in virtue of their being British subjects. It claimed rights as belonging to the Americans in virtue of their status as "beings naturally free." Here the justification of the claim to rights lies not in legal precedents established in the past but in the very nature of men as beings of a certain kind. Such rights are natural rights. They belong to men as men. They apply to Americans, to all other British subjects, to Frenchmen, to Chinese to all men. Agreements such as the Magna Carta can create special rights, but natural rights are not created by any human agreement. They belong to men as beings having a certain nature.

In the years leading up to the American Revolution, the American colonists often appealed to the ancient rights of Englishmen embedded in the unwritten constitution that had supposedly governed English life from time immemorial. They appealed to the Magna Carta. They appealed to the specific rights guaranteed to the colonists in the charters granted by British kings in founding the American colonies. They also appealed to natural rights possessed by Americans simply in virtue of their nature as men. For example, a resolution adopted by the town of Lexington maintained that the keeping of a standing British army in the colonies to enforce the acts of Parliament was an infringement of the "natural, constitutional and chartered rights" of the colonists. These different arguments were mutually supporting, but the natural rights argument was fundamentally different in scope and kind. Appealing to neither history nor legal precedent, it raised directly philosophical reasons for resisting the authority of the British government, reasons that implied rights that were universal in scope, applying to all men everywhere. It was this directly philosophical claim to universal natural rights that made the shot on Lexington green, in the words of Ralph Waldo Emerson, "the shot heard round the world."

Not only for Americans, but also for people in all corners of the world, the Declaration of Independence, adopted by the Second Continental Congress in 1776, provides an inspiring and powerful formulation of the philosophy of natural rights.

We hold these truths to be self-evident, that all men are created equal, that they are endowed by their Creator with certain unalienable Rights, that among these are Life, Liberty and the pursuit of Happiness. That to secure these rights, Governments are instituted among Men, deriving their just powers from the consent of the governed, that whenever any Form of Government becomes destructive of these ends, it is the Right of the People to alter or to abolish it, and to institute new Government.

In these words the American colonists appealed directly to rights endowed upon all men by their creator, to rights held by all men in virtue of their God-given nature as men. The American colonists did not invent this idea. The theory of natural rights has a long history running back to the works of the ancient Greek and Roman philosophers. Particularly influential on the thinking of the American colonists was the English philosopher John Locke, whose *Second Treatise* on government used a theory of natural rights to defend the English revolution of 1688. Indeed, the phrases of the Declaration so closely parallel passages from Locke that a fellow Virginian accused Thomas Jefferson, the principle author of the Declaration, of copying directly from Locke *Second Treatise*. In the discussion that follows we will sometimes turn to Locke and other philosophers in an attempt to make sense of some of the basic concepts of the philosophy of natural rights found in the Declaration.

Rights

The Declaration of Independence claims that men have certain rights. This idea of rights is clearly one of the basic ideas of the philosophy of natural rights. We Americans often argue about what rights there are. Is there, for example, a right to die? We also argue about who has certain rights. Does the fetus in the womb have a right to life? However, despite these differences, we tend to take the idea of rights for granted. We rarely stop to ask just what a right is or what it is for a person to have a right. Now, in fact, contemporary philosophy recognizes several different kinds of rights. Here, though, we will focus on a particular conception of rights that is central to the philosophy of the Declaration and to the historical core of the philosophy of natural rights.

According to this conception, a right is a moral claim belonging to an individual that prohibits all other persons from acting in certain ways toward that individual. For example, your right to life prohibits all other persons from killing you. Similarly, your right to liberty prohibits all other persons from enslaving you, kidnapping you, or holding you prisoner against your will. Such rights are often said to be moral fences. They surround people and protect them from outside interference. They are said to be "negative rights" in that they stipulate things that other people may *not* do in their interactions with some individual. Your right to life says that I may not kill you. My right to liberty says that you may not enslave me.

Rights protect people from outside interference. But, of course, the protection afforded by rights is not always effective. People have been murdered. People have been enslaved. The natural rights theory does not deny these unfortunate facts of life. What it does say is that murder and slavery are serious moral infractions. This is what is meant by saying that rights are moral claims or moral fences. They stipulate things that other people *should* not do to you. They specify limits on how we may rightly or justly interact with one another. They also provide the basis for complaints of unjust treatment, as when the American colonists in the Declaration of Independence pointed to a series of actions by the king of England as transgressions of their rights, transgressions that justified resistance to English rule.

Natural Rights

The rights to life and liberty claimed by the Declaration prohibit people from killing or enslaving one another. In this respect these rights are like rights created by human beings. Human laws often prohibit certain kinds of actions. Murder and kidnapping are illegal. Human law forbids them, though of course this does not prevent their happening from time to time. Like the rights proclaimed in the Declaration, legal rights say how we should behave, which is not always how we do behave. Legal rights, like the rights of the Declaration, are prescriptive, not descriptive. Both prescribe certain behaviors. But since we humans sometimes fail to live up to these prescriptions, neither accurately describes how we invariably will behave. In these ways the rights claimed by the philosophy of natural rights are like legal rights. Nonetheless, there are some important differences. These differences are central to the idea of certain rights as *natural* rights.

The fundamental difference between natural rights and legal rights is that legal rights are created by human beings and natural rights are not. Human law may give me certain rights. For example, human law gives me the right to drive a car provided I meet certain requirements. Supposing I have met those requirements, no one may interfere with me in the lawful driving of my car. However, the legislature might decide to restrict night time driving for people with poor night vision, or it might, because of life-threatening problems of pollution, decide to ban automobile driving for all but emergency purposes. My right to drive a car is created by human law and may be modified or abolished by the action of a legislature composed of human beings. My natural rights are not like this.

Consider, for example, my natural right to life, a right I have independent of any human action. The Declaration says that I am endowed with this right by my creator. It belongs to me simply in virtue of my being a human being who, like all human beings, is created equally with a certain nature. It belongs to me by nature, not by human artifice. My natural right to life does not depend upon any human act of creation and cannot be taken away by any human action. Legal rights are created by human action and can be taken away by human action. An evil legislative body might pass a law denying me a legal right to life. The legislature might, correctly following the rules of parliamentary procedure, amend the human law to permit the killing of human beings of a certain kind. Something like this happened in Germany in the 1930s, when the law was changed to deny civil rights to Jews. In America, of course, any such action would violate the written constitution that governs what our legislators may do. Such an action would be illegal because it violated my constitutional rights. But suppose a constitutional amendment is passed excluding human beings with my ethnic background from the protections of the Constitution. It would then be within the power of a human legislature to take away my right to life and the right to life of all people like me. However, according to natural rights theory, while the legislature may have stripped me of my legal right to life, it would be wrong for it to do so.

The idea of a natural right to life can be easily grasped by reflecting on the debate over abortion that has divided Americans for the last quarter century. On one side, the state legislatures and the courts have said that abortion, subject to some restrictions, is legal. The law does not recognize a fetal right to life. On the other side, opponents of abortion argue that abortion is a great moral evil because it involves the violation of a natural right to life that belongs to every human fetus. Now, not all natural rights theorists would agree that human fetuses do have a natural right to life. Here there is important disagreement about who is included among the class of beings that have a right to life. However, thinking about the abortion controversy can help us see what is involved in claiming such a right. The fetal right to life is supposed to be a natural right. Such rights do not depend upon human creation, and while they may be violated, they cannot be destroyed by any human action.

Natural Law

We have already seen that natural rights are in some ways like legal rights. Both prohibit other people from interfering with us in certain ways. Both involve a complex network of responsibilities corresponding to the rights they claim. My natural right to life imposes a duty on you and all others to refrain from killing me. My right to drive a car imposes a duty on you and all others to refrain from interfering with my lawful exercise of that right. Legal rights exist as part of a system of laws. My legal right to drive a car and the corresponding duties of other persons are precisely spelled out by the laws governing the use of motor vehicles. In a similar way, natural rights theorists conceive of natural rights as existing within a system of natural laws. The Declaration of Independence itself mentions "the laws of nature and nature's god" as the basis for those rights to life, liberty, and the pursuit of happiness it goes on to claim.

These laws of nature are moral laws. They are not like the laws of nature discovered by physics and chemistry, which tell us how things invariably do act but say nothing about how things *should* act. Unlike the laws of chemistry and physics, but like human created legal laws, moral laws of nature are prescriptive rather than descriptive. They tell us how we ought to behave, not how we invariably do behave.

Like many, natural rights theorists, the authors of the Declaration of Independence saw the laws of nature as God's laws. The Declaration conceives of natural rights as part of a larger system of natural law, a body of moral law coming from God rather than from any human legislators. It is important, however, to distinguish this "natural law" from what philosophers and theologians have traditionally called "revealed law." The biblical text known as the Ten Commandments serves as an excellent example of revealed law. According to the biblical story, these commandments were given directly to Moses by God in an encounter on the top of Mount Sinai. In this story God reveals the commandments of the moral law to Moses and through him to all of God's chosen people. Preserved in the holy scriptures of the Jews, Christians, and Moslems, these commandments are then revealed to all who read them. The appearance of God before Moses on Mount Sinai is an example of a special revelation, an instance of God's speaking to a particular individual or group of individuals at a particular point in time. The revelation of God's message in the scriptures, available to all who can read them or hear them read, is an example of general revelation. Revealed law is based upon the general or special revelations of God's commandments that have appeared in the course of human history. In revealed law God's moral law appears to humans in the form of commandments given by a divine law-giver.

While philosophers and theologians have generally agreed that the content of revealed law and the content of natural law are the same, the idea of natural law includes within it the idea that the moral law can be known by the use of human reason unassisted by either special or general revelation. For this reason natural-law philosophers have often spoken of natural law as the law of reason. Natural law is a system of moral laws that human beings can come to know by observing the nature of things and thereby discovering the right use of those things.

An example may help make this clear. It is of the nature of something that is a knife to have a sharp edge. Without a sharp edge suitable for cutting, a thing would not be a knife. Now, it is possible to use a knife in many different ways. It could be used to pry nails or as a doorstop, for example, but such uses would tend to damage the blade of the knife. For this reason they might be said to be contrary to the nature of the knife. Such uses are not the uses for which the nature of the knife is suited. On the other hand, to use the knife for cutting is to use it in accordance with its nature. The general idea of natural law theory is that the right use of a thing is the use that is in accordance with its nature and that any use of a thing that is contrary to the nature of the thing is a wrong use of the thing.

Now, in this example there is surely no great moral wrong in using a knife to pry nails. But the example should help us see how important moral laws might be discoverable by examining the natures of things. Consider, for example, the nature of human beings. We are animals, and in this respect our nature shares some features with other animals. But human beings also have a capacity for thinking about what they are doing. Unless forced to change by changes in their environments, other animals replicate the ways of life of their ancestors. Humans, on the other hand, are constantly changing their ways of life. They think about their way of life and try to find better ways to satisfy their needs and better ways to express their thoughts and feelings. It is this capacity to think about what they are doing, to reflect upon their way of life, and to guide their lives by their thoughts that many philosophers have considered to be one of the distinctive features of human nature. Human beings are animals, but they are rational animals. Every normal human being has this capacity for thinking about his or her life and guiding that life by this thinking. This is a capacity that appears to be unique to human beings.

If this is so, we can begin to see how certain moral principles might be based on this human nature. How should we live our lives? What is the right use of a human life? Natural law theory holds that we can begin to answer this question by studying our nature as human beings. Suppose we do that and, like the ancient Greeks, arrive at the conclusion that the nature of a human being is to be a rational animal. Then, according to the general principle that the right use of a thing is in accordance with its nature, it follows that the right use of our life requires us to think about our life and what we are doing. While it might be possible for a human being to live his or her life without ever stopping to think about it, such a life would fail to correspond to human nature. Even if it produced a life of success and great happiness, such a life would be, in some sense, sub-human. It would not be a life in accordance with our human nature. For this reason the philosopher Plato said in his *Apology* that "the unexamined life is not worth living for man."

Consider also the implications of this way of thinking about human nature for the institution of slavery. Suppose again that it is true that every normal human being has a capacity for thinking about his or her life and guiding that life by his or her own thinking. When we enslave human beings, we make them the subject of our will. We tell them what to do. In doing this we treat them as mere animals, lacking the power of rational self-direction. But, in doing this, we treat human beings contrary to their nature as human beings. In this way the natural law thinker can argue that slavery is contrary to the law of nature. In this way also we can see how the natural right to liberty can be understood as a requirement of the natural law. Every normal human being has a capacity for rational self-direction. Consequently it is contrary to natural law to deprive a human being of the opportunity to exercise that capacity. We have a duty to refrain from such violations of the natural liberty of a person, and this, of course, is just what is meant in saying that a person has a natural right to liberty.

Natural Equality

We are now in a position to understand one of the most puzzling phrases in the Declaration of Independence. The Declaration says that "all men are created equal." But this seems to be patently untrue. Some men are wise; others are not. Some men are strong; others are weak. Isn't it obvious that human beings are very different from one another in these and other respects? How can the Declaration say not just that all men are equal but that this equality is self-evident? One common response here is to say that all the Declaration means in saying that all men are created equal is that all men have equal rights. But this response makes obscure the Declaration's two separate claims: one that all men are created equal and another that all men have certain rights. Further, this response misses entirely the connection between these two claims, the connection between human nature and natural rights discussed above. This connection is central to the whole idea of natural law.

In considering the idea of natural law, we saw how the right use of a thing is supposed to be connected to the nature of the thing. According to this view, slavery is wrong because it involves treating a human being with a capacity for rational self-direction in the way that one would treat an animal that lacked this capacity. In this view, the right to liberty that slavery violates is a natural right inherent in the very nature of a human being as a rational animal. It is this conception that lies behind the words of the Declaration. All men are created equal in the sense that all men have the capacity for rational self-direction, and it is because all men have this capacity that all have the equal right to liberty. This connection between an equality of rights and a prior equality of nature upon which the equality of rights depends is clearly formulated by Locke in the *Second Treatise*, where he says that there is "nothing more evident than that Creatures of the same species and rank promiscuously born to all the same advantages of Nature, and the use of the same faculties, should also be equal one amongst another without Subordination or Subjection." The same idea, that an equality of rights is based upon a prior equality of nature, is also clearly present in the draft of the Declaration of Independence written by Thomas Jefferson. There the key philosophical section reads as follows:

> *We hold these truths to be self-evident; that all men are created equal & independent, that from that equal creation they derive rights inherent & inalienable, among which are the preservation of life, & liberty & the pursuit of happiness.*

The equality of men is an equality of kind. All men are equal in the sense that they are all members of one kind and as such share in the nature of that kind. Because a capacity for rational self-direction is part of our nature as human beings, natural law requires that we be treated in accordance with that nature. Our natural right to liberty is thus a consequence of a distinct equality of nature, an equality of kind.

Inalienable Rights

Inalienable rights are often thought to be rights that cannot be taken from us. A more accurate view would be that inalienable rights are rights that we may not relinquish. In the legal terminology of the eighteenth century, to alienate a thing was to transfer one's rights over it to some other person. To have property rights in a thing was to have the exclusive rights to use, sell, bequeath, or destroy the thing. Some or all of these rights could be transferred to another person. Thus the rights of ownership over a horse might be alienated by selling the horse or giving it away. While in those days laws of entailment restricted the transfer of some landed property, these restrictions were created by human law and applied only with respect to some property. For the most part, property other than land could be alienated by its owner at will. Alienation of one's rights over a horse involves the alienation of legal rights of ownership, rights that are created by human laws. While many interesting moral problems may arise in considering the rightness or wrongness of specific transfers of property rights, there seems to be no fundamental difficulty in the idea of the alienability of such rights. But when we come to our natural rights, there does seem to be a fundamental difficulty.

Consider my natural right to liberty. May I alienate this right? May I give up this right and transfer it to some other person? May I sell myself into slavery? If I do so, am I not treating myself contrary to my nature? The law of nature is based on the nature of things. Partaking of the nature of human kind, I share the capacity of rational self-direction. According to the natural law, I have a moral obligation to live in conformity to this nature. I have a moral obligation to use my capacity for rational self-direction. If I sell myself into slavery, I fail to live up to the requirements of the law of nature. For this reason, I may not alienate my right to liberty. Unlike the property rights I hold in a horse, my right to liberty is an inalienable right. By similar reasoning, it would seem that all my natural rights are inalienable. Since I have those rights in virtue of my God-given nature, I, like everyone else, am obliged by the law of nature to respect those rights in myself. Thus the Declaration of Independence holds that when a people confronts a despotic attempt to rule over them, "it is their right, it is their duty, to throw off such Government."

Self-Evident Rights

The Declaration of Independence holds that it is "self-evident" that all men are created equal and that they are endowed by their creator with certain inalienable rights. With this idea of "self-evident" truths we encounter one of the more esoteric aspects of the philosophy of natural rights embedded in the Declaration. We can begin to see what is involved in the idea of self-evidence by considering systems such as the geometry developed by the ancient Greek astronomer Euclid. In Euclid's system a certain theorem of geometry is proven to be true by showing that it follows necessarily from theorems that have already been proven to be true. If we ask how we know that these earlier theorems are true, the answer is that they follow from other theorems that already have been proven to be true. In this way the truth of each theorem can be shown to follow from what has already been proven to be true. But it is obvious that such reliance upon prior results cannot be continued indefinitely. The whole system must begin somewhere. In the geometry of Euclid it begins with certain axioms. These axioms state the fundamental principles from which the truth of all other theorems are ultimately derived. But how can we know that these axioms are true? If we appeal to some other principles as evidence for the truth of our axioms, we merely postpone the difficulty, since now the question arises as to how we know that these other principles are true.

One way of solving this difficulty, of bringing the demand for justification to an end, is to say that these axioms are self-evident. What is meant by this is that anyone who truly understands what an axiom is saying will see that it simply must be true. It requires no evidence outside itself to support it. Its truth is manifest in itself. Consider, for example, the principle that equals added to equals give equals. The truth of this principle is transparent to anyone who understands what it says. It needs no proof, no external evidence. It is self-evident. Its truth is so clear and certain that no additional evidence could make it more evident to us than it already is.

Like many other philosophers, John Locke believed that in principle it was possible to construct a system of ethics that, like the mathematics of Euclid, would begin with self-evident axioms and derive from them a complete account of the principles of morality. He described the knowledge of such self-evident truths as being "like bright sunshine" that "forces itself immediately to be perceived, as soon as ever the mind turns its view that way; and leaves no room for hesitation, doubt, or examination, but the mind is presently filled with the clear light of it." Despite his repeated assurances that such a project was in principle possible, that the laws of nature could be known by the methods of geometry, Locke himself never provided us with anything like a deductive system of ethics. Nonetheless, we have already considered some comments he made in the Second Treatise that throw some light on the claim to self-evident truth found in the Declaration of Independence.

Recall that in the Second Treatise Locke claimed that there was "nothing more evident" than that creatures of the same species "should also be equal one amongst another without subordination of subjection." In the section that immediately follows this remark, Locke goes on to cite the similar view of Richard Hooker, another philosopher of the natural law, that it is "evident in it self" that the equality of men by nature is the foundation of our moral obligations to one another. In effect Locke and, in Locke's view, Hooker are saying that it is self-evident that men are equal by nature and self-evident that because men are equal by nature they have equal rights. These two claims about self-evident principles are the same two claims made by Jefferson in the rough draft of the Declaration, where he held that it was self-evident that "all men are created equal & independent" and self-evident that "from that equal creation they derive rights." The revised final version of the Declaration to some extent obscures the connection between these claims, saying only that two truths are self-evident: that all men are created equal and that all are endowed by their creator with certain inalienable rights. Nonetheless, it seems fairly clear that an understanding of the claims to self-evidence made by the Declaration will require an understanding of how the claim to natural equality could be thought to be self-evident and an understanding of how it could be thought to be self-evident that such an equality implied an equality of rights.

The first claim, that it is self-evident that all men are created equal, can be understood in a relatively straightforward way. If we think that men are by nature rational animals, then only those things that are rational animals are men. To say that all men are created equal is just to say that everything that is a man has the nature of being a rational animal. But this is like saying that all bachelors are unmarried males. Just as no thing could be a bachelor without being an unmarried male, so no thing could be a man without being a rational animal. "All men are created equal" is self-evident in the way that "All bachelors are unmarried" is self-evident. Once we understand what is being said, we see that it must be true.

The view that it is also self-evident that because all men are created equal they therefore have equal rights can be understood as a special instance of the fundamental idea of natural law. According to natural law theory, given an understanding of the nature of a thing, we can derive from that how that thing should be used. But if this is true, since all men have the same nature, it would follow that all men should be treated in the same way—that all men have equal natural rights.

Universal Rights

The natural rights claimed by the American revolutionaries were claimed on behalf of all men. They belonged to Americans, English men, Frenchmen, and Chinese. In this sense, the rights claimed were universal rights, as opposed to the particular rights of Englishmen, rooted in the particular traditions of the English people. But in another sense, the rights claimed were not truly universal. They did not include women or males of African descent who labored as slaves in the land of freedom. We will consider the implications of these exclusions later in this book. Still, in a world largely ruled by tyrannical minorities, the Declaration's claim that every man had both a right and a duty to resist tyranny, despite its false universality, had revolutionary implications. From the great upheaval of the French Revolution, which soon followed the American example, to the massive demonstrations by students in Tiananmen Square in Beijing two hundred years later, the philosophical doctrine of natural rights has been a powerful force in history. Indeed, even those excluded by the American revolutionaries, such as women and Africans, would eventually appeal to the philosophy of natural rights to support their own claims to freedom and equality. In the chapters that follow we will examine some criticisms of the theory of natural rights. We will also look at some alternative ways of thinking about the fundamental issues of political life, and we will explore some of the ways that the theory of natural rights has been revised or expanded in response to these criticisms and alternative ways of thinking.

Legal rights are rights conveyed by a particular polity, codified into legal statutes by some form of legislature (or unenumerated but implied from enumerated rights), and as such are contingent upon local laws, customs, or beliefs.

In contrast, natural rights (also called moral rights or inalienable rights) are rights which are not contingent upon the laws, customs, or beliefs of a particular society or polity. Natural rights are thus necessarily universal, whereas legal rights are culturally and politically relative.

Blurring the lines between natural and legal rights, U.S. statesman James Madison believed that some rights, such as trial by jury, are social rights, arising neither from natural law nor from positive law but from the social contract from which a government derives its authority.

The existence of natural rights has been asserted by different individuals on different premises, such as a priori philosophical reasoning or religious principles. For example, Immanuel Kant claimed to derive natural rights through "reason" alone. The Declaration of Independence, meanwhile, is based upon the "self-evident" truth that "all men are endowed by their Creator with certain unalienable Rights".

Likewise, different philosophers and statesmen have designed different lists of what they believe to be natural rights; almost all include the right to life and liberty as the two highest priorities. H. L. A. Hart argued that if there are any rights at all, there must be the right to liberty, for all the others would depend upon this. T. H. Green argued that "if there are such things as rights at all, then, there must be a right to life and liberty, or, to put it more properly to free life." John Locke emphasized "life, liberty and property" as primary. However, despite Locke's influential defense of the right of revolution, Thomas Jefferson substituted "pursuit of happiness" in place of "property" in the United States Declaration of Independence.

Thomas Hobbes included a discussion of natural rights in his moral and political philosophy. Hobbes' conception of natural rights extended from his conception of man in a "state of nature". Thus he argued that the essential natural human right was "to use his own power, as he will himself, for the preservation of his own Nature; that is to say, of his own Life; and consequently, of doing any thing, which in his own judgement, and Reason, he shall conceive to be the aptest means thereunto."

According to Hobbes, to deny this right would be absurd, just as it would be absurd to expect that carnivores might reject meat or fish stop swimming. Hobbes sharply distinguished this natural "liberty", from natural "laws" (obligations), described generally as "a precept, or general rule, found out by reason, by which a man is forbidden to do, that, which is destructive of his life, or takesth away the means of preserving his life; and to omit, that, by which he thinketh it may best be preserved."

3

Rise of Modern Science and Philosophy

Introduction

The philosophers that I shall discuss Shaftesbury, Hutcheson and Butler belong to the 'Enlightenment'. In the first flush of scientific confidence, the thinkers of the Enlightenment tried to carry over into every human intellectual endeavour the search for first principles which, in Newton's physics, had been attended with such success. This search brought with it a sceptical attitude towards authority, rejecting everything that had no secure foundation in experience. In history, morals, metaphysics and literature the Enlightenment attitude briefly prevailed, giving rise to the phenomenal ambitions of the French encyclopaedists, and to their materialist, almost clockwork, vision of the universe. It produced the political theories which motivated the French and American revolutions, and the systematic explorations in chemistry and biology that were to find fruition in nineteenth century evolutionism. It also brought about the technical achievements which precipitated modern industrialism, and while thus preparing the way for the miseries of revolution and factory labour, it infected the minds of the educated classes with a serenity of outlook, and a trust in human capacities, that weathered the assaults of Hume's scepticism, of Vice's anti-rationalism, of the growing introversion and doom-laden mysticism of the romantics. This was the Augustan age of English poetry, the age of Johnson and Goldsmith, of Voltaire, Diderot and Rousseau, of Lessing and Winckelmann. From the point of view of the historian it is perhaps the richest and most exciting of all intellectual eras, not because of the content, but because of the influence, of the ideas that were current in it.

The two major Enlightenment thinkers that I shall discuss Hume and Kant are among the greatest of philosophers. But I shall discuss them independently of the intellectual ferment from which they grew, both because they were superior to it, and also because their thought has a philosophical significance that is wholly misunderstood when they are seen merely as manifestations of a spirit which, being common to so many, retains the individual mark of no one in particular. I shall ignore the encyclopaedists, the French materialists and the great tradition of German academic philosophy which created the bridge between Leibniz and Kant. In all these cases philosophical ideas which were elsewhere given complete elaboration found more confused expression. The astonishing fact is not the depth of the thinking involved, but rather the remarkable character of an age that could generate the appearance of depth in so many.

But while it is possible to study the history of epistemology and metaphysics in such a way, concentrating only on the greatest thinkers, it is necessary to stray a little from the path of genius in order to discuss the history of philosophy's subordinate branches. This is particularly true of ethics, aesthetics and political philosophy. I shall touch on the first of these in the present chapter, and the third in chapter 14. In both cases I shall be representing a characteristic aspect of Enlightenment thought.

With the advance of science came the hope for a 'moral' science. This hope achieved early expression in Descartes'

Treatise on the Passions (1649), a work which profoundly influenced Spinoza. Spinoza's own deductively conceived system of ethics, with its startling conclusions and its remote, noble vision of human things, served as a model for many later thinkers. Its appeal rested not merely in its reinstatement of a Platonic ideal of man as freed and fulfilled in thought, capable of rising above the vicissitudes of nature through understanding alone; but also in the fact that its conclusions seemed to depend on no appeal to revealed religion, or to any other moral authority that was not already contained in human reason. The vision of 'each man his own moralist' was to achieve its most profound and powerful statement in the philosophy of Kant. Before then, other thinkers were radically to change the subject of ethics, by recasting it in empiricist terms. They attempted to combine this outlook with the ideal of a science of human nature from which the precepts of ethics would follow, not as a matter of willing obedience, but as a matter of course. In other words, there arose the general impetus towards an ethical 'naturalism'. Naturalism is the theory that the ideal of the good life is to be derived not from divine precept but from a description of human nature. Such a theory aims to show that evil is against nature, while good fulfils it.

Ethical naturalism found its most important expression in Britain, giving rise to the school of 'British Moralists', whose modesty of style and lack of metaphysical pretension to some extent conceal the seminal character of their philosophy. Their thoughts began to take shape under the influence of Locke, and in the writings of a man whose family had already enjoyed the intimacy and instruction of that philosopher. Anthony Ashley Cooper, third Earl of Shaftesbury (1671–1713), published his *Inquiry Concerning Virtue or Merit* in 1699 and his *Characteristics* in 1711. The latter was one of the most popular philosophical works of the eighteenth century and saw eleven editions before 1790. Shaftesbury was the founder of the empiricist 'moral science' and of the modern study of aesthetics. His influence on the French and German Enlightenment was considerable. Even at the end of the eighteenth century Herder could write that 'this virtuoso of humanity has had a marked influence on the best minds of our century, on those who have striven with determination and sincerity for the true, the beautiful and the good'. However, the aspect of his thought which is now of greatest interest is not that which was most immediately influential. In his earlier work Shaftesbury attempted to combine the Lockean theory of the workings of the human mind with many of the arguments of Aristotle's *Nicomachean Ethics,* and it is this aspect of Shaftesbury's philosophy which we need to consider.

In Aristotle the project of deriving an account of the good life from a description of human nature had found its finest ancient expression. At first sight it may seem that Shaftesbury was by no means original in his attempt to revive the outlook (if not all the conclusions) of Aristotle. The few philosophical achievements of Renaissance humanism had been in the field of ethics, and in almost every case the inspiration had been Aristotelian. Even Aquinas had advocated ethical ideas which stemmed directly from the conceptions of Aristotle, and when Count Baldassar Castiglione (1478-1529), in his *Book of the Courtier* (1528), gave to these ideas the humanistic bias which they naturally favour, he changed the morality of scholasticism only in two particulars. He neglected to mention God, and at the same time he shifted the aims of ethics away from a description of the good, towards a description of the noble.

Shaftesbury's Aristotelianism was, however, new. It shared the sceptical temper, and the search for rigorous foundations, which characterise empiricism. It also sought to detach the conclusions of ethics from this or that particular style of life, this or that set of manners, these or those protective institutions. It was, in intention, 'institution-free', in a way that the ethics of the humanists was not. Hence Shaftesbury's description of the good life was derived from qualities of human nature which he regarded as more or less common to all, and definitive of a human norm. Like Aristotle, he was concerned to found his moral system not so much in a conception of the 'right' or 'wrong' of particular actions, as in a notion of the 'goodness' or 'badness' of the characters which generate them. And, again like Aristotle, he regarded good character, or virtue, as the sole and sufficient cause of happiness. Happiness is the state in which our nature is in harmony with itself; the whole character is involved in this harmony, which is a form of proportion in the soul. Our love of beauty is therefore as much excited by the perception of happiness (or virtue) as is our natural sympathy, and it is as much given to human nature to admire virtue in others as to find fulfilment in pursuing it oneself.

But what does virtue consist in? Again Shaftesbury's account is Aristotelian: virtue consists in a certain disposition of character, in which reason has governance over the passions (the 'affections'). This governance is not the *suppression* of passion but the securing of its 'right application'. The virtuous person is not the one who feels no hatred, love, anger or contempt. He is the one who is disposed to feel these passions only towards their appropriate objects towards those things which are worthy of hatred, love, anger and contempt. Such a disposition requires a steady will and resolution, but it is not a form of unfeelingness, or blind obedience. The whole character is involved in virtue; hence any truly wicked act, since its wickedness displays the vice which was its motive, implicates the character of the agent.

What is this 'reason' that has or should have governance over the affections? Shaftesbury's answer to this question is not clear, but his awareness of the need for an answer, and the terms in which he posed the question, were to provide the structure of moral philosophy as it developed to its culmination in Kant. The principal operation of reason in this respect is connected with 'conscience'. Shaftesbury argued that no morality could be founded in religious obedience, or piety. On the contrary, a person is motivated to such obedience only because conscience tells him that the divine being is worthy of it. Shaftesbury wavered between seeing the origin of conscience in reason, and seeing it in a specific moral feeling. This feeling he also regarded as natural, being a kind of internal reflection of our social sense. It is because we are social beings that we acquire the sense of right and wrong. Conscience therefore reflects the nature not of this or that particular human agent, but rather of our common humanity. The dispositions of the virtuous are the fulfilment of this common nature, and must therefore form themselves in harmony with it. The principle of harmony is sympathy, which is the ability to feel the sufferings and joys of each individual as a part of some greater whole.

This shift in emphasis from reason to sympathy as the ruling principle in moral thought was characteristic. It shows Shaftesbury's reluctance to carry his arguments through, or fully to define his terms. It also shows his awareness of the complexity of the moral and emotional life of human beings. This awareness was to gain strength and vitality in subsequent thinkers. Shaftesbury had perceived two important truths: first, morality is both peculiar to rational beings and also integral to their entire nature; secondly, morality has an intimate relation to the emotions, at the heart of which lies man's perception of his nature as a social being. To which sphere, then, should morality be assigned: the rational or the emotional? Shaftesbury's hesitation is in part an expression of a tardy perception that the distinction between these is as unclear as the definition of either, and that no advance in the 'moral sciences' will be possible without a clearer account of how reason and emotion interact.

As Kant was later to perceive, Shaftesbury's problems arose in the course of an attempt to recapture and delimit the conception of 'practical reason' which had troubled Aristotle. But it was not until Kant that this notion was once again fully to come into the foreground of moral thought. The intervening period, which led from Shaftesbury to Hume, was characterised by further attempts to explore the structure of the 'human nature' from which morality derives.

Francis Hutcheson's *Inquiry Concerning Moral Good and Evil* was published in 1725. It shows everywhere the influence of Shaftesbury, adopting a neo-Aristotelian view of human virtue, and directing many of its individual arguments against the seventeenth-century moral sceptics (such as Hobbes and Mandeville) whose writings had equally called forth the opprobrium of Shaftesbury. Nevertheless it is marked by certain important original features. Hutcheson saw in ethics the basis of a new epistemological problem. Putting the point in terms of Lockean empiricism, he notes that, since our language contains terms like 'moral good' and 'moral evil', we ought to be able to locate the ideas which such words stand for, and the qualities in objects which those ideas represent. We must ask ourselves what foundation there is in nature for this distinction of words. As he recognised, such a question generates a problem of epistemology which for the empiricist is particularly acute. What is the experience, or set of experiences, from which our moral ideas derive? If we can say nothing about those experiences, then we have a problem not just about the truth or falsehood of moral judgements, but about their very meaningfulness.

Hutcheson began from the distinction between self-interest and morality. He argued that Shaftesbury's view that self-interest alone suffices to persuade the reasonable person to virtue is fallacious. Shaftesbury had ignored the completely different character of the motives of morality and self-interest, and the different manner in which we are affected when we perceive the moral and the non-moral reality of things. Hutcheson now faced a question: how do we know that some action, or character, is morally good, if this is not revealed to us by the calculations of self-interest? He felt that he could not derive an answer by referring merely to ordinary capacities of sense-perception: goodness is not, as one might say, a 'perceivable property' of the world, in the way that redness is. For one thing, as Shaftesbury had also observed, only rational beings have moral views. Yet there is nothing absurd in supposing that a non-rational being should have all the sensory capacities—sight, touch, hearing, etc. —which characterise us. On the other hand, Hutcheson was reluctant to allow that reason alone could determine what is good or bad. He anticipated Hume's view that reason can deliver to us no more than the relations among ideas. Hence it provides no insight into the ends of our conduct, however useful it might be in calculating the means to them. Moreover, Hutcheson was thoroughly persuaded not only of the falsehood of rationalist metaphysics, but also of the falsehood of an implication contained in it. This implication is almost explicit in the ethics of Spinoza (whose 'systematic' approach to ethics Hutcheson nevertheless sought to emulate). It seems that, on the rationalist view, the ordinary unthinking person could only have confused and indefinite moral convictions, and that it is an unlikely accident if the opinions of the normal active majority happen to coincide. This consequence of rationalism was rejected by all the British moralists as palpably absurd.

Hutcheson, despite his empiricist bias and the consequent emphasis on the question 'How do I know?', shared with other eighteenth-century naturalists the view that there is a common body of moral knowledge, and that it is available to everyone whatever the state of their education. It is part of human nature to acquire and exercise this body of moral knowledge. How then is it acquired? Hutcheson's answer is that we each possess a moral sense, which compellingly delivers to us, through experience, the moral ideas that prompt our actions. Hence these ideas are intelligible in the manner of all ideas by virtue of an intrinsic connection with the experience from which they derive. This postulation of a moral 'sense' explains various facts which would otherwise be mysterious. First, it explains why moral opinions are common to people of all periods and cultures, local variations being explicable not as fundamental differences of outlook but as reflections of the varying circumstances with which the common moral outlook is combined. Secondly, it explains why these opinions are aroused in us spontaneously upon the perception of good or evil acts. They are aroused, as it were, against our will: faced with an outrageous act I am stirred to indignation. This is not something I *do* but something that *happens* to me. ('Passivity' is a feature of sensory perception made prominent by Berkeley and later by Hume.) Moreover it seems that the moral sense cannot be overcome by self-interest or passion: it always tells me what is right or wrong, much as my eyes always tell me what is there, whatever my individual desires, projects or emotions.

It is clear that the moral-sense theory is able to reconcile the objectivity of moral judgement with empiricist conceptions of meaning. Nevertheless it leaves many questions unanswered. For example, it seems odd to speak of a 'sense', when there is no particular organ involved in the perception. Moreover, the problem remains of explaining why only rational beings with certain non-sensory powers are capable of exercising moral judgement. What is it about a dog that makes it impossible for it to perceive these apparently evident properties of the actions which we call right and wrong? Moreover, how is it that we can engage in and be persuaded by moral argument? We do not argue someone into perceiving the colour of a thing, nor would we try to do so. What is the force, then, of referring to a 'sense' when the rational capacities seem so integral to its exercise?

Hutcheson did not address himself to all those problems: nevertheless, he rightly felt that the moral sense could not be taken as a brute capacity like the capacity to hear, for example which we might have lacked while being in every other respect rational. He recognised that the moral sense has a further basis in rational nature, and its fundamental working can be understood only in terms of that basis. Hence Hutcheson, like Shaftesbury, had recourse to a general theory of benevolence. He argued that the disposition of human beings to feel pained at each other's sufferings and to rejoice at each other's delights is, in so far as it exists, the motivating force behind both the perception of moral qualities and the actions which are precipitated by it. The disposition to sympathise in these and all the many other ways with which we are familiar is part of what later philosophers were to call the 'social' nature of humankind. The British empiricists deserve credit for this, if for no other thing, that they so described the moral life as to make it clear that there could be no moral theory, whether sceptical or otherwise, that treated the individual as an isolated unit, in only accidental relation to his fellows. The concepts of 'sympathy' and benevolence became basic to moral theory, until Kant suddenly swept them aside in a theory of ethics that made not only these, but every other variety of emotion, utterly irrelevant.

It is at this point that the moral-sense theory becomes unsatisfactory, however. Benevolence may be a natural disposition, but it is not clear how it can provide the foundation of a *sense.* There are no objects, states of affairs or whatever which it is proper to benevolence to perceive, even though it may be proper to benevolence to act on them. At least, if we do say that there is a perception of right and wrong and it is benevolence which leads us to it, we also need to meet Hume's later charge that this, which we interpret as a 'perception', is but another example of the mind's capacity to 'spread itself upon objects'. There is neither right nor wrong in the world, but only a collective hallucination born of good will. It does not really alter this fact that by nature we all agree on what is right or wrong. That only shows that our sympathies are naturally in tune. It does nothing to persuade those who are out of tune with the spirit of benevolence that there is a respect in which they perceive the world wrongly.

The moral-sense theory waned, was revived, waned again, and still continues its spasmodic life, under the guise of ethical 'intuitionism'. But the immediate contemporary of Hutcheson, and the philosopher who did most to gather together the insights of Lockean moral philosophy into a system, was not persuaded by it. Bishop Butler, whose *Sermons* first appeared in 1726, kept closer to Shaftesbury's strategy. That is to say, he put aside questions of moral epistemology and of the meaning of moral terms in favour of a description of human nature which would show, in Aristotelian fashion, not that the evil perceive things wrongly, but rather that they act and feel against nature. Hence, however we answer such questions as 'To what idea does the word "right" refer?' or 'Is there an objective property of things which constitutes their moral value?', we shall be in a position to argue that there is as much reason to act in accordance with the precepts of morality as there is to act in accordance with any other part of ourselves which is essential to the harmonious functioning of our nature. It was from reflections inspired by this thought—and in particular from those delivered by Butler—that much of the modern philosophy of mind was born. If Butler is admired now it is as much because of his acute understanding of the peculiar philosophical problems posed by the nature of appetite, will and emotion, as on account of his answers to the questions of morality.

Butler argued against a certain species of hedonism. According to this theory, no one does anything unless prompted by desire. Since the satisfaction of desire is pleasure, the ultimate end of all action is pleasure. It does not matter that the original desire was to do good: the fulfilment of the action lies in the pleasure that accompanies its success. Hence it is this pleasure that is *really* wanted. Butler felt that this thought, or some variant of it, lay behind most moral scepticism, as well as behind many accepted accounts of the nature of emotion. Since he also thought that it makes morality either impossible, or at best no more natural or respectable than its opposite, he was led to explore the nature of motivation, in order to refute hedonism in this and every other form. At the same time he developed a subtle and in many ways persuasive theory of rational agency.

First, Butler argued that hedonism rests in a fallacy. Even if it were true that whenever I act, I act from a desire, and true that pleasure is the natural or even essential consequence of the satisfaction of desire, it does not follow that my desire is always for pleasure. On the contrary, Butler argued, pleasure presupposes the existence of desire, and is obtained not because we pursue it, but because we pursue something else. The pleasure of drinking wine comes through the satisfaction of the desire for wine. Had it been pleasure alone that we sought, then the wine would have been replaceable as a means to it. I might have said, to someone who asked for a glass of wine, 'Take this, it will do just as well,' and thereupon handed them some other object a book, a pistol, a plate of fish—the possession of which brings pleasure. To put the point succinctly, hedonism overlooks the specific nature of the objects of our appetites and passions.

Moreover, Butler argued, hedonism rests on an over-simple view of the nature of desire. It assimilates all desires to those of immediate impulse. It fails to distinguish the desires which are peculiar to reason from those which have their basis in animal nature. A rational being can reflect on his predicament and see that the satisfaction of this or that desire might conflict with his long-term interests, bringing discomfort, restlessness, debility or grief. A modern philosopher might speak here of the rational being's capacity for 'second-order' or 'long-term' desires. Some of my desires involve, as part of their object, that I should or should not act on some other short-term, or first-order desire. Butler spoke in this connection of 'cool self-love'; meaning the general capacity to step outside the sphere of present impulse and reflect on one's existence as it extends through time, to see what kind of disposition or character it would be most satisfactory to acquire, and so to act accordingly, encouraging some appetites and discouraging others, in the interest of one's ultimate well-being.

Shaftesbury had argued that common morality can already be generated by cool self-love, without reference to any other principle. His was the Aristotelian view that, properly considered, reflection on the nature of human fulfilment or happiness will lead us to see that a certain long-term disposition that of virtue is uniquely suited to produce it. Butler was not persuaded by Shaftesbury's conclusion, but accepted many of his premises. In particular, he accepted that the motivation of a rational being must be understood in terms of a principle of self-knowledge, which takes long-term satisfaction and fulfilment into account and which may overrule the urgings of more specific appetites or desires. Moreover he accepted the view that the principal objects of this 'second-order' principle are not particular or momentary things, but rather general dispositions of character. And he further agreed that, among these dispositions, benevolence is one of the most, perhaps the single most, important. Hence it is true that cool self-love already points us in the direction of a virtuous life. However, Butler thought that the picture of rational motivation was still too simple. There is a further principle which must be mentioned if rational agency is to be intelligible the principle of conscience:

> *The very constitution of our nature requires, that we bring our whole conduct before this superior faculty; wait its determination; enforce upon ourselves its authority, and make it the business of our lives, as it is absolutely the whole business of a moral agent, to conform ourselves to it.*

Butler's description of conscience is extremely interesting, partly because it foreshadows, and to some extent gives content to, Kant's later reflections on the nature of practical reason. It also shows a concern to avoid the usual simplifications of empiricist thought, while remaining free of the contentious claims made in opposition to them on behalf of the powers of reason. As Butler put it, inspired by a remark of St Paul's, man is by his very nature a law to himself. What deters us from evil when we act out of conscience is not the fear of punishment, nor even the natural dispositions which self-love would foster, but something altogether higher, which is the obnoxiousness to us of violating a known obligation. Conscience is steady, immovable, and makes itself felt even in the act of disobedience. It is therefore both the maker of law and the motive to obedience; it has (and here Butler borrows from political thought an old Ciceronian distinction) both power and authority, telling us what is good while at the same time motivating us towards the good. Conscience, unlike self-love, is a motive which can overcome passion. While cool self-love can tell us, in reflection, that we should indeed cultivate the disposition of temperance, say, and while this may be of the utmost consequence in persuading us to amend our lives accordingly, self-love is of little use in the actual moment of passion, and is as soon overcome by lust, gluttony or transient passion, as that passion itself might be overcome by rival affections or desires. Conscience, on the other hand, continues quietly to command us even in the frenzy of desire, and can therefore prevent the *subjection* of human nature to the appetites which conflict with it.

Butler's description of conscience is subtle and distinctive. He remained in part a naturalist, committed to the view that all of ethics, even that part which was the responsibility of conscience alone, was but an exploration of human nature, and of what is necessary for that nature to act in harmony with itself. He was able, therefore, to incorporate into his outlook many of the ancient and interestingly argued doctrines that had appealed to Shaftesbury. For example, he held that there is no such thing as love of injustice, oppression, treachery, ingratitude; but only eager desires after such and such external goods; which, according to a very ancient observation, the most abandoned would choose to obtain by innocent means, if they were as easy, and as effectual to their end.

Indeed, it often seems as though the claims that Butler makes for conscience are nothing but descriptive; they derive their authority from that same dispassionate argument about the true nature of rational agency that had surprised and delighted the Greeks with its results—in particular with the result that vice is self-defeating and virtue its own reward. In fact, however, Butler's invocation of this new principle of authority in the moral life represents a departure from naturalism. Even if we attribute to conscience a motivating power adequate to ensure its obedience, we need also to show that what it commands is in fact justifiable. This would seem to raise precisely those epistemological questions which Hutcheson felt he could answer, and which Hume later argued that he could not.

The naturalist's investigation of the moral life was continued by Adam Smith, in an interesting discussion of the moral sentiments. It led eventually to utilitarianism, and to the study of political economy as a natural science, so providing historical foundations to some of the principal traditions of nineteenth-century thought. At the same time and again under the original influence of Shaftesbury empiricist philosophers began to interest themselves in the subject of aesthetics. The Lockean theory of the association of ideas seemed to give a new basis to the view that beauty is not a subjective sentiment, but something that precipitates connections of thought which reach into our innermost feelings. Beauty must therefore have a significance which is greater than that of any appetite or sensual delight. The empiricist philosophers began to be aware of the great lacuna left in their philosophy of mind by the failure to speak of beauty, and by their fumbling efforts towards an account that would distinguish true taste from mere sensory preference. This awareness, expressed in the works of Lord Kames, Archibald Alison and Edmund Burke (*On the Sublime and the Beautiful,* 1750), was to provide the concepts from which Kant invented anew the philosophical discipline of aesthetics.

Charles Darwin published "The Origin of Species" in which he explained that life on earth evolved through a slow process of random mutation and natural selection.

Darwin understood that his theory would provoke serious controversy, and so he did not dare to discuss the evolution of humankind or the philosophical implications that evolution might have on ideas of human purpose or morality. But as the theory of evolution slowly gained acceptance, other thinkers did begin to speculate.

The idea soon became popular that because evolution led to the rise of intelligent life, it was a process that generated something of value, and could therefore be equated with "progress for the better". It was believed that continued human evolution would lead to further progress, and so anything that aided this process could be thought of as 'good'.

It was believed that evolution would benefit from increased competition. The capitalist free market economy favored individual resourcefulness and was therefore considered to be good. Social welfare was seen as helping the sickly and feebleminded to survive and multiply, thereby working against natural selection and decreasing the future survivability of the entire species.

These kinds of ideas were promoted by conservative political elitists, not only as a way of justifying the inequalities between races, sexes, and classes, but also as a way of arguing for more aggressive economic policies that would favor their own special interests. Many conservatives argued that society's interests were best served by individuals acting out of pure self-interest.

4

Logic and Critical Thinking in Philosophy

Introduction

In the ancient world things were not so different. After the establishment of Plato's Academy, philosophical schools devoted to different philosophical traditions were the major places where philosophy was learnt, taught and passed on. Wealthy individuals might have philosophy tutors in their homes, but these would typically have been trained in some philosophical school. Each school would belong to a definite tradition, within which certain texts (typically Aristotle's, or the Stoics') were privileged. And from fairly early on the philosophical curriculum consisted of three parts: logic, physics and ethics. This happened early enough for it to be ascribed (unconvincingly) to Plato, though it is clear that neither Plato nor Aristotle wrote with such a curriculum in mind; it fits the interests of later schools, like the Stoics and Epicureans, far better. So far we have looked at an important topic in the ethics part of the curriculum, and also at theory of knowledge, which was considered part of logic, since logic was construed broadly, so as to cover what we call epistemology and philosophy of language. But there was also logic as we generally understand the term, more narrowly. And there is the topic that sounds oddest to us, 'physics'.

Logic

Why is logic needed as part of philosophy? This topic was controversial then as now, some holding that logic was a part of philosophy in its own right, others that it was only a 'tool' that we use in order to improve our study of philosophy proper. Either way, we need logic to ensure that our arguments are sound ones, with no lurking fallacies for opponents to exploit, and also to enable us to detect weaknesses in the ways our opponents argue. In ancient philosophy logic has the function of sustaining philosophical truths and demolishing philosophical mistakes. Logic developed for its own sake was often regarded as a potential distraction from the central concerns of philosophy.

Logic is one of the more impressive achievements of Aristotle. Finding no given systematic techniques for classifying and distinguishing arguments that just persuade people from arguments which lead to true conclusions by valid inferences (and also finding, as today, many influential people glorying in conflating the two), Aristotle systematized the notion of valid argument and constructed an extensive logical system.

The centre of Aristotle's logic is the idea of a *deduction*, in Greek *sullogismos*. He defines it quite generally: a deduction is an argument in which, some things having been laid down, something other than the things laid down comes about by necessity, because these things are so. More formally, the conclusion of a deduction follows necessarily from the premisses. Aristotle adds that the conclusion must be something *different* from the premisses; hence he is not trying to capture what modern logicians are after when they hold that 'If p then p' is a valid argument. He also holds that the truth of the conclusion must come about in a way that is *through* the truth of the premisses, thus excluding redundant premisses making no contribution in establishing the truth of the conclusion. Here too he diverges from modern notions of purely formal inference. There has been a large amount of (unsettled) modern discussion as to what Aristotelian deductions are, in terms of modern formal logic, and hence as to how his logic should be classified.

In modern terms Aristotle's is only a fragment of logic, since, despite the wide scope of his definition of a deduction, he systematically studies only a much narrower range of deductions, those that have come to be known as Aristotelian syllogisms. He considers statements, positive and negative, that have the form of claiming that a predicate *P*, 'belongs to' or does not 'belong to' a subject *S*, in all, some or no cases. (As developed since the Middle Ages, these statements take the more familiar form of 'All *S*s are *P*', 'Some *S*s are *P*', 'Some *S*s are not *P*', and 'No *S*s are *P*'.) Aristotle's greatest contribution is the use of schematic letters, which enables him to study the form of an argument regardless of its particular content. He systematizes the ways in which two statements in one of these forms, which share a common term (the 'middle' term) lead to a conclusion. Some of these combinations will give valid arguments, others not. Aristotle devotes great ingenuity to showing which forms are valid, and which are not.

Various suggestions have been made as to why Aristotle should have limited himself in this way. Fairly plausible is the idea that, although he is interested in arguments as such, Aristotle is most concerned to formalize the type of argument which finds its home in his model of a completed science or body of knowledge, one in which what is at stake is the relations of kinds of thing, and claims about what holds universally are particularly important. Arguments involving individuals find no place in this logical system (though they appear in fleeting thoughts on Aristotle's part about a 'practical' logic of arguments that lead to action).

Aristotle hints at ideas, developed further by his pupil Theophrastus, of systematizing arguments where what is studied are the relations between the statements, rather than the terms which form part of them. Real progress here, however, was left to the Stoics, in particular Chrysippus. Stoic logic concerns statements or *axiomata*, which assert or deny something. Compound statements are produced by joining simple statements by various connectives, such as 'and', 'or' and 'if'. Stoic logic studies arguments which are made up of premisses and conclusion, where these are all statements; much of it overlaps with modern 'propositional logic', though there are differences. Five argumentschemata are taken as basic (the schematic letters *P* and *Q* stand in for statements). These are: (1) If *P*, then *Q*, *P*; therefore, *0* (still familiar, as 'modus ponens'), (2) If *P*, then *Q*, not-*Q*; therefore not-*P* ('modus tollens'), (3) Not both *P* and *Q*, *P*; therefore not-*Q*, (4) Either *P* or *Q*, *P*; therefore, not-*Q*, (5) Either P or *Q*, not-*P*, therefore *Q*. From this basis Stoic logic developed in sophisticated and powerful ways.

As with Aristotle, the Stoics were not merely interested in argument for its own sake. They were concerned to produce arguments which were also 'proofs' — arguments which, as they put it, 'by way of agreed premisses, reveal by deduction an unclear conclusion'. Logical form is studied in the service of representing our claims to knowledge, in this case the way we claim to reach knowledge of 'unclear' or theoretical matters by way of what we can agree on in our experience.

Epicurus and his school affected to despise formal logic as a trivial waste of time. But they also spent energy on studying what were called 'signs' on the basis of which we make inferences from what we experience to matters that are beyond our own experience; so they engaged other schools in discussion about logic to some extent.

Students of philosophy in the ancient world could (unless they were Epicureans) expect to study both Aristotelian and Stoic logic, which were seen as complementary, although there could be disputes as to which was the more important. By historical accident, Stoic logic was lost, along with much early Stoicism, at the end of antiquity, whereas Aristotle's logic not only survived but became regarded as all there was to logic. It was elaborated in the Middle Ages, regarded as complete by Kant and dislodged from its place in the syllabus only by the rediscovery of propositional logic by Frege and Russell at the beginning of the twentieth century.

Nature and Science

The third part of the philosophical curriculum, 'physics', no longer sounds as though it even belongs to philosophy. This is partly because of our narrowing of a term which originally meant the study of *nature* or *phusis*. Nature is just everything that there is, or the world (including humans, who are part of the world). Hence the study of nature can cover a number of very different things, and 'physics' covers a range of enquiries which for us have got segregated into different subject-matters and taught in very different ways.

One type of enquiry seeks explanations for the puzzling things we see around us and are exposed to. What explains the regularities of the sun and the moon? What brings about the seasons, so crucial for farmers? Why are there hurricanes, earthquakes, eclipses? In the ancient world these were regarded as issues which were part of the study of nature as philosophers undertook that. As philosophy developed, however, and especially after Aristotle, these questions lost much of their interest, since there were numbers of theories about them, but no decisive ways of deciding between these, and so no convincing way of showing any given answer to be correct. They became regarded as suitable material for dinner-party discussion rather than live philosophical questions. In the modern world, of course, the advances of science, whatever their other drawbacks, have provided us with firm answers to questions like these. They no longer seem remotely philosophical, and ancient discussions of them are often put into the history of science.

The study of nature narrowed in another way also, especially in the period after Aristotle, with the development of bodies of scientific knowledge separate from philosophy. Medicine, though crude by modern standards, developed as a specialized science, with differing schools. It was the mathematical sciences, however, which made the greatest strides, with Euclid *Elements a high point.* Archimedes was not only a great mathematician, but developed astronomy and also applied branches like engineering. Historians of science sometimes lament the fact that sophisticated technical ideas were applied in trivial ways; Heron of Alexandria describes a machine for making figures mechanically pour libations on an altar. But basic facts about the ancient economies precluded anything like the development of our industrial technology. Whether we are obviously the winners here is another matter.

Physics and Metaphysics

The study of nature, or 'physics' in the ancient sense, however, covered more than what became narrow scientific enquiries. From the beginning, 'nature' could be used for 'what there is', everything that there is to be studied. Hence much of ancient 'physics' is so broad as to correspond to what we think of as metaphysics. Is change a necessary feature of our world? What is change, anyway? In the world around us, what are the real entities, the things that are basic to a true view of the way the world *really* is? Are living things, like animals and humans, such basic entities? They seem to be the subjects of changes, the things changes happen to. But if what is real is the subject of change, then perhaps in looking for what is real we should not stop with the living things, but look for whatever it is which in them is the subject of change. Perhaps this is the material they are made out of. Issues like this are central to the philosophical enquiries of many of the so-called Presocratics and of Aristotle, who engaged with their ideas and is our major source for many of them. They are not part of modern science, but of more abstract philosophical enquiries, generally called metaphysical. Often the dividing-line between Aristotle's 'physics' and his 'metaphysics' is a thin one.

Such questions were thought to arise naturally in the context of a general view of the world as a whole. Given the less ambitious scope of modern metaphysics, they are often studied in relative isolation. Thus we tend to see Plato's 'theory of Forms', for example, as a metaphysical theory that has nothing to do with what we think of as physics or the study of nature. In the ancient world, however, it was mostly seen as one aspect of Plato's 'physics' or theory of the world, which was primarily studied in the *Timaeus*, a dialogue not very popular today which contains Plato's cosmology or account of the universe and its structure.

What you studied as 'physics' or metaphysics in the ancient world would depend a great deal on what tradition of philosophy you primarily belonged to. Epicureans, for example, held that physical and metaphysical questions mattered only to the extent that getting the answers to them wrong led us to be disturbed and unhappy; getting interested in them for their own sake was a misuse of time that would be better employed learning more directly how to live well. The Stoics thought it important to get right the major metaphysical points about the world: it is governed by providence, and a rational appreciation of it will discern how everything in it is for the best. But they were not much more interested than the Epicureans in getting the details right for their own sake.

Aristotle on Nature

Among ancient philosophies it is the Aristotelian tradition which has the broadest and most generous conception of what the study of nature is. Aristotle had the reputation of being the philosopher most interested in causes and explanations.

Plato's 'Theory of Forms'

Plato has no explicit theory of Forms. In some dialogues, especial *Phaedo*, *Republic*, *Symposium*, *Phaedrus*, and *Timaeus*, there are passages, some with argument and others more expressive and metaphorical, which introduce in various ways items we usualty call Forms, but for which Plato never develops a standard terminology.

In contrast to the things in our experience which are beautiful, Plato introduces the idea of the 'beautiful itself, which is beautiful in a way not relative to context or time or perspective. Unlike all the beautiful things and people in our experience, the beautiful itself is never not beautiful. This idea is developed with value terms Like *beautiful*, just, and qood, and with mathematical terms Like *double* and *half*. It is notoriously unclear how Plato's arguments could be extended beyond terms with opposites. Despite a widely misinterpreted passage in the *Republic*, Plato does not think that there is a Form for every general term; Forms are not what came to be called universals. There is a Form only where there is an objective nature that can be known by being intellectually grasped; Forms are always associated with using your mind to reason, as opposed to relying uncritically on your sense experience. The most famous passages about Forms stress this contrast between the mindless assumption that what experience impresses on you is just what there is, and the critical use of reason to grasp realities, the Forms, that are accessible only to the enquiring mind.

In the dialogue *Parmenides* Plato shows that he is aware of apparent inconsistencies in what he has said about Forms. The right response, however, he holds, is not to abandon Forms but to continue to argue on both sides until a defensible position is reached. He continued in this spirit, never successfully producing a definitive theory of Forms. Later philosophers have often simplified the issues, but Aristotle and Late twentieth century philosophers have explored the different arguments Plato employs for and against the existence of Forms.

For Aristotle, nature is the world made up of things that have natures. What is it to have a nature? It is to be a thing which has a source internal to itself of changing and being changed. We can understand what a lion is only by looking at lions themselves and at the way they interact with their environment and other species. To understand an artefact like a shield, by contrast, we have to appeal to something external to the shield itself the designs of humans that made it. Things with natures are primarily living things, such as plants and animals, including humans. For Aristotle, then, nature is, right from the start, not just whatever happens, the undifferentiated totality of what there is (as it is for Mill and others from the nineteenth century on). Nature is already a world of things that organize themselves and live characteristic lives, and to understand nature is to come to understand what kind of lives these are. Nature is active, a system of living and changing things. There is no hint in Aristotle of the view, notorious in many scientists since the early modern period, that nature is passive, lying out there to be mastered by the scientific mind.

Still less is there the even more notorious idea that nature is there for us to exploit. For Aristotle, skill and expertise take further what nature has begun. He is thinking of farmers who breed grasses to produce food crops, and of cooking as a process of predigestion to enable us to consume otherwise inedible foods. It never occurs to him to think of technology as invasive of nature. (Doubtless this is partly because he is not aware of any technology sophisticated enough to do this.) Nor does it occur to him that human activities might upset nature's established balances. Humans hunt and eat animals and fish in the way these hunt one another and eat plants; it is all part of a self-regulating system. Many of Aristotle's ideas are, tragically, bound to sound quaint in our world, where humans have intervened disastrously in the workings of nature, wrecking ecosystems and exterminating species. For Aristotle the species, including humans, have always been there and always will be; what we want is to understand how they all fit in overall. That is why, in a famous passage, he defends the study of the 'lower' animals and how they work as being as worthy a human study as the grander study of the heavenly bodies. 'For in all natural things there is something wonderful.'

For Aristotle, we want to understand nature, including ourselves as parts of nature, because it is natural for humans to want to understand things. Isn't this circular, though? Yes, but the circularity does not matter. Aristotle's theories are naturalistic in the modern sense; they accept that the processes by which we come to understand nature are themselves a part of nature. They are not something mysteriously exempt from the conditions they study. Philosophy, including the study of nature, begins in wonder; we are puzzled and interested by what we find around us, and do not feel satisfied until we have adequate explanations for it. The search for explanation thus does not point beyond itself; for Aristotle it would be beside the point, as well as foolish, for us to try to understand nature in order to exploit it for our own ends. Hence, although different methods are appropriate for studying different areas of nature, we are puzzled, and seek explanations, in our own case in the same way as happens with other living and non-living things.

Explaining is finding out *why* things are as they are, and for Aristotle there are four basic ways of doing this, his so-called 'four causes', which appeal to what he calls form, matter, the moving cause, and the final cause, what the thing is for.

Teleology without Design

Aristotle is aware that his demand for teleological explanations, explanations in terms of final causes or what something is for, is contentious. He knows of previous thinkers who held that there are no goals in nature, and that we and the world around us are the contingent products of random events. Animals' teeth, for example, were held by some to be the product of random combinations of material, some of which turned out to be suited to animals' needs while others were not.

Aristotle's 'Four Causes'

Aristotle insists, against what he sees as the narrowness of previous philosophers, that there are four 'causes' which the enquirer into nature should make use of. What he has in mind is the different ways in which we explain natural processes and things, and he is insisting that there is not just one type of explanation, but many, which do not exclude one another. Aristotle's theory, though, is about the way the world is and not just the way we explain it; the four so-called 'causes' are different kinds of item which figure in what he thinks are the four fundamental types of explanation of nature.

One is the material cause or matter, the physical make-up of the thing, which puts considerable restrictions on what it can be and do. The second is the form. Aristotle gives examples of artefacts where the form is the shape, but in the case of a Living thing the form is more complex: it is, very roughly, the way of being alive which defines that kind of thing. The form of an oak tree is whatever it is which explains why the tree lives and *grows as an oak* from acorns, for example, and only in certain climates. Thirdly is the moving cause, the item initiating a change. Fourthly is the final cause or end, what the thing or process is for, something that has to be cited in showing how it functions.

Modern theories of causality have very different aims and assumptions, and would count only Aristotle's moving cause as a cause (and only with qualifications).

Aristotle, as often, does not think that this story is *completely* wrong; we do need the right kind of physical embodiment. But on its own it is inadequate to explain why we *always* (or nearly always) find that animals are well adapted to the lives they lead, and that their parts are formed in a way which performs the appropriate function. Teeth, for example: we find the sharp incisors at the front of the mouth, for tearing, and the blunt molars at the back, for chewing. We always find this, because it is a good arrangement for the animal. Unless something has gone wrong, we don't find animals struggling with bad arrangements (molars at the front, for example). Random happenings, Aristotle thinks, are quite inadequate as an explanation of how we get to the universal well-adaptedness to environments and lifestyles that we find among animals. Thus, he concludes, our explanations have to include what the thing is for. Aristotle does not think that this is always appropriate: there is nothing, for example, that horses or camels are for. The level of explanation that concerns him is that of the parts of animals. Hearts, for example, are for pumping out the blood to the rest of the body; blood, in turn, is for carrying nutriment to the body.

Aristotle's is an especially interesting position, because we can now appreciate both that he is wrong, and that at the time he had the better of the argument. In the absence of any plausible mechanism for getting to (almost) universal well-adaptedness from random happenings, as well as the absence of any idea of geological time, Aristotle is right in thinking that present well-adaptedness cannot be accounted for merely by random happenings. After Darwin's work, we can see why we are not compelled to an Aristotelian view by the kind of consideration that Aristotle stresses.

Aristotle's teleological approach is the source of his most sympathetic insights. In plants, he comments, the roots have the function that the head has in animals; but we should not think of plants as growing upside down, since what is up and what down depends on the kind of thing we are talking about. Crabs are the only animals which move sideways; but in a sense they are moving forwards, since their eyes are so positioned that they can see where they are going. In these and many other cases Aristotle frees himself from human ways of thinking of things like nutrition and movement to observe how well the species functions from its own point of view.

Aristotle's thoughts about teleology have nothing to do with the idea that purposes in nature are the product of design indeed, for him this would be inappropriate projection of human concerns onto nature, shaping nature in our image in an absurdly pretentious way. But Aristotle's was not the only version of teleology available in the ancient world.

Teleology with Design

In his dialogue *Timaeus*, Plato presents an account of the universe as created by God, who is a craftsman and who produces our universe in the way that a craft worker creates an artefact, by imposing form and order on materials which are more or less satisfactory for the task. Plato holds that the materials available to God for making the world are inherently unsatisfactory and perhaps even refractory, since our world is created to a good plan, but contains failure and evil.

It is uncertain, and was much discussed in the ancient world, whether Plato had in mind an actual creation or was merely giving an analysis of the ways things are, but certainly the overall picture is one in which our world is not just created, but created to carry out an intellectual design on the part of a creator. Moreover, not merely the general principles of cosmology, but some quite specific details, particularly concerning humans, are explained in terms of overall design. The fact that humans walk upright, and have roughly spherical heads, is explained by reference to our being rational in a way that other animals are not; the explanations, as we might expect, are extremely fanciful.

The *Timaeus*, however, presents itself not as serious cosmology but merely as a 'likely story', an example of the kind of account that Plato thinks is the right one to give; it is poetic and grandiose in style. And the account it gives is also very openly 'top-down', working through the consequences of a few very general principles; Plato shows no interest in satisfying the observations we make in our experience, or in making any himself.

The Stoics picked up on Plato's account of the world as the creation of a designer God, and developed it, though in a somewhat different direction. Their conception of God is different; for them God is to be thought of not as a creator of the world, but in a more impersonal way. God is simply the rational organization of the world, and so should not be thought of on the model of a person (though the Stoics allow that popular religion, which accepts several gods, is a dim grasp of the idea that the world is structured by reason and intelligence).

The Stoics therefore take a different tack from Plato's appeal to the idea that God is like a craftsman. They appeal to evidence in the world that suggests that it is the product of design and rational ordering. They reject the idea that the world is the product of random events and forces, on the grounds that it is implausible like, they say, the idea that random distribution of letters of the alphabet could produce a poem.

Some of their arguments for design in the world appeal to the sheer complexity of natural objects. Suppose, one argument goes, that a complicated mechanism like a clock were shown to people unfamiliar with it; they would still recognize it as the product of a rational being. Hence, natural objects, which display a greater complexity and suitability for their function than artefacts, must be the product of reason clearly a reason greater than ours, one embodied in the universe as a whole.

Other arguments appeal to the complexity of the world's organization, seen as a huge ecosystem in which all the parts are mutually interdependent. The Stoics also appeal to the way that animals are well suited to their environments and mutual interrelations, but they are not interested in these for their own sakes, merely for the indication they give that the world is a well-organized whole.

Thinking of the world as designed, the Stoics often compare it to a house or a city, and since these are obviously designed for the sake of their inhabitants, this makes prominent the point that for the Stoics the world is rationally designed for the obvious beneficiaries, namely rational beings that is, gods and humans. As far as humans are concerned, therefore, the rest of the world plants and animals is designed for our benefit. This leads the Stoics to a very anthropocentric view of the world, in which grain, olives and vines are for us to consume, sheep for clothing us with their fleeces, oxen for pulling our ploughs and so forth. Such a world-view is almost guaranteed to kill the curiosity about nature's wonders that we find in Aristotle, and it leads to an exploitative attitude to the rest of the natural world, a strikingly ugly contrast to the humanitarian attitude we find in Stoic thought to all humans, whatever their social roles.

No Teleology?

Epicurus alone among the ancient schools denies that in nature we find any teleological explanations. Nothing in nature is for anything, neither the world as a whole nor anything in it.

Positively, Epicurus asserts that our world, and in the course of time infinitely many worlds, have grown up as a result of random collisions of atoms in empty space. This is, he claims, a sufficient explanation, given enough time. We have seen that given the state of other beliefs about the world in ancient culture (for example the absence of any indication of the real age of the world), Epicurus' position here was bound to seem weaker than it does to us, and one reason that one or other form of teleology was so common in ancient thought was just the implausibility of the alternative.

Epicurus also argues against the opposition, and here appeals to the idea that an unbiased view of our world does not make it look like the product of design, or at any rate of a very good design. Most of the world is not habitable by humans, for example; human attempts to survive are constantly threatened by the unpredictability of natural factors (droughts, hurricanes and so on) and by hostile environments and other species that render human life a struggle. Humans, with their helpless babyhood and lack of natural weapons, do not seem particularly well-adapted to compete for survival with other species. And so on.

Epicurus' arguments are effective only against the view that the world was providentially designed for the benefit of humans. Even so, there are responses: perhaps the problems humans encounter are due to the fact that rational design in the universe has only inferior materials to order. And Epicurus never really meets the point that with no appeal to any kind of purpose in nature he has a hard time explaining how random collisions of atoms result in the *regular* well-adaptedness of species to their environments.

Ancient Theories and The Modern World

The legacy of these ancient disputes became greatly simplified. Already in the ancient world both Jews and Christians found Plato *Timaeus* acceptable as a philosophical explication of the creation story in Genesis. This is not surprising, since the Judaeo-Christian God is the creator of the world, and designed it so as to be good. Moreover, humans have a privileged place in it. In the Middle Ages the view that prevailed was the design view: everything in the world, including us (indeed especially us) was created to fulfil its place in the world, which is to be found in God's design for it. Humans are the special beneficiaries of this plan, and the rest of creation is designed for us to put to our use.

In the Middle Ages, when Aristotle's views were rediscovered, they were fitted into the design view, since they were fitted into a theological framework in which the world is the creation of a designer God. Aristotle's own more subtle position was not appreciated; the only alternatives were seen as being that the world is the result of divine design or that it is the product of mere random happenings. The latter view was not taken seriously until the Renaissance, when Epicurus' views again became influential and inspired some philosophers to reject the entire medieval world-view.

This world-view included, and indeed had itself largely come to be formed by, the philosophy of Aristotle. But that itself had become greatly altered in the process. Aristotle's view of nature, including his ideas about ends in nature, had become part of a large theological system. In the process, his own tentative and co-operative methodology was forgotten as his ideas were hardened into a system, increasingly seen as a complete and all inclusive system, with answers to everything. The medieval poet Dante calls Aristotle 'the master of those who know' in other words, the great know-it-all, something very different in spirit from Aristotle's own enquiry in a spirit of curiosity and wonder.

The new learning of the Renaissance replaced the system of Aristotelianism, but because this had become deeply entrenched in the universities it hung on for surprisingly long, and became associated with self-protective and reactionary rejection of new kinds of thinking. A similar phenomenon happened with Aristotle's ethical and political thought, which was elevated to a central place by the Roman Catholic Church. This rigidification of Aristotle's thinking has led to equally unsubtle rejections of his ideas, and to refusal to engage with them in detail. In periods when Aristotle was regarded as The Great Authority, intelligent thinkers have often rejected that authority, while Aristotle's own attitude has been lost. Because Aristotle's own works are quite difficult to read, hostile attitudes to his ideas get passed on from book to book, and get accepted by people who have never actually engaged with him as a philosopher. Even today, it is quite common to find sometimes paranoid hostility to Aristotle on the part of people who have never read more than a few quotations pulled out of context and who think of him simply as an authority to be rejected.

This is an extreme example of the way in which ideas from ancient philosophy can get used and reconfigured by subsequent traditions, in a way which pulls them out of their original context of argument. Sometimes this can be invigorating, and produce a new and fruitful engagement, as happened when Plato *Republic* became a political text in the nineteenth century.

Aristotle and Authority

'The investigation of the truth is in one way hard, in another easy. An indication of this is found in the fact that no one is able to attain the truth adequately, while, on the other hand, no one fails entirely, but every one says something true about the nature of things, and while individually they contribute little or nothing to the truth, by the union of all a considerable amount is amassed. Therefore, since the truth seems to be like the proverbial barn door, which no one can fail to hit, in this way it is easy, but the fact that we can have a whole truth and not the particular part we aim at shows the difficulty of it. It is just that we should be grateful, not only to those whose opinions we may share, but also to those who have expressed more superficial views; for these also contributed something, by developing before us the powers of thought.'

'When a Schoolman tells me Aristotle hath said it, all I conceive he means by it, is to dispose me to embrace his opinion with the deference and submission which custom has annexed to that name. And this effect may be so instantly produced in the minds of those who are accustomed to resign their judgement to the authority of that philosopher, as it is impossible any idea either of his person, writings or reputation should go before. So close and immediate a connexion may custom establish, betwixt the very word Aristotle and the motions of assent and reverence in the minds of some men.'

Bishop George Berkeley century and with Aristotle for much of the Middle Ages. But if the interpretative tradition goes on too long (especially without serious competition) and gets too rigid and institutionalized, the result can become stultifying, and can end with hostile unthinking rejection. And this makes it harder to get back to the original and engage with it from our own perspective.

Many people have turned expectantly to the beginnings of Greek philosophy, only to find that the first philosopher they meet, Thales in the sixth century BC, held, apparently, that 'everything is water'. Anyone teaching ancient philosophy has to cope with the bafflement that this discovery tends to produce. It is an odd beginning to a philosophical tradition. Yet *something* happens in the sixth century, later to acquire the name *philosophia* or love of wisdom, which we can recognize as philosophical. What exactly is it?

It is in keeping with what we have seen of the varied and disputatious nature of ancient philosophy that this question is quite hard to answer. There is little that non-trivially unites philosophers from Thales to the end of antiquity. There is a tradition, but a mixed and contested one.

In view of the great cultural prestige of Greek philosophy, it has at times been resented, and sometimes groups that have felt themselves culturally marginalized by it have claimed that Greek philosophy is nothing new at all, but just a tradition taken over without acknowledgement usually, it is claimed, from the group in question. The early Church fathers held that the pagan philosophers stole their ideas from the Jewish scriptures.

Afrocentric writers in the twentieth century have made the same claim for Egyptian mystery religion. These claims, however, are historically non-starters.

Differing Views on the Greeks' Originality

'What provokes admiration is the mental vigour and independence with which these people sought after coherent systems and did not shrink from following their Lines of thought to astonishing conclusions. It may well be that contact with oriental cosmology and theology helped to Liberate their imagination; it certainly gave them many suggestive ideas. But they taught themselves to reason. Philosophy as we understand it is a Greek idea.'

Martin West, 1986

'What is Plato but Moses writing in Greek?'

Numenius of Apamea (second century AD).

'We should not be surprised to say that the Greeks are capable of filching the beliefs of the Jews, given that they have not only plundered their other sciences from the Egyptians and Chaldaeans and other foreign nations, but even now can be caught robbing one another of their Literary reputations.

It is reasonable to think that the Greeks, who contributed nothing of their own in wisdom (only verbal facility and fluency) and filched everything from foreigners, should also have been aware of the sayings of the Jews and Laid hands on these in turn . . . Not just my words but their own establish them as thieves.'

Eusebius, Bishop of Caesarea (AD c.260–339)

The Greeks themselves did not think that philosophy was original with them; they thought of it as coming from a variety of sources outside Greece, usually Eastern. But then, they did not value originality as such very highly, and they certainly did think that philosophy was something that they did distinctively and well. And indeed, when we read the fragments even of an author as elusive as Thales we can see an interesting and distinctive way of thinking emerging.

Tradition of Reasoning

What makes it philosophical? Usually this is characterized as explicit appeal to *reason* and *argument*. Stated as generally as this, the claim is undoubtedly true. Philosophers are distinguished by arguing for their conclusions and against other philosophers' conclusions, and by demanding reasons for others' claims and giving reasons for their own. But while this may mark philosophy off from poetry and the like, it does not give us a very determinate way of proceeding, or of marking philosophy off from other intellectual endeavours. There are many kinds of reason and argument which is to count? When we look at the different kinds of project that the Presocratics produced, we are hard put to find a single kind of reasoning at work, or a demand for a single kind of argument.

The first Presocratics, Thales, Anaximander, and Anaximenes from Miletus in Asia Minor were concerned to provide cosmologies, reasoned accounts of the world we live in. As Aristotle acutely saw, they focused on what he called the material cause the question of what our world is composed of. This is the question to which we find answers in terms of water, air and 'the boundless'. These answers show a very striking degree of simplicity and economy, and bring with them explanations of a wide variety of puzzling physical phenomena. Because of this, these philosophers have at times been seen as precursors of science, with its explanatory hypotheses. It is clear, however, that there is little in these very speculative theories that can be usefully compared with any precise concept of scientific enquiry. A just account has to see these Presocratic figures as transitional, with an intellectual impulse to render our world explicable which has much in common with later philosophy and science.

Other Presocratics are anything but scientific. Heraclitus of Ephesus writes in aphorisms of notorious obscurity, uniting an account of the world as fire with concern for the individual's self-knowledge. His account of both appeals to reason (*logos*), both your individual reason and the big Reason in the universe that your reason should try to conform to; yet there is little reason or argument to convince us of this. Xenophanes of Colophon uses reason and argument to undermine naive beliefs about the gods. In him we see clearly for the first time reason being used to fault and replace ordinary beliefs by something the philosopher argues to be more

New Way of Thinking

'My aim has been to show that a new thing came into the world with the early Ionian teachers the thing we call science. It is quite wrong to took for the origins of Ionian science in mythological ideas of any kind. It is to these men we owe the conception of an exact science which should ultimately take in the whole world as its object.'

John Burnet, 1892

'I have tried to show how the philosopher retains his prophetic character. He relies for his vision of divinity and of the real nature of things on the assumed identity of his own reason with a portion of the cosmic consciousness. The intuitive reason replaces that supernormal faculty which had formerly been active in dreams and prophetic visions; the supernatural becomes the metaphysical. It would have been a miracle if the wise men of the sixth century should have swept their minds clean of all mythical preconceptions.'

Francis Cornford, 1952 rationally adequate. Anthropomorphic views of God are shown to be defective in a convincing way: every people, Xenophanes says, makes gods in their own image (and so would animals, if they could). But his allegedly more rationally adequate conception of God is so peculiar God seems to be a kind of sphere that the issue is bound to arise of what the authority is of the reasoning that overthrows our beliefs and gets us to this point.

This question arises extremely sharply for Parmenides and Zeno of Elea, authors of some of the most notorious arguments in antiquity. Parmenides produced an abstract argument to a conclusion that nobody could accept: namely, that there is really only one object we can think of or refer to, which cannot without absurdity be said to be pluralized, qualified or divided. Thus our experience of a varied and changing plurality of objects is totally misleading. Zeno produced many arguments reducing to absurdity our everyday assumptions about plurality and change. The problem here is that the arguments are hard to fault, but the conclusions cannot be accepted. This creates a discomfort about reasoned argument: what do we do when its results conflict with our beliefs?

Responses to this differ. Some thinkers continue to produce big explanatory theories of the world, taking on board the point that their theories undermine common-sense beliefs. Anaxagoras of Clazomenae tells us that 'the Greeks are mistaken' in saying that things come into and go out of existence; in terms of his theory what emerges was there already. Similarly Empedocles of Acragas and the Atomists Leucippus and Democritus of Abdera produce theories which revise our commonsense beliefs about reality and change in accordance with their own hypotheses. None of them doubt that their reasoning has the power to do this. None of them deal adequately with the question of how we get to their theories from the beliefs we all start with—indeed Democritus recognizes a problem in that we get from our experience to the deliverances of reason, which then devalues our experience.

Other thinkers, however, including some of the sophists, fasten on the point that there is something suspicious about the way that philosophical reasoning leads by arguments that you can't fault to conclusions that you can't accept. Cleverness in argument becomes something to be feared and envied, and seen as a technique in its own right. Seen this way, there is little distinguishing philosophical reasoning from the amoral cleverness of the effective speaker in politics or the law courts.

This situation can reasonably be seen as rather a mess, and goes some way to explain why these philosophers have come to be called 'Presocratics', implying that Socrates is the crucial reference point. Whatever their individual accomplishments, they do not clearly belong within a unified tradition in which reasoning has a clear philosophical role. That begins with Socrates.

Reason and Understanding

Socrates seems an unlikely figure to characterize the philosophical tradition. He is the perpetual amateur, who refuses to do any of the things which philosophers of his time did. Moreover, he utterly despises all these things producing theories of the world, giving displays of oratory, winning debates as being a pretentious waste of everybody's time. So what made him such a founding philosophical figure?

Socrates, as we have seen, argued against the views of others, showing them by their inability to withstand his arguments that they lacked understanding of what they were talking about. To have understanding of something, it emerged, you have to be able to 'give an account' of it, where this means giving reasons, and ultimately a rational account of what the subject in question is. But this will not be possible until you have rigorously asked yourself what reasons there are for the belief you hold. Thus, when you ask someone what reasons they have for what they say, you can show that they lack understanding if they have none, or have reasons that are confused or inconsistent. But, particularly if you are good at this sort of questioning (as Socrates undoubtedly was), you will realize that the same applies to you; you may have developed views, but you cannot be said to understand them, and hence have the right to put them forward authoritatively, unless you can withstand the challenges of others by giving reasons for them.

From Socrates on, reasoned argument is the lifeblood of philosophy because it is only in the give and take of argument that we achieve understanding of the positions we hold and want to put forward to others. Hence the emphasis on reasoning and arguing that we find in all schools of philosophy. Now we find emerging a clear sense of *philosophical* reason and argument, distinguished from merely arguing others down and linked to the search for truth and understanding.

From the outside, then as now, all the arguing can seem aggressive and unattractive, and to those with no gift for philosophy it can seem pointless. (There is a story of a Roman bureaucrat who summoned all the Athenian philosophers and offered conflict mediation so as finally to settle all their disputes.) But from now on the importance in philosophy of reasoned argument lies in its crucial role for understanding. Figures who dismiss argument like the Pythagoreans, who reverence their Master and want only to treasure his words are always seen as philosophically marginal. And Epicurus' relative de-emphasis of argument led to criticism by other philosophical schools.

Philosophy as a Subject

Plato has a claim to be the first philosopher to establish philosophy as a subject. He did so by taking over from Socrates two elements: argument as crucial for understanding, and positive views on a variety of matters. Plato added three other important elements. One is system, a variety of ideas seen as holding together. A second is seeing philosophy as self-consciously demarcated from other ways of thinking. And a third is the institutionalization of philosophy as a subject for study.

In the ancient world Plato was seen as a pivotal figure, the first philosopher who was concerned to systematize his ideas and thus to hold views on a wide variety of topics as holding together in a mutually supportive way. It is unclear whether it is quite fair to see Plato as the pioneer here – Democritus the Atomist also had views on a range of topics but Plato is certainly the first to do it whose works we have. Later writers ascribed to Plato the honour of being the first to see philosophy as a system of ideas with three parts logic, ethics and physics. This is anachronistic, but it is true that Plato held positions over most of the range that later thinkers were to cover.

Plato does not tell us how his positive systematic ideas relate to the need for understanding to be grounded by argument. But he shows us clearly enough, in writing dialogues in which he is personally never a speaker, thus detaching himself from the positions put forward, that what matters is not just having the right position, but holding it in the right way understanding it on the basis of reasoned argument. For it is up to the reader to think about the positions put forward and test her own understanding of them. Plato, even where it is clear that he believes a position strongly, never puts it forward authoritatively. If the reader accepts it on Plato's authority, she is missing something crucial. It has to be tested and argued for before she understands it.

Plato's legacy has been a divided one. His own school, the Academy, for most of its life took philosophizing in Plato's way to be arguing against the views of contemporaries *ad hominem*, without commitment to a position of your own. It was not till after the end of the school, in the first century BC, that philosophers started to study and promote Plato's own ideas as a system. Interpretations of Plato perpetually risk overstressing one side at the expense of the other seeing him as throwing the argument over to us, and seeing him as passionately concerned to put forward certain positions.

It is modern rather than ancient interpreters who have stressed Plato's evident desire to establish philosophy as a distinct way of thinking. When he has Socrates tell us at the end of the Republic that there is an old quarrel between poetry (or literature more generally) and philosophy, he seems to be projecting his own view back. For one of the most striking things about Plato is the way that he is willing to use his own brilliant literary gifts to establish that philosophy is crucially about 'dialectic', sheer argument which does not rely on rhetorical or literary skill. Philosophy, he keeps insisting, is just for this reason *different* from what other people, such as orators, poets and sophists do.

Whatever the tensions this produces in Plato's own work, one of his lessons was well learned. Later philosophy develops for itself a professional style: straightforward, transparent, relying only on the force of rational argument. Unsurprisingly, this is often unattractive to ordinary readers, and we find that a gulf comes about between easier, more literary works written for the general public and 'real' philosophy, written in an uncompromisingly professional and technical way.

This gulf is also strengthened by philosophy's institutionalization. We know almost no detail about the organization of Plato's school, the Academy, though in every age philosophers have interpreted it on the model of their own university or college. But it was something new, a philosophical school, to which young men like Aristotle came to study philosophy. They probably learned Plato's ideas; they also learned how to argue. When, later in life, Aristotle set up his own philosophical school, this was seen by some as an uppity gesture, but it established the pattern whereby an original philosopher would set up his own school, finding pupils and disciples who would learn, further and spread his ideas. Hence Plato's philosophy and Aristotle's philosophy came to have a history in their own schools; they became objects of study to other philosophers.

Once we get schools of philosophy the Stoic and Epicurean schools getting established on similar principles we can see the activity of ancient philosophers as astonishingly like the activity of modern philosophers. Although Plato, who was rich, refused to take fees for teaching, payment by pupils soon became a necessary feature of the system. Young men (and occasionally young women) would join a philosophical school as part of their education. (Or they might have a trained philosopher as a tutor at home.) They were educated to understand and appreciate important philosophical ideas, many of which were already part of their cultural heritage. In the schools, they were also trained in argument, acquiring abilities which had more practical application when they left, in politics and law, for example. Those most gifted at philosophy, and committed to it, would stay and become part of the school's permanent philosophical community. This does not sound so unlike the picture of philosophy teaching in universities today. (Or rather, in the less rigid university system that existed before degrees and grades came to be important as credentials.) This idea of philosophy as a kind of university education continued on until late in the ancient world, throughout vast political and cultural changes.

The similarity extends to many of the specific ways in which philosophy was carried on. We find philosophers writing treatises and essays, and also books of arguments against other philosophers' treatises and essays. We find commentaries on texts of past philosophers, especially Plato and Aristotle. We find controversies within a school, for example as to which of two contemporaries has got Epicurus right. We also find extensive arguments against other contemporary schools. In their style and purpose many of these works are quite like modern philosophy journal articles and books. Indeed, modern philosophy students can find it easier to relate to works of this kind, the products of philosophical professionalism, than to Plato's dialogues, which are in form unlike any modern kind of philosophical writing.

Philosophy after Plato is, then, the history of philosophical schools (with two exceptions, to which we shall return). There is an interesting shadow side to it—a running complaint till the end of antiquity about bogus philosophers, who use philosophy's prestige to further their private agenda, whether money or reputation. The bogus philosopher, high minded in class and money-grubbing outside it, is a stock figure of ridicule. This brings home the fact that in the ancient world philosophy was taken to offer people not only intellectual challenge but also practical help in living a better life and finding answers to the search for the meaning of life. Philosophers were expected not only to convey intellectual skills but also to provide in their own persons examples of the search for living well.

Nowadays we are more likely to seek the latter in religion, or in less intellectual pursuits. Ancient philosophers did not offer just one subject among many, but a subject that was uniquely close to the hearts of their audience.

A Diverse Range of Schools

Although Aristotle was Plato's pupil, in some ways his is the least representative of the schools which formed after the Academy. This is because of Aristotle's own huge range of interests. He studied, furthered or invented a wide range of subjects, from literary theory to logic, from economics to biology. The works he left behind are vast, some of them theoretical treatises and others more like records of research. In this respect Aristotle's school differs from the philosophical schools that come after him, which had narrower interests.

The Stoics' school began, as the earlier ones had, in a public place; Epicurus was unusual in holding his school in a private residence, the Garden. And Epicurus was unusual also in requiring his views to be held deferentially and memorized. But before very long the Epicurean school and its offshoots in other places were doing very similar things to the Stoics and other schools arguing and counter-arguing, commenting on founding texts, generally continuing the philosophical activity of the founders. Every generation of students needs to learn afresh and understand philosophical positions for themselves, and hence even philosophical schools dedicated to teaching the thought of the founders will develop philosophically in the give and take of philosophical interpretation. Moreover, with changing political and social circumstances new issues had to be dealt with and new challenges met. When the Romans became rulers of the Mediterranean, for example, Greek intellectuals started educating unintellectual Romans.

From the first century BC we find that the continuing debates between the schools give rise to some schools which are hybrids, or 'eclectic' combining positions from different schools to form a new stance. One who was influential in his day was Antiochus, who thought that the core views of Plato, Aristotle and the Stoics on a number of issues were compatible, and that the differences had been overplayed. Histories of philosophy tend to rank these schools lower in interest than those founded by more original thinkers. But we can sympathize with their position. Once philosophy has formed a teaching tradition, it can well seem foolish to seek originality at all costs, and sounder to argue from and build on what are already going positions. This is what most philosophers do today, so we should pause before turning up our noses.

In the late Roman republic and early Empire, ancient philosophy arguably had a heyday. There were no more great original thinkers, but a variety of philosophical schools flourished and interacted. A serious student would have widespread opportunities to learn and think about the ideas of a variety of philosophical schools spread throughout the Roman Empire. (By this time Athens had lost its previous dominance as a centre of philosophy, which it had held from Plato to the first century BC, and cities like Alexandria and Rome itself were as important intellectually.) Philosophy was familiar and accessible to educated people throughout the Empire. It has seldom been the case that so rich and varied an intellectual tradition has been so culturally widespread and so important to many people. Until the end of antiquity the only significant new school was a third century AD reformulation of an old one — Plotinus' rethinking of Plato's ideas in a new and original synthesis, giving rise to the school we call Neoplatonism, one which flourished in later centuries.

In the mix were two philosophical movements mentioned earlier, which were anti-schools rather than schools. But in its own terms it is self-defeating for a Pyrrhonist to set up as an authority on anything, even the nature of Pyrrhonism. For this would convict him of firm enough commitment to some beliefs to threaten sceptical tranquillity. Hence Pyrrhonism could never coherently be an institutionalized school. This is one reason why we know so little about its spread and influence.

The second 'anti-school' movement is the Cynics, deriving from the fourth-century figure Diogenes of Sinope, who set a model which was followed rather than setting up any formal institution. Cynics took their name from dogs (the ancient symbol of shamelessness), went in for street preaching and lived in ways which deliberately flouted social norms, the aim being to 'return to nature' by rejecting social convention. Some Cynics did teach informally, but as a philosophy it remained a way of life, attracting moralizing drop-outs. It could never be a philosophical school, since Cynics rejected reasoned argument, taking it that there is really nothing difficult to understand and that the answers to life's problems are simple.

The Final Break

The end of ancient philosophy as a living tradition is hard to date, especially since the end of antiquity the culture of Greece and Rome is also not something to which a neat date can be given. When the Roman Empire split, the Eastern, Byzantine empire retained political and cultural unity, and philosophy remained there as an academic study, though in partial and restricted form. In the Western part all such unity crumbled, and philosophical texts were (some of them) preserved in monasteries by people who were no longer part of the tradition they contained. Even knowledge of Greek, the language of the major texts, was lost. When philosophy developed again, some of the tradition, mainly Aristotle and some Plato, became part of it, but within a different, theological framework. Not until the Renaissance did it become possible to study the ancient texts independently, and study of Aristotle still has to contend with the after-effects of his medieval transformation.

There is therefore something to be said for dating the end of ancient philosophy, as a living tradition, in AD 529, the year in which the Christian Emperor Justinian closed the schools of pagan philosophy in Athens. Like many famous historical moments, this one crumbles somewhat under historical investigation. Athens had long ceased to be the major philosophical centre; it is not clear that any philosophical schools were functioning there other than the Platonists; Justinian did not actually close the schools, but at most seems to have forbidden pagans to teach, and the decree does not seem to have been effective. Pagan philosophy was in trouble before 529, and trickled on to some extent afterwards.

Yet there is a rightness to the idea that it was intolerance by a Christian Emperor that marked the tradition's end. Jews and Christians in the ancient world had always faced a choice between rejecting philosophy entirely in favour of faith and loyalty to scripture, and trying to incorporate at least some philosophy into their own traditions. They did this by claiming that philosophy was a development in distorted form of some of the deep truths in Judaism and Christianity. Such an approach, however, is not only selective but curtails drastically the space for reason and argument, always so central to the activity of ancient philosophers. Jewish and Christian writers in the ancient world have by and large served as transmitters to us of (parts of the philosophical tradition, rather than as participants in it. With Christianity a single intellectual view of the world was imposed, and philosophy was mostly unable to continue its task of questioning and reasoning about our beliefs.

Ancient Philosophy and Philosophy Today

Since its recovery, ancient philosophy has played a mostly respected and occasionally influential role in the development of philosophy in Western European countries, which have seen themselves as the inheritors of the culture of the ancient Greek and Roman world, and also in philosophy in countries culturally influenced by Western Europe, such as North America and Australia. Different parts of the hugely varied ancient tradition have been found compelling at different times. The Stoics were influential in the eighteenth century, relegated to specialist studies in the nineteenth; exactly the opposite happened to Plato. At times the idea of Great Thinkers has led to a view of 'the canon' as a parade of Great Thoughts, to the neglect of their argumentative context. The tradition has been capacious enough to give rise to an variety of differing engagements — all, for the last three centuries at least, appreciating the importance to it of reasoned argument for philosophical understanding.

There has, however, been one unfortunate result of this stress on reason and argument. It has sometimes given rise, in the later ancient world and also in the twentieth century, to a simplifying tendency to see other philosophical traditions, particularly 'Eastern' ones, as radically different and 'other', characterized by lessened emphasis on argument and a greater stress on mysticism and a search for wisdom by non-rational means. This has sometimes led to the view that they are more primitive than the 'Western' tradition, because it honours reason. But it has also led, by reaction, to the view that they are more profound than the 'Western' tradition, which prizes what gets seen as superficial squabbling. In the late twentieth century especially, sweeping attacks have been mad on reason and its place in the 'Western' tradition, and ancient philosophy has often been the subject of (usually ill-informed) attacks.

Both tendencies have been unfortunate; they lead to crude contrasts which are unhelpful and in large part untrue. This holds particularly with respect to the philosophy of India. Ancient India produced a large and wide philosophical tradition, encompassing materialism, scepticism and empiricism as well as schools tending to mysticism and forms of idealism a tradition which is comparable to ancient Greek and Roman philosophy in extent and variety. Yet both Westerners and many Indians have (unless they are specialists) emphasized only those schools that form a contrast to Western philosophy. Students often think that 'Eastern' philosophy, including Indian, will be all similar and nothing like the 'Western' tradition. We have yet to reach a completely post-colonial view, which can get beyond the false contrast of 'Western rationalism' and 'Eastern mysticism' and recognizes the strong affinities between some of the Indian traditions and ancient Greek and Roman traditions more familiar in the West. (It has been suggested, for example, that there are affinities between Pyrrhonian scepticism and the Madhyamika school of North Indian Buddhism, whose founding figure is Nagarjuna, who was perhaps contemporary with Sextus Empiricus. In view of the story that Pyrrho earlier visited North India with Alexander's army, there is even the possibility of historical influences on both sides, particularly given the continued Greek presence in Northern India.)

I shall close with a view of ancient philosophy by an intellectual insider with an outsider's perspective Lucian of Samosata, a second century AD satirical author. In his essay *The Runaways* he has Philosophy remind her father, the chief god Zeus, of the reason he sent her down to earth in the first place, namely so that humans, hitherto ignorantly and violently mismanaging their lives, would do better. First, she continues, she went to India, to the Brahmans, then to Ethiopia, Egypt and Babylon, and then to Thrace, the wild north. Finally she went to the Greeks, which she had thought would be the easy part, given their intellectual reputation. But it turned out to be harder than she expected. After a promising start, the Sophists mixed philosophy up with — well, sophistry. And then the Athenians executed Socrates! Philosophy goes on to complain about the less than wonderful time she went on to have in Greece. Most people respect her, she says, though without much understanding her, and there are genuine philosophers who love and strive for truth, and this makes it all worth while. But there are also bogus philosophers who aim only at money and status, and bring her into discredit, and they drive her crazy. She needs a bit of divine help to improve the situation.

In the ancient Greco-Roman world philosophy, for better and worse, became a subject, with its own practices, texts and institutions. It was a more urgent matter to its practitioners and its audience than it is for us now. Philosophy was seen as a natural extension of an ordinary good education, given the importance of living well, and the importance of philosophy for doing that. For us there is more of a tension than there was for the ancients between the idea that philosophy enables us to understand ourselves and the world, and the idea that it is a rigorous and intellectually demanding matter. The important role in life played by philosophy in the ancient world has been taken over by a variety of other interests and pursuits. But philosophy still matters, and in many ways we can still relate our concerns to those of the ancients, and find that our study of them leads naturally to direct philosophical engagement. We still have Philosophy's problem and, lacking divine help, we still have to do the work, search for the truth, and expose the bogus for ourselves.

5

Libertarian Challenge for Modern Philosophy

Introduction

The income should correspond to contribution, others say that it should correspond to effort or need, and still others say that it should correspond to a more abstract criterion such as the maximization of average utility or the distribution specified by Rawls's difference principle. In an important book published in 1974, Robert Nozick offered a radical challenge to any such "patterned" theory of justice.

In the real world, of course, it is highly unlikely that any society would ever achieve a distribution of income that would perfectly match the ideal pattern stipulated by some philosophical theory of distributive justice. But, just for the sake of argument, suppose that some society somewhere did do just that. This society has achieved a state of perfect justice in distribution, and accordingly each individual in this society is justly entitled to hold the income that he or she holds. Now a disturbing thing happens. Michael Jordan, having retired from professional basketball, offers to play exhibition basketball for the public in exchange for a $2 admission fee. Millions of fans are delighted at the chance to see Jordan play again and consider the admission fee a real bargain. Each of these fans pays for his admission fee out of his own, on our own view, just holdings. But the resultant distribution of wealth, involving the transfer of millions of dollars from the fans to Michael Jordan, violates the perfect pattern of justice that had been achieved. Must we then deny that the fans and Jordan had a right to enter into their mutually satisfying agreement?

Any pattern of distribution, once achieved, is likely to be upset by acts of individuals with respect to the dispersement of the income they hold. A harmless gift between lovers would lead from a distribution satisfying the pattern of justice to a distribution not satisfying that pattern. Hence, any patterned theory of justice seems to require an extensive and continuous interference with the liberty of individuals to do with their income what they like. Liberty upsets patterns, and any political philosophy that attempts to realize on earth some ideal pattern of justice will be forced to pervasively interfere with the liberty of individual persons. Libertarianism, the political philosophy defended by Nozick, rejects ally such interference with individual liberty. It is a political philosophy based on the consistent and inviolable defense of individual liberty as the fundamental principle of all political and social life.

Liberalism and Liberty

The libertarian challenge to theories of distributive justice can serve as the basis for a re-examination of the place of liberty in the liberal tradition. There can be no doubt that liberals, both classical and new, have always proclaimed their love of liberty, but the libertarian challenge raises deep concerns about the centrality of liberty in the liberal vision and the strength of the philosophical commitment to liberty within liberalism.

Within classical liberalism, liberty was understood as negative freedom, as the absence of interference with the individual. John Stuart Mill's great defense of liberty in *On Liberty* clearly had such a negative conception of liberty in mind. The harm principle, which Mill claims should rightly govern all relations between the individual and society, says that "the sole end for which mankind are warranted, individually or collectively, in interfering with the liberty of action of any of their number, is self-protection." As we have seen, by "self-protection" Mill means the prevention of harm to other people. So long as an individual's action harms no one else, Mill argues that society may not interfere with that individual. Non-interference, or negative freedom, is thus the central idea of liberty in the Mill's classical liberalism.

In contrast, as we have seen, new liberals championed a positive conception of freedom, defined by T.H. Green as "a positive power or capacity of doing or enjoying something worth doing or enjoying." In the view of Green and the new liberals who followed his philosophical lead, freedom understood as the mere absence of interference by other people is not sufficient. For the new liberals, just as a negative freedom of movement is useless to a paraplegic who lacks the resources to get around, so too negative freedom without resources is empty for the poor and socially disadvantaged. In this way the new liberals sought to bring a concern for improving the lot of the poor and disadvantaged within the compass of the traditional liberal concern for freedom.

Mirroring the distinction between negative freedom and positive freedom is a distinction between negative rights and positive rights. As we have seen, classical liberalism incorporated into its conception of how political and social life should be organized the array of individual rights proclaimed by the American and French revolutionaries on the basis of their theories of natural law and natural rights. Liberals, even those who followed the dominant utilitarian thinking in rejecting the ideas of natural law and natural rights, believed that in a good society the primary function of government was the protection of such rights.

For the most part, these rights can be understood as

negative rights. That is, they are rights against the interference of other people or the interference of governments in our lives. Thus, for example, understood as negative rights, the right to life is a right not to be killed, and the right to liberty is a right not to be enslaved, imprisoned, or in any way held captive against one's will. The Bill of Rights, consisting of the first ten amendments to the Constitution of the United States, lists the familiar freedoms of religion, speech, press, assembly, and so on as rights that belong to the people and upon which the government may not infringe. Understood as the freedom to practice one's religion, to speak and write as one likes, and to assemble with others, all without interference by any other person, these rights are negative rights.

But, just as the new liberals added positive freedoms to negative freedoms, so too they added positive rights to negative rights. While negative rights are rights not to be interfered with, positive rights are rights to have some resource provided that is deemed necessary to living a morally acceptable form of life. Rights to education, housing, and medical care are all examples of such positive rights. They demand not just that governments and other individuals refrain from interference, but that positive steps be taken to provide schools, housing, and medical care to those who are too poor to provide them for themselves.

In the long period during which the philosophy of the new liberalism dominated thinking in most of the advanced industrial countries, from the closing decades of the nineteenth century until the 1970s, it was taken for granted by most political philosophers, and most practicing politicians, that securing positive freedoms and positive rights were the legitimate aims of good government. The "Four Freedoms" proclaimed by the administration of Franklin D. Roosevelt in 1942 included alongside the negative freedoms of speech and worship a clearly positive "freedom from want." And the same planning document that proclaimed this freedom from want also listed a "new bill of rights" that included positive rights to food, clothing, shelter, medical care, rest, and recreation. Similar commitments to positive freedoms and positive rights can be found in the United Nations Universal Declaration of Human Rights, adopted in 1948, and in many other national and international documents concerning human rights and the rights of citizens.

We have already seen how the new liberalism's extension of liberalism to include positive freedom and positive rights disturbed some of those thinkers who claimed allegiance to classical liberalism and its understanding of freedom and rights in terms of negative freedom and negative rights. In their view, the use of the concepts of positive freedom and positive rights to justify an increasingly large and increasingly intrusive welfare state marked a dangerous betrayal of classical liberalism's commitment to individual liberty. A.V. Dicey, a distinguished English legal scholar and a follower of the classical liberalism of James Mill during the middle of the nineteenth century, became a sharp critic of the new liberalism by the end of the century. Writing in 1896, Dicey pointed out that T.H. Green's positive definition of freedom was "unnatural" and that it lent support to a growing current of state intervention in the affairs of individuals and to "social despotism." In a similar vein, in *"From Freedom to Bondage,"* an essay published in 1891, the classical liberal Herbert Spencer attacked the new liberalism for its betrayal of liberty.

Similar criticisms of new liberalism as the enemy of liberty surfaced here and there throughout the long hegemony of new liberal philosophy. Prominent among these critics were F.A. Hayek, who argued in *The Road to Serfdom* that new liberal dreams of using the power of the state to eliminate poverty and injustice threaten individual liberty, and Milton Friedman, who argued in *Capitalism and Freedom* that the growing welfare state posed a threat to individual liberty. One might also mention here the many books of the novelist and essayist Ayn Rand, who vividly portrayed the totalitarian implications of Communism in her native Russia and championed individual liberty against the claims of government, society, and other individuals. Each of these thinkers shared the idea that the welfare state threatened individual liberty and each contributed to the critique of the new liberalism and to the development of libertarianism as an alternative to new liberalism in political philosophy.

Classical liberalism was born of the confluence of natural-rights theory and utilitarianism, with utilitarianism gaining ascendancy by early nineteenth century. For the most part, liberal thinkers followed Bentham in viewing the ideas of natural law and natural rights as "metaphysical" concepts, not verifiable by any experiential test, and tainted with theological presuppositions. Utilitarianism, which made no theological assumptions and dealt with the experientially confirmable states of human pain and pleasure, appeared more acceptable to the scientific outlook that came increasingly to dominate modern thought. Unfortunately, that utilitarianism provided at best only a shaky foundation for liberty and the rights of individuals championed by classical liberalism.

As we have seen, in *On Liberty* John Stuart Mill explicitly relinquishes "any advantage which could be derived to my argument from the idea of abstract liberty," and bases his case for liberty on the grounds that liberty is conducive to happiness. In a similar way, Adam Smith argues for freedom of trade on the grounds that free markets will maximize the wealth of nations and, consequently, the total amount of happiness produced. For utilitarians such as Mill and Smith, liberty is valuable only as a means to happiness; liberty has extrinsic value but not intrinsic value. While the arguments offered by Smith and Mill are powerful ones, resting on broad appeals to human nature, social science, and human experience, they leave room for possible abridgments of liberty.

For example, one might argue, as does a character in Dostoyevsky novel *The Brothers Karamazov*, that ultimately liberty brings greater suffering to human beings than they are able to bear. Were this true, the consistent utilitarian would have to abandon liberty, since for the utilitarian it is happiness, not liberty, that is the ultimate goal of political philosophy.

Such a wholesale abandonment of liberty was never a part of the thinking of the new liberalism. Indeed, leading new liberals such as Green, Hobhouse, and Dewey remained as convinced as Mill and Smith that there was a strong connection between liberty and happiness. Nevertheless, because they viewed liberty as a means to happiness, in principle they were willing to sacrifice specific claims to liberty where doing so could be shown to actually contribute to maximizing happiness. In particular, the new liberals were willing to restrict the liberty of property owners to do what they wanted with the property they owned in order to advance the positive freedoms of workers, and to tax the rich to support programs aimed at helping the poor for the sake of advancing the welfare of society as a whole. For utilitarians, the commitment to liberty was not absolute, but only conditional on liberty's conduciveness to happiness. For a political philosophy such as libertarianism, which makes an inviolable commitment to individual liberty its fundamental principle, utilitarianism is an unreliable ally.

Rights-Based Theories

In the very first sentence of *Anarchy, State, and Utopia*, Robert Nozick says, "Individuals have rights, and there are things no person or group may do to them (without violating their rights). So strong and far reaching are these rights that they raise the question of what, if anything, the state and its officials may do." The rights that Nozick claims here are not rights that are created by any government or any human agency. In this sense, they are natural rights, rights that human beings have simply in virtue of their existence as human beings. Among the rights central to Nozick's view is the right to liberty, a right to do what one wants with one's life without interference from government or any other person so long as one's actions do not interfere with the like liberty of others.

Nozick believes that the right to liberty forms a "side constraint" on what governments or other people may do. Suppose there is something the government would like to do that would greatly increase the total happiness of society as a whole but which involves violating my right to liberty. In saying that my right to liberty is a side constraint, Nozick means that it blocks any such governmental project. My right to liberty may not be violated even if doing so would achieve greater overall happiness. Further, suppose some dictator agrees to release a hundred political prisoners on the grounds that you capture me and turn me over to him to be his prisoner. By capturing me and achieving the release of the hundred political prisoners, you would maximize non-violations of the right to liberty. But by calling the right to liberty a side constraint, Nozick means to prohibit even this. My right to liberty may not be violated even if doing so minimizes total violations of rights to liberty. My right to liberty is, in a sense, an absolute right, not violable for any reason.

This idea of a strong right to liberty, understood as a negative right not to be interfered with that belongs to every normal adult human being and which may not be violated to achieve some other purpose, is fundamental to libertarian political philosophy. For the libertarian, this absolute or near-absolute right to liberty is the cornerstone upon which the edifice of economic, social, and political institutions must be built. In an essay published in 1974, *"What Libertarianism Is,"* the libertarian philosopher John Hospers says, "Every human being has the right to act in accordance with his own choices, unless those actions infringe on the equal liberty of other human beings to act in accordance with their choices." In a later essay with the same title Hospers says that, "The essential ingredient in all this is freedom from coercion by others. This is one's basic and inalienable right." The libertarian philosopher Jan Narveson makes an even stronger claim about the centrality of the right to liberty, saying that "the only relevant consideration in political matters is individual liberty."

Unlike utilitarianism, which makes the right to liberty a means to the end of social happiness, libertarianism conceives of the right to liberty as an independent foundation for political philosophy. It, not the maximization of happiness nor any other end, is the "bottom line" for political philosophy.

Further, in conceiving of the right to liberty as inviolable, as a side constraint on all other economic, social, and political institutions, libertarians raise the independently grounded right to liberty above all other considerations. For these reasons, libertarianism is said to be a "rights-based" theory. In this respect, and in its conception of the right to liberty as one belonging to human beings by nature and not by human convention, libertarianism agrees with the older natural-rights tradition and disagrees with utilitarianism.

This shift away from utilitarianism to rights-based theories was characteristic of a broad movement in ethics and political philosophy in the 1960s and 1970s. This shift was largely motivated by imagined cases that seemed to show that utilitarian principles led to morally unacceptable conclusions. In chapter 6 we considered the case of the utilitarian surgeon faced with five patients needing transplants and one patient whose organs happened to provide the needed matches for the five needing transplants. Utilitarianism, consistently applied, would seem to require the surgeon to painlessly kill the one in order to harvest organs for the five, thereby maximizing the total amount of happiness in the world, but also grossly violating our sense that such an action would be a morally unacceptable violation of individual rights. Faced with a number of such examples, most philosophers have come to the conclusion that utilitarianism is not tenable as a fundamental theory of morality, and consequently not tenable as the foundation for political philosophy. Though utilitarians have mounted some interesting defenses of their position, most philosophers have felt that these defenses ultimately fail and have turned to rights-based theories or mixed theories as more adequately accounting for our fundamental moral judgments.

As a rights-based theory, libertarianism built upon this shift away from utilitarianism in ethics and political theory. However, libertarianism represents only one current within the wider family of rights-based theories. Rawls's theory of justice, for example, also lies, broadly speaking, within the family of rights-based theories. Utilitarianism is often called a teleological or consequentialist theory. Such theories identify some quality or state of affairs as what is intrinsically good and then define morally right actions as those actions that aim at maximization of this good. In the case of utilitarianism, the good is happiness and right action is action that maximizes happiness. In contrast, Rawls's theory is a deontological theory, one that determines the rightness or wrongness of an action in terms of the kind of action that it is, and not in terms of the conduciveness of that action to the maximization of some good. Thus, for example, according to Rawls's theory, any suppression of liberty is morally wrong. In this, Rawls too accepts a strong right to liberty. Other political philosophers have also supported the shift from utilitarianism to rights-based theories but do not adopt libertarian positions.

One characteristic of libertarians is that they reject claims to positive rights. We will examine the implications of this position more fully below. Here it suffices to note that the shift from utilitarianism to rights-based theories need not include the rejection of positive rights. Nor need the rights-based theorist agree with the libertarian that negative rights always override other moral and political considerations. For example, the philosopher Michael Freeden presents a complex theory that includes negative rights, positive rights, and considerations of utility. Libertarianism is a particular current within the broader family of postutilitarian rights-based theories. It is, in a sense, a radical rights-based theory, one that challenges much of the fabric of law and practice that has come to govern economic, social, and political life in developed industrial societies. Having seen how libertarianism makes the right to liberty the cornerstone of political philosophy, it is to these radical implications of libertarian theory that we now turn.

Radical Implications of Libertarian Theory

Libertarians reject all positive rights. At the heart of libertarian theory is the right to liberty that belongs to every normal adult human being. Libertarians understand this right as a negative right, a right not to be interfered with in the conduct of one's life so long as one does not interfere with others in the free conduct of their lives. The libertarian understands this non-interference in terms of the absence of coercion. If I am walking down the street and a tourist from out of town stops me and asks for directions, there is a sense in which the tourist has interfered with me. By stopping me and asking for directions, the tourist interrupts the flow of my life. But I remain free to ignore this request. If I am in a hurry, or lost in thought, or just don't want to be bothered, I am free to go on my way. So far the libertarian has no objection to the actions of the tourist. But were the tourist to grab me by the arm and prevent my moving on, or threaten me with a gun and demand an answer, then the intervention of the tourist takes on a coercive aspect that aims at removing my freedom. It is such coercive intervention that the libertarian sees as interfering with my liberty in a morally objectionable way. Libertarians argue that positive rights inherently involve such coercive interference with liberty. To see why this is so, we must briefly consider the libertarian view of property rights.

To have a right of property in or over some thing is to have the right to use the thing; the right to sell, bequeath, or give away the thing; and the right to prevent others from using the thing. In this way, property rights are often said to be bundles of rights over objects. Now, each of these rights can be understood as involving a right of liberty with respect to the thing. To say that I have a right to use the thing is to say that I am free to use the thing and others may not coercively interfere to prevent me from using it. In the same way, to say that I have the rights to sell, bequeath, and give away the thing, is to say that I have a right of liberty to do these things that prevents others from coercively interfering in my doing so. And, finally, to say that I have a right to prevent others from using the thing is to say that the question of whether or not others may use the thing is one that falls within the domain of my free choice. You may not take my car without my consent. Your use of my car is up to me. It is a matter of my free choice. In this way the exercise of property rights over things that we own can be understood as inherent in our right to liberty. It is for this reason that for the government to forbid the basketball fans from spending their own money to see Michael Jordan play exhibition basketball appears to be a violation of liberty. Similar reasoning will also show that the right to life, understood as the right not to be killed, is also implicit in the right to liberty. After all, to kill someone is to coercively interfere with that person's freedom to do with her life as she wants.

Given this understanding of property rights, and the view that the right to liberty is inviolable, the libertarian argument against positive rights is straightforward. Negative rights, such as the right to life, the right to liberty, and the right to property, require nothing more of me than noninterference with the possessor of those rights: I must not kill, enslave, or take what is not my own. Negative rights require nothing further from me. They do not take from me anything that is my own. On the other hand, positive rights, such as the rights to food, clothing, housing, education, and medical care, all require the provision of resources to people who need them. Who is to provide these resources? In practice, of course, it is governmental agencies, supported by taxpayers that bear the responsibility for meeting those needs. But taxpayers are not free to decline to pay their taxes. The government has a coercive power over individual taxpayers. Refusal to pay will be met with fines, imprisonment, and the forced confiscation of property. This is the fundamental difference between public assistance and private charity from the libertarian's point of view. Donations to private charities are voluntary donations. They are given without coercive intervention or the threat of coercive intervention. Taxes, on the other hand, are extracted under a coercive threat. Positive rights claim rights to the provision of resources. But if A has a right to X, then B or someone else, must provide X. The provision of X has ceased to be B's voluntary contribution.

The case against positive rights is neatly summed up in this passage from Ayn Rand:

> *Jobs, food, clothing, recreation, homes, medical care, education, etc. do not grow in nature. They are man-made values goods and services produced by men.* Who *is to provide them?*

If some men are entitled by right to the products of the work of others, it means that those others are deprived of rights and condemned to slave labor.

Any alleged right of one man, which necessitates the violation of the rights of another, is not and cannot be a right.

No one can have a right to impose an unchosen obligation, an unrewarded duty or an involuntary servitude on another man. There can be no such thing as *the right to enslave.*

A right does not include the material implementation of that right by others; it includes only the freedom to earn that implementation by one's own effort.

The argument is simple and powerful. Since positive rights inherently require the provision of resources, they inherently violate the freedom of at least some persons by requiring those persons to pay whether they want to or not.

The libertarian's rejection of positive rights has broad implications. Under the sway of new liberal thinking, more or less extensive welfare states were constructed in all of the advanced industrial countries. Typically, governments have supplied resources to provide food, shelter, education, and medical care to persons in need. All of these things are financed by taxation. In a libertarian society, all such programs would be eliminated and would be replaced by private, voluntary charities. A libertarian society would even do away with many public services that antedate new liberalism. There are a number of other services paid for by coercive taxation that are not directly targeted at poor people. For example, in the United States, public schools and public highways are financed by taxation and have been for the entire history of the republic. In a libertarian society none of these things would be provided by governmental agencies. All would be privatized and paid for by those who use these services. Also gone from a libertarian society would be public support for art, science, and recreation. Museums, libraries, and parks would be privatized and financed by fees assessed upon those who use them. In short, from the central claim of an inviolable right to liberty, libertarian philosophy reaches conclusions that would require radical changes in how we have traditionally understood the public realm and the proper role of government.

Libertarian philosophy also requires a radical change in how we view trade unions. As we have seen, during the hegemony of the new liberalism, trade unions gained the power to force employers to bargain collectively with employees in entering into contracts governing wages and terms of employment. From a libertarian point of view, this is an unacceptable interference with the rights of liberty of employers and employees alike. Libertarians have no objection to trade unions. Workers may voluntarily join any organization they like so long as they do not attempt to use that organization to impose their will contrary to the liberty of others. Employers are also free to bargain with unions if they choose to do so. What the libertarian finds objectionable is not the existence of unions or collective bargaining, but the existence of a body of law that compels employers to bargain with unions. Here the right to liberty of the employer is clearly violated. The libertarian also finds objectionable any attempt by unions to impose their will on workers who, for whatever reason, choose not to join a union or go along with a union action. If a union chooses to strike, the libertarian has no objection. Workers are free men, not slaves. They have the right not to enter into a contract with their employers. But if a union does strike, its members may not impose their will on employees who want to work. If a strike is called and other people, either former employees or outsiders, desire to enter into a contract on terms acceptable to the employer, the union does not have any right to try to prevent these other people from working. From the libertarian perspective, violence, threats of violence, and intimidating picketing all involve unacceptable violations of the liberty of those people who do want to work. Here too, libertarian philosophy would require a radical change in the laws that have been developed regarding unions, the obligation of employers to bargain with unions, and the right, in some countries and in some states of the United States, for unions to organize closed shops, which legally exclude non-union members from employment.

Libertarian Theory of Justice

We began with consideration of Robert Nozick's libertarian critique of patterned theories of distributive justice. We saw how any attempt to maintain some ideal pattern of distribution must necessarily violate the liberty of individuals. Now, with some understanding of the core ideas of libertarianism, we can ask what a libertarian theory of justice regarding the distribution of wealth and income would look like. In a sense, the answer to this question is that a just distribution of wealth and income might look just about any way, according to libertarian principles. The key thing about the libertarian theory of justice is that it does not aim at preserving any pattern at all. For the libertarian, any pattern of distribution is just provided it arises in a morally acceptable way. Let us suppose that some initial distribution of property exists and that it is just. Now each person owns some property. Accordingly, each person has the right to keep, sell, trade, bequeath, or give this property away, and no one may coercively intervene to prevent the owner from doing anything he or she chooses with it. Now, suppose a sequence of sales, trades, bequeathments, and gifts takes place and that each of these transfers is freely done without any coercive intervention. From a libertarian point of view, each of these transfers is morally acceptable. This being so, since by hypothesis the initial distribution of property was also just, the libertarian argues that it follows that the resulting distribution of property is just. From this perspective what counts is not the nature of the end pattern of distribution, but the moral purity of the history by which this end distribution is reached. In *Anarchy, State,* and *Utopia*, Nozick defends this "historical" conception of justice against all patterned theories of justice. Unlike the various patterned theories, such a historical conception is consistent with the strong right to individual liberty championed by Nozick and his libertarian allies.

A number of very interesting problems remain. Among these is the problem of how to specify what makes for justice with respect to any possible initial distribution of resources.

However, we shall postpone consideration of this and other difficulties to the following chapter. Here our aim has been only to understand what libertarians say, some of the considerations that lead them to say these things, and the implications of libertarians' ideas.

6

Anarchists and Socialists in Modern Philosophy

Introduction

At the heart of this utilitarian argument was the idea that free markets would deliver the goods. Adam Smith argued that the best way to advance the wealth of a nation was to organize its economic life according to the principles of free trade. Though aware of the need for governmental authority to be on guard against the attempts of entrepreneurs to monopolize markets or prevent competition, Smith claimed that truly free markets would, in the long run, benefit nearly everyone. With an increase in the overall wealth of the nation, the portion falling to each individual would grow. In the long run, ordinary working men and women would be better off than they would be under any alternative economic system.

By the middle of the nineteenth century, this optimistic prognosis seemed to be contradicted by the grim realities of the new capitalist order. To be sure, the young capitalist system had produced astonishing wealth in a very short period of time. In England, parts of continental Europe, and parts of the Americas, mines, factories, canals, and railroads had been built. Great cities devoted to manufacturing, trade, and commerce appeared in what just decades before had been a largely rural landscape. But, at the same time, the new system had produced a world of squalor and grinding poverty. This world was inhabited by the newly created working class, a class of people who lived by selling their labor power to the owners of the mines and factories of the emerging industrial world. The men, women, and children of this working class labored fourteen, sixteen, and even eighteen hours per day, six days per week, in places that were dangerous, poorly lit, and polluted by dust and fibers that filled the air. For this they received wages barely sufficient to pay for meager food and for crowded rooms in the urban slums that grew up in the new industrial towns. Family life deteriorated. Children grew up unchurched and unschooled. Men and women turned to the consolations of alcohol and drugs. Begging, vagabondage, prostitution, and crime became familiar aspects of working-class life. Respiratory diseases caused by the polluted and crowded conditions brought many to an early death. This is the world depicted in the novels of Charles Dickens. It was a world of wealth and poverty standing side by side, divided by the fences of private property. Accordingly, it is not surprising that questions about the rights of private property came to play a central role in the political philosophy of the nineteenth century.

Property Rights

To hold a thing as a piece of property is to have a bundle of rights with respect to that thing. The owner of a piece of land has the right to use that land, the right to exclude other people from using the land, the right to sell the land, the right to bequeath the land, and the right to give the land away. It is possible for an individual to hold one or more of these rights without holding all of them. For example, in England and much of Europe, private property in land was often restricted. The system of entailment stipulated the succession of heirs to a landed estate, in effect removing the right of bequeathment from the bundle of rights held by the owner of the land. Medieval law and tradition sometimes also recognized the right of peasants to forage for firewood on the estates of their feudal lords, thereby limiting the right of exclusive use belonging to the owner of the land. As the new capitalist order emerged from the feudal past, owners of property sought to remove these restrictions and secure full property rights over land, rights like those held by the new capitalist class with its wealth in industrial and commercial property. For the most part, owners of property were successful in this, and by the end of the nineteenth century nearly all of the land, mines, forests, factories, means of transportation, and means of communication were privately owned. The owners of these productive resources, the capitalists, formed a relatively small portion of the population, with the vast majority of men and women belonging to the working class, a class of individuals who owned no productive resources and who made their living by selling their labor power to the capitalists who did own these things. Ownership of such private property brought wealth. For those who lacked such property, poverty and its attendant miseries was a constant threat.

Natural Rights and Property Rights

As legal rights, property rights are clearly human creations, but are there any natural moral rights to private property? On the face of it, it might seem that there are not. After all, how could a person come to have, by nature, rights over some particular piece of land or some particular object? People normally acquire property by purchase, bequeathment, or gift. But each of these means presupposes a prior right of property belonging to the person who sells, bequeaths, or gives away whatever piece of property it might be. To account for a natural right of ownership of the one who acquires property formerly belonging to another, it will be necessary to give some kind of account of how natural rights of property can originally be acquired in some object.

How is it that human beings, finding themselves on the face of the earth either by the hand of God or by some process of evolution, come to have a right over some portion of the earth or some object on it?

In his *Second Treatise of Government*, John Locke attempts to provide an account of original acquisition by which a person can come to have a natural right of ownership over some piece of land or some object even though originally God has given all things to men in common. Locke says this:

> Though the Earth, and all inferior Creatures be common to all Men, yet every Man has a *Property* in his own *Person*. This no Body has any Right to but himself. The *Labour* of his Body, and the *Work* of his Hands, we may say, are properly his. Whatsoever then he removes out of the State that Nature hath provided, and left it in, he hath mixed his *Labour* with, and joyned to it something that is his own, and thereby makes it his *Property*. It being by him removed from the common state Nature placed it in, hath by this *labour* something annexed to it, that excludes the common right of other Men. *Labour* being the unquestionable Property of the Labourer, no Man but he can have a right to what that is once joyned to, at least where there is enough, and as good left in common for others.

In this famous passage, Locke provides an account of how a piece of property belonging in common to all human beings legitimately could come to be the private property of some individual person. At the center of Locke's account is the idea that every person has a natural right over his or her own labor and that it is by mixing labor with something in its natural state that a person comes to ownership rights over property. Assuredly, there are some odd features to this account. If a man plows some previously uncultivated soil, mixing his labor with it, just how much land does he thereby acquire? Does he gain rights to minerals far below the surface? However, for now at least, we will set this difficulty aside and assume that Locke has succeeded in providing a tenable account of how legitimate rights over property might be acquired and consequently also how legitimate rights over property might come to be held by purchase, bequeathment, or gift. Still, some interesting difficulties remain.

The Anarchist Critique of Private Property

In 1840 Pierre-Joseph Proudhon, son of a cooper and himself a printer by trade, published a book entitled *What Is Property?* Proudhon answered this question in a single word: "theft." His argument was simple. If one traces actual ownership claims backward in time, Proudhon argued, one eventually comes to a point of origin, and that point of origin in fact invariably rests upon an act of force in which some individual claimed something as exclusively his own and by force excluded others from their common right of use. Since this is so, and since violent exclusion of others from the use of that to which they have a right is an act of theft, it follows that all original claims of property ownership rest on a primitive act of theft and are therefore illegitimate. Of course, it also follows that all subsequent rights over property, based on transfer by sale, bequeathment, or gift from those original violent seizures, are also illegitimate, since the person who transferred the property to another never had a legitimate title in the first place.

Anarchism

Proudhon was a revolutionary anarchist. He viewed all coercive power over human beings as a violation of their natural right to liberty. The exclusive claims of private property, grounded in original acts of violence and backed up by the coercive power of law, became the means by which peasants and workers were crushed and oppressed. The state and the whole system of law were at bottom nothing more than instruments of oppression, incompatible with the natural liberty of hunian beings. "To be GOVERNED," said Proudhon, "is to be watched, inspected, spied upon, directed, law-driven, numbered, regulated, enrolled, indoctrinated, preached at, controlled, checked, estimated, valued, censured, commanded, by creatures who have neither the right nor the wisdom nor the virtue to do so." In place of the coercive principles of law and the state, Proudhon proposed a revolutionary reorganization of the whole of society, based upon the principle of contracts mutually agreed upon by all parties. The illegitimate ownership rights claimed by the capitalists who controlled the land, mines, and factories were to be swept aside, and these productive resources be given over in common to the control of the workers who labored in them.

The Ricardian Socialists

There is a curious passage in *The Second Treatise*. Having introduced the idea that it is by mixing labor with a part of nature that one comes to have a right over that part of nature, Locke goes on to say, "Thus the Grass my Horse has bit; the Turfs my Servant has cut; and the Ore I have digg'd become my *Property*." Now, leaving the horse aside, why is it that the turfs Locke's servant cut come to belong to Locke and not to the servant? By nature, surely, it is to the servant they belong.

The idea that the by natural right the fruits of labor belong to the laborer serves as one of the premises for a simple but powerful argument for the conclusion that capitalism was unjust. The other premise upon which this argument rests comes from the science of economics created by Adam Smith and developed by Smith's successor, David Ricardo. According to Smith and Ricardo, the value of a thing is proportional to the amount of labor necessary to produce it. This idea, known as the labor theory of value, reduces the value of all things to the labor contained in them. Smith and Ricardo used the labor theory of value to explain the relative exchange rates of commodities: why a pair of shoes cost as much as two shirts, for example. But in the 1820s certain critics of capitalism combined Ricardo's labor theory of value with Locke's labor theory of property rights to produce a simple but powerful argument against capitalism. According to Locke's principle, the laborer had a right of ownership in the products of his labor. According to Ricardo's labor theory of value, the value of all commodities was a product of the labor necessary to produce them. From these two premises it followed that everything should belong to the laborers. But in the capitalist system it was the capitalist, the owner of the factory who employed the laborer, who claimed the product of the laborer as his own. This, the Ricardian socialists argued, was an injustice inherent in the very nature of the capitalist system of production.

Although they possessed a clear and powerful argument that capitalism was unjust, the Ricardian socialists were less clear about how society ought to be organized. They did, however, contribute to a number of experiments aimed at establishing islands of justice in the sea of supposedly unjust capitalism. Labor exchanges were organized, in which craftsmen could bring the objects they had produced and exchange them for other objects of equal labor value. More ambitious projects aimed at establishing whole alternative communities, separated from the surrounding capitalist system, and organized on the principle of reward according to the amount of labor performed.

Christian Socialism

Other utopian communities were organized on the basis of the principles of Christianity. Etienne Cabet, a French Christian socialist and author of the popular utopian novel *Voyage to Icaria*, inspired the foundation of a number of communist communities, most of them located in the New World, where land was plentiful and cheap.

Cabet blamed the social problems of his time on greed. He preached an austere ethic of the renunciation of desire and diversity. All property was to be owned by the community as a whole, and each member was to receive equal food, clothing, and shelter. Where the Ricardian socialists had appealed to the principles of Locke and Adam Smith to justify their socialist ideas, Cabet claimed to base his ideas on the commandments of God as revealed by Jesus Christ. After all, did not Christ tell the rich young man to give away all that he had to the poor? And does not scripture tell us that the disciples of Christ practiced communism?

Now the company of those who believed were of one heart and soul, and no one said that any of the things which he possessed was his own, but they had everything in common. There was not a needy person among them, for as many as were possessors of lands or houses sold them, and brought the proceeds of what was sold and laid it at the apostles' feet, and distribution was made to each as any had need.

The Socialism of Marx and Engels

When the *Manifesto of the Communist Party* appeared in the spring of 1848, Karl Marx and Frederick Engels were obscure German socialists living in exile in London. By the end of the nineteenth century their ideas had come to dominate the radical labor movement aimed at the overthrow of capitalism. In the twentieth century their ideas inspired the creation of Communist states in Russia, Eastern Europe, China, and elsewhere.

At the center of Marxist thought was Marx's theory of capitalism. Marx began this work in the mid-1840s. An unpublished draft of his theory, now known as the *Grundrisse*, was written during the winter of 1857-58. A second version of the theory was published in 1859 under the title *Contribution to the Critique of Political Economy*. A third version appeared in 1867 with the publication of the first volume of *Capital*, a projected multi-volume study of capitalism. Despite its unfinished nature, this work on capitalism, occupying nearly forty years, filling several thousand pages of text, and informing all of his other works, was the major theoretical achievement of Marx's lifetime.

In many ways Marx shared the theoretical outlook of the classical economists Adam Smith and David Ricardo. Like Smith and Ricardo, he sought to analyze the workings of a capitalist system characterized by free markets and private ownership of the means of production. Like his classical predecessors, he used the labor theory of value, according to which the value of a commodity was determined by the amount of labor necessary to produce it, as the basis for a theory of relative prices of commodities and for a theory of the relative shares of total wealth going to the owners of land, labor, and capital. And, like Smith and Ricardo, Marx was tremendously impressed with the productive powers of capitalism:

> *The bourgeoisie [the class of capitalists], during its rule of scarce one hundred years, has created more massive and more colossal productive forces than have all preceding generations together. Subjection of Nature's forces to man, machinery, application of chemistry to industry and agriculture, steam-navigation, railways, electric telegraphs, clearing of whole continents for cultivation, canalization of rivers, whole populations conjured out of the ground what earlier century had even a presentiment that such productive forces slumbered in the lap of social labour?*

Nonetheless, unlike Smith and Ricardo, Marx was also highly critical of capitalism. In *The Wealth of Nations*, Adam Smith argued that capitalism would benefit the vast majority of the population. The invisible hand of the free market would yoke the self-interest of each agent to the cause of increasing the total wealth produced, thereby increasing the share available to each individual person. Smith offered an optimistic prognosis for the future of capitalism, foreseeing peaceful competition, a steady increase in the production of goods and services, and a steady increase in the share of those goods and services going to everyone willing to put his hands or head to work.

Marx argued that this optimistic prognosis rested upon important errors in Smith's economic theory. Marx's own theory of capitalism offered a pessimistic prognosis. Though he agreed with Smith about the productive power inherent in capitalism, Marx's economic theory differed from Smith's theory about the likely effects of capitalism on the lives of ordinary people. Marx saw capitalism as a "contradictory" social system. As capitalism developed over time, it did produce greater and greater productive forces. But it also produced a greater and greater concentration of wealth. In the competitive world of free markets, successful firms grew larger and larger, gradually eliminating their less successful rivals. Competition gave way to monopoly. The vast productive power produced by capitalism gradually came under the control of fewer and fewer people. Over time, the bourgeoisie, the class of capitalists, those who owned the means of production, became smaller, and the proletariat, the class of workers, those who owned no land, mines, or factories and lived by the sale of their labor power, grew larger. Marx also argued that over time, as the new productive machinery produced by capitalism displaced human labor, capitalism resulted in an ever-growing pool of unemployed workers. Faced with intense competition, each individual capitalist was forced to reduce the costs of production as much as possible. Wherever possible, the capitalist sought to replace human labor with the less expensive labor of machines. Wherever human labor remained necessary, the capitalist sought to increase the output and reduce the costs of that labor as much as possible. With increasing numbers of unemployed workers competing for jobs, workers were forced to take jobs that provided little pay and demanded long and arduous effort. The working class, far from benefiting from the increased powers of production produced by capitalism, found itself riveted to drudgery and poverty.

There was also a historical dimension to Marx's theory of capitalism that was missing from the economic theory of Adam Smith. Smith conceived of capitalism as involving a system of competitive markets. He thought of this competitive system as stable, persisting over time as capitalism grew and developed. Marx, however, saw the system of competition as inherently unstable. In the sea of competition, the big fish eat the little fish. Over time, markets come to be dominated by a few large firms that exercise monopolistic or oligopolistic control. The class structure that is fundamental to capitalism also changes over time. Gradually the small capitalists are eliminated, falling prey to larger and stronger capitalists, who are better able to finance investment in more productive new technologies and better able to withstand the stresses produced by hard times. As capitalism develops, wealth and power come to be concentrated in the hands of a very few, and the vast majority are reduced to the role of impoverished wage laborers. Where Adam Smith saw capitalism as a stable system, gradually reproducing itself on a grander and grander scale, Marx saw capitalism as inherently unstable, gradually transforming itself, by its own innate logic, into something quite different from the competitive system of free producers envisaged by Adam Smith.

This historical dimension to Marx's conception of capitalism finds a place in a broader understanding of history suggested by Marx in a number of places. Marx sees capitalism as a distinctive form of life. In his view, capitalism emerges at a particular moment in history, evolves in the ways suggested above, and eventually will pass away. Marx saw capitalism as emerging out of feudalism in western Europe in the sixteenth and seventeenth centuries. He held that capitalism would grow and expand to all comers of the globe, gradually transforming itself into ever more concentrated forms of wealth as it did so. Marx also predicted that eventually the working class would come to see that capitalism was inimical to its interests, would organize itself into a revolutionary agent for change, and would overthrow capitalism, replacing it with a system of socialism.

Marx had relatively little to say about what this system of socialism would be like. He seems to have thought of a decisive battle for political power and control of the state between workers and capitalists. After the victory of the working class, there would follow a transition period of indeterminate length during which the working class would use its control of the state to pass laws that would, step by step, transform monopolistic capitalism into a fully socialist form of social organization. Fully developed socialism would involve the collective and democratic ownership and control of the means of production, would operate according to the maxim "From each according to his ability and to each according to his need," and would provide the conditions necessary "for the free development of all."

Despite their sketchy nature, Marx's descriptions of socialism are sufficiently outlined to make clear important differences between the Marxist vision and the visions of the future advanced by other socialists and by the anarchists. Nineteenth century socialists such as Robert Owen, Etiennie

Cabet, and Charles Fourier saw socialism as emerging through the formation of experimental communities by the voluntary association of like-minded persons. These communities would first exist as islands of socialism within the sea of capitalism. It was hoped that these socialist communities would demonstrate to all that socialism was better for human beings than capitalism and that, having seen the proof of socialism, more and more people would join together to create a network of communal societies so vast that it would eventually displace capitalism as the dominant form of social organization.

Marx and Engels viewed this vision as utopian. The productive powers created by capitalism could not be utilized in a society consisting of such communities. Railroads, canals, and telegraph lines spanned vast geographic distances and, even in the nineteenth century, trade had taken on truly global dimensions. How were these resources to be managed in the society of the future? Marx and Engels were convinced that the conditions necessary for the free development of all presupposed the ability to effectively use the productive powers created by capitalism for the good of all human beings. But to effectively manage the productive resources created by capitalism, the socialist society of the future would require national and even international forms of cooperation. For the Marxists, gaining control of the political power of the nation-state was critical for creating the forms of cooperation necessary for the socialist society of the future. This emphasis on the importance of obtaining control of the political apparatus of the state also distinguished the Marxists from the anarchists. The Marxists contended that it was only by obtaining political control of the state that the working class could gain the means by which the socialist society of the future could be created. The anarchists, convinced that all forms of the state were inimical to individual liberty, viewed the Marxists with suspicion. They feared that the Marxian brand of socialism would only increase the oppressive powers of the state.

Like the anarchists and like all socialists, Marxists viewed the reign of capitalist private property as oppressive to the vast majority of humankind. It is in their conception of capitalism as a necessarily transient form of life embedded within a larger process of historical development, and in their conception of the role to be played in the creation of a more humane world by working-class control of the state, that Marxists differed from other socialist and anarchist critics of capitalism. In the closing decades of the nineteenth century this Marxist understanding of capitalism and the way to its overcoming came to dominate the growing movement of the working class, a movement that called for the revolutionary transformation of the whole social system.

Ideology of Socialism

The Marxist variant that came to dominate the socialist movement late in the nineteenth century formed an ideological alternative to both conservatism and classical liberalism. In several important respects, socialist ideology shared key ideas with the ideology of classical liberalism. Like classical liberalism, socialist ideology appealed to the ethical norms of freedom and human happiness. It also placed a great deal of faith in the power of human reason to understand human social existence and, on the basis of this understanding, construct a social system radically different from the social systems of the past. Also like classical liberalism, socialist ideology was generally optimistic about the course of history, believing in not only the possibility but also the actuality of a generally progressive direction to the historical process. The chief point of contention between socialist and classical liberal ideologies pertains to the assessment of the likely consequences of capitalism as a way of life. Where classical liberals were optimistic, expecting the growth of total production produced by capitalism to benefit the vast majority of people, socialists were pessimistic, expecting the growth of total production produced by capitalism not to benefit the vast majority of people. It is important to see that this central point of disagreement concerns a question of social science: What would be the long-term consequences of capitalism? In terms of its underlying ethical values, socialist ideology shares the values of the liberal tradition.

Socialist ideology has less in common with conservative ideology. It rejects conservative beliefs in the wisdom of tradition and the dangers of radical change. It also rejects conservative religious views that subordinate the human ends of freedom and happiness to transcendent ends and purposes. Socialists do agree with conservatives about the alienated character of human existence within a capitalist mode of production. Like conservatives, socialists deplore the dehumanization resulting from the supposed capitalist reduction of all human relationships to relationships of mutual use. However, where conservatives looked for at least a partial restoration of precapitalist restraints on the forces of the free market, socialists looked forward to the abolition of capitalism and its replacement with socialist forms of life based on humane relationships grounded in democracy and solidarity among people. On the whole, then, socialist ideology is much closer to the humanistic, rationalistic, and optimistic outlook of classical liberalism than it is to the divine-centered, traditionalist, and cautious outlook of conservative ideology.

Socialism and Communism

In the *Manifesto,* Marx and Engels conclude a brief overview of the course of capitalist development with a prediction of a class war "where the violent overthrow of the bourgeoisie lays the foundation for the sway of the proletariat." These words were published in the spring of 1848, at a time of acute economic and political crisis within the capitalist world of England and western Europe. At the time they were written, the working class lacked the right to vote. Violent rebellion seemed to be the only avenue for change. Decades later, with the male working class having gained at least in part the right to vote in several European countries, Marx allowed that, where the working class did have the right to vote, the revolutionary overthrow of the bourgeoisie might be achieved by peaceful means.

Marx's recognition of a possible peaceful path to socialism is significant in at least two respects. First, it indicates the important point that the Marxist idea of a revolution should not be confused with the idea of violent change. Marx conceived of the transition from capitalism to socialism as revolutionary because it constituted a fundamental change in the way social life was to be organized. Whether this revolutionary change was to be violent or peaceful was a separate issue. Second, with the extension of the right to vote to much of the male working class in various European countries in the last quarter of the nineteenth century, socialists of the decades after the deaths of Marx and Engels, even those who considered themselves orthodox Marxists, almost uniformly embraced the peaceful, electoral path to socialism. Social Democratic political parties appeared in most European countries, claiming to be guided by the "scientific socialism" of Marx and Engels and pinning their hopes for the future on the votes of their working-class followers.

In Russia things were different. Russia, and the greater Russian Empire, were ruled by an autocratic monarch, the tsar. In Russia there was no elected parliament, and freedom of speech, freedom of the press, and freedom of assembly were severely truncated. The Social Democratic party was illegal in Russia, and spies and police agents infiltrated the party at every level, reporting party activities and party members to the tsar's agents. Union organizers and Social Democratic activists were arrested and deported to Siberia. Under these conditions it was suicidal to attempt to emulate the Social Democratic parties of western Europe, developed to follow the electoral path to socialism. Responding to the repressive and backward conditions found in Russia, V.I. Lenin proposed a "party of the new type," made up of committed revolutionaries. The party would be a secret organization, with membership at each level known only to those party functionaries necessary to coordinate the activities of the party. The party would be organized according to the principles of democratic centralism. Whenever the party was faced with an important issue, there was to be democratic debate among members of the party about what action should be taken. This debate would occur at whatever level was necessary to deal with the issue and would often take place in secret meetings of small groups or in large meetings outside the borders of Russia and beyond the repressive control of the tsar's agents. Once a decision was reached by democratic vote, all members of the party were to be bound to obey the decision reached. The party was also to be hierarchically organized, with decisions reached at the highest levels being binding on party members at all lower levels. Lenin proposed such a party structure as a way of making maximally effective use of revolutionary activists under conditions of tsarist repression. He advanced his proposal for a new type of party in *What Is to Be Done?* in 1902. One year later, at a congress of the Russian Social Democratic Labor Party in London, the majority, or Bolshevik, faction of the party adopted Lenin's proposals, creating a Marxist, secret, disciplined, and highly centralized revolutionary party. Until World War I, this Leninist form of party organization was largely unknown outside Russia. However, the war and the events that followed the war would change this.

For Marxists around the world, World War I was no surprise. Marxian socialists had predicted the war and had long debated how the working-class parties should respond to it. At international conferences in Stuttgart in 1907 and Basel in 1913, Social Democrats pledged to work against war and to push for revolutionary change in the event that war broke out. When war did come, the great Social Democratic parties of Germany and western Europe betrayed these commitments, fearing to make the revolutionary attempt. But in Russia the Bolsheviks did lead a successful revolutionary attempt, seizing power and successfully holding that power through the course of a long and terrible civil war. In 1919, in the aftermath of the war and the revolution in Russia, the international Marxist movement split into two camps: Communists, who followed the proposals of Lenin for forming parties of the new type, and Socialists, who continued to follow the electoral model of the prewar Social Democratic parties. In Russia itself, the Communist Party, organized according to the Leninist principles of democratic centralism, became the ruling party of the land, justifying its role as necessary to preserve and develop the socialist revolution in Russia. It was this Russian version of communism as a dictatorship of the Communist Party that came to serve as a model for Communist regimes in other parts of the world as well, a model that combined the Marxist idea of central planning with the decidedly un-Marxist idea of a dictatorship by a ruling elite. With the collapse of Communism in the Soviet Union and Eastern Europe, this model has been discredited and with it, rightly or wrongly, much of the appeal of the whole socialist tradition.

Anarchism is a political philosophy which considers the state undesirable, unnecessary and harmful, and instead promotes a stateless society, or anarchy. It seeks to diminish or even abolish authority in the conduct of human relations. Anarchists may widely disagree on what additional criteria are required in anarchism. The Oxford Companion to Philosophy says, "there is no single defining position that all anarchists hold, and those considered anarchists at best share a certain family resemblance."

There are many types and traditions of anarchism, not all of which are mutually exclusive. Strains of anarchism have been divided into the categories of social and individualist anarchism or similar dual classifications. Anarchism is often considered to be a radical left-wing ideology, and much of anarchist economics and anarchist legal philosophy reflect anti-statist interpretations of communism, collectivism, syndicalism or participatory economics. However, anarchism has always included an individualist strain supporting a market economy and private property, or morally unrestrained egoism. Still some individualist anarchists, like Pierre-Joseph Proudhon, were also socialists.

Socialists advocate a method of compensation based on individual merit or the amount of labor one contributes to society. They generally share the view that capitalism unfairly concentrates power and wealth among a small segment of society that controls capital and derives its wealth through a system of exploitation. They argue that this creates an unequal society that fails to provide equal opportunities for everyone to maximise their potential, and does not utilise technology and resources to their maximum potential in the interests of the public. Socialists characterize full socialism as a society no longer based on coercive wage-labor. Reformist and revolutionary socialists disagree on how a socialist economy should be established.

Modern socialism originated in the late 18th–century intellectual and working class political movement that criticised the effects of industrialisation and private ownership on society. Utopian socialists such as Robert Owen (1771–1858), tried to found self-sustaining communes by secession from a capitalist society. Henri de Saint Simon (1760–1825), who coined the term socialism, advocated technocracy and industrial planning. Saint-Simon, Friedrich Engels and Karl Marx advocated the creation of a society that allows for the widespread application of modern technology to rationalise economic activity by eliminating the anarchy of capitalist production. They argued that this would allow for economic output (or surplus value) and power to be distributed based on the amount of work expended in production.

7

Cartesian Revolution in Philosophy

Introduction

It has been said of the scientific revolution of which Descartes was a part that since it overturned the authority of the science not only of the Middle Ages but of the ancient world—since it ended not only in the eclipse of scholastic philosophy but in the destruction of Aristotelian physics it outshines everything since the rise of Christianity and reduces the Renaissance and Reformation to the rank of mere episodes, mere internal displacements, within the system of mediaeval Christendom.

And it is impossible to doubt now that the predilection of cultural historians to find the great divide between medieval and modern at the Renaissance has obscured and to some extent misrepresented the true development, not only of Western philosophy, but of Western thought as a whole. From ancient times until the mid-eighteenth century science and philosophy went hand in hand. For the historian of ideas, it is impossible to separate the development of philosophy from that of scientific thought, and, when taken together, it becomes apparent that the most significant point in the development of each occurred, not at the Renaissance, but in the early seventeenth century, in the intellectual turmoil that to some extent caused, and to a large extent was caused by, the thought of Descartes.

Already in the sixteenth century the problems of scientific method had been vigorously discussed notably at the University of Padua, where it was recognised that experiments are of the first importance in scientific investigation, and also that experimental results can be fully understood only by a science of quantity and not by one of quality. Bacon had attempted to describe the form of such a science and the logic which would govern it, and such men as Harvey and Galileo had exemplified it in their writings and researches. But Descartes, partly because of his deep epistemological preoccupations, introduced with a novel explicitness the suggestion that there must be fundamental physical laws, of a kind so general as to provide the explanation of everything, and yet so abstract as to be the outcome not of experiment but of *a priori* reflection. He enunciated such laws in his *Principles of Philosophy* (1644), showing both their deductive dependence on metaphysics and their power to generate comprehensive explanations. Much of the content of the *Principles* was influenced by what Descartes had understood of the work of Galileo. But Descartes was perhaps the first to give clear prominence to the law of inertia. This law says that a body continues at rest or in motion in a straight line until something intervenes to halt, slacken or deflect its movement. The law makes movement into a basic fact of the physical universe, which may sometimes neither require nor permit further explanation. It reverses the traditional physics, which had postulated a 'mover' for every movement, believing motion as such to stand in need of an explanation. By accepting the law of inertia, and also embedding it at the heart of what he considered to be a rigorous, axiomatic system, Descartes changed the aspect of physical science and prepared the way for Newton.

However important Descartes' contribution to science, he gave only a subordinate role to experiment, and a far more elevated role than would now be considered acceptable to metaphysical speculation. He wished to deduce the nature of the whole universe from the nature of God, with each step bound to its predecessor in an unbreakable chain of 'geometrical' reasoning. Everything was to be accounted for mathematically, either by configuration or by number, since mathematics gives us the most complete tabulation of 'clear and distinct perceptions' that we could ever hope to arrive at. No rival explanation therefore could compete with it. Any science that started from the mere evidence of the senses must be inferior in its conclusions to a science that began from principles so abstract that their persuasive power would be apparent to reason alone. It was not until Newton's *Principia* that it was definitely established that the geometrical method could not prove the propositions of physics, and that it was only through a new, and previously unthought of, alliance of geometrical reasoning and experimental method that significant progress could be made. It is fair to say, however, that without Descartes Newtonian physics would have been impossible, and that since Descartes' physics was the child of his philosophy there is a further historical reason for thinking that the Cartesian philosophy marks the birth of much that we would recognise as peculiarly 'modern' in the spirit of scientific investigation.

In philosophy itself the immediate impact of Descartes was enormous. The lucidity of his style, his contempt for scholastic technicalities, the clarity, honesty and unassuming objectivity of his approach, made it impossible to resist the appeal of his writings. Many of the greatest thinkers of the time felt called upon to respond to Descartes' *Meditations,* offering their objections either directly to the author, or else indirectly, to the tireless impresario Father Marin Mersenne (1588–1648), who, with a humility remarkable in a man of less than total genius, acted as go-between among the scientists and philosophers of his age, achieving for the France of his day what the Royal Society was later to achieve for England. The objectors included

Thomas Hobbes, Pierre Gassendi and the young priest Antoine Arnauld (1612–1694), who put forward the objection referred to in the previous chapter, arguing that Descartes' proof for the existence of God must be circular. The interest of this objection lies in the suggestion that a search for method as absolute as Descartes' must in the end rely not only upon 'self-verifying' truths such as the 'cogito', but also, and more generally, upon some characteristic of our mental processes whereby we recognise the intrinsic validity of ideas. The 'clear and distinct perception' of Descartes must itself be immune from Cartesian doubt. If this is so, then the faculty which governs clear and distinct perception, the 'natural light', of reason, is our ultimate guarantee of knowledge. It is in the recognition of this commitment that Cartesian rationalism is born, out of a sceptical epistemology that seemed at first to make rational enquiry as dubious as our other claims to knowledge.

Arnauld is significant not only as a critic of Descartes but also as expressing the spirit which arose, partly in opposition to Cartesian enlightenment and partly as its natural corollary, in the philosophy of Jansenism. Cornelius Jansen (1585–1638) was bishop of Ypres and an enthusiastic exponent of doctrines which, while seemingly compatible with the new findings of science, exalted the act of faith above the conclusions of reason as our guide to theological and metaphysical truth. He joined with the Abbé de Saint-Cyran in founding what is known as the Port-Royal movement, after the abbey where its activities were located. Arnauld was a member of this movement, and was associated with two decisive thinkers of the time: the moralist Pierre Nicole (1625–1695) and the famous mathematician and philosopher, Blaise Pascal. Together with Nicole, Arnauld wrote a textbook of logic for the Port-Royal School, under the title *La Logique ou l'art de penser* (1662), usually known as the Port-Royal logic. This work exemplifies the profundity of the Cartesian revolution in philosophy, and also anticipates the difficulties which the Cartesian 'geometrical method' was soon to encounter.

Judged from the historical point of view, the Port-Royal

logic is merely one among a multitude of manuals designed to abbreviate and restate a discipline that had become too deeply overlaid by the pernickety squabbles of the scholastics to recommend itself to the new man of science. In 1556, Petrus Ramus had published his *Animadversiones Aristotelicae,* in which he claimed to discredit the whole science of logic as Aristotle had invented and the scholastics embellished it. By the mid-seventeenth century faith in Aristotelianism was so much shaken that it seemed vital to achieve some rival logic with which to record and validate the 'method' of the new philosophy. In fact no systematic alternative to the Aristotelian logic was to emerge until the nineteenth century, and, despite many attempts (culminating in some notable ones from Leibniz), the seventeenth century logic was less new than it claimed to be. It served partly to mask the old Aristotelian theories in Cartesian jargon. Without Aristotelian logic the rationalist conception of substance is, after all, scarcely intelligible; and yet it is this concept which lies at the heart of the philosophy of Descartes, Spinoza and Leibniz, surviving, in modified form, even in the works of Kant.

There are, however, important philosophical reasons for noticing the Port-Royal logic at this juncture. First, it represents an attempt to examine the nature of human reasoning in the light of the Cartesian theory of ideas. Traditional logic had spoken of the relations between judgements or propositions. It was unclear to Arnauld and Nicole how this logic bore on those more important relations without which there could be no such thing as the Cartesian 'method': the relations among ideas. The Cartesian 'idea', seeming to be both concept and proposition at once, has no claim to be the true subject matter of logic.

There are two further respects in which the Port-Royal logic deserves recognition. First, because of its quasi-mathematical development of part of the medieval logic. This development must have seemed natural to any follower of Descartes, but it contained the first premonition of modern formal logic. Secondly, because of its distinction, again novel at the time but now considered fundamental to logic, between the 'comprehension' and 'extension' of a general term. The word 'comprehension' denotes that which is understood in understanding a term in other words, the idea that the term expresses. The extension of a term, on the other hand, is the set of things to which it is applied. Following the nineteenth century Scottish philosopher Sir William Hamilton, the distinction is now often expressed as that between the intension and the extension of a term. It was important to Arnauld and Nicole, since they wished to isolate the former (the realm of 'ideas') as giving the true subject matter of logic; it is important in modern thought for the opposite reason, because logicians have come increasingly to realise that logic is the science not of the intension, but of the extension of terms.

The Port-Royal school projected a manual on mathematics, and, as a preface to this, Blaise Pascal (1623–1662) wrote his *De l'esprit géometrique,* an investigation into the philosophy of mathematics designed to display not just the nature of the 'geometrical' method, but also its limits. Pascal, like Descartes, was a great mathematician and a deeply religious man. But his faith, which he acquired by conversion, took the passionate form characteristic of Jansenism, according to which the claims of reason could never suffice as foundations for so great a thing as religious doctrine. Pascal argued that the indefinability of terms and the need for axioms in the 'geometrical method' showed not the absolute validity of the 'clear and distinct idea', but rather the imperfection of finite minds, which must always rest content with indefinables. Our reason may give us some guarantee of the methods of the geometer, but it could never provide the same guarantee for his axioms.

In the famous *Pensées* (published posthumously) Pascal takes further his strictures on the use of reason, arguing that, since God is hidden from mortal view, it is futile to attempt to discover his essence through rational enquiry. 'We know truth not only by reason but more by the heart. ' And it is from the heart that we sense the meaning of life and its divine eschatology. Pascal stopped short of total scepticism, believing it to be self-defeating, and qualified his strictures against rational theology with a curious argument for the existence of God: 'Pascal's wager'. The argument goes roughly as follows: 'If God exists He will reward belief in Him: while if He does not exist, such belief leads to no harm. Hence the best bet is to believe in Him. ' The argument reflects Pascal's concern with the concept of probability; it is interesting because it offers practical reasons (rather than theoretical reasons) for an article of faith, so connecting the logic of religious belief not with that of science but with that of practice. This singularly modern idea which resurges periodically in later philosophy, for example in Kant's conception of the 'ideas' of reason, in Kierkegaard's notion of the 'leap' of faith, in the neo-Marxist theory of *praxis* and in the existentialist concept of commitment possesses less philosophical merit than rhetorical impact. For while it is indeed a striking suggestion that religious belief may be constituted by a form of voluntary activity, and so be inaccessible to metaphysical doubt, it seems hard to reconcile with the obvious fact that the question of the existence of God is a question about what is true, and not a question that could be resolved by mesmerising ourselves into a state of unfounded belief in Him.

Perhaps the greatest of the many philosophers who could reasonably be called Cartesian was Nicolas Malebranche (1638–1715), a priest of the Oratory who engaged in a vivid and at times bitter controversy with Arnauld over matters of theology and metaphysics. Like Pascal, Malebranche was distinguished by his literary gifts and produced in his *Dialogues on Metaphysics* some of the finest philosophical prose since Plato. But he did not share Pascal's distrust of metaphysics and conceded to mysticism only a narrow region of carefully circumscribed darkness. Malebranche had thoroughly absorbed the principles and proofs of the Cartesian philosophy, but, like many who were convinced that Descartes' method was both valid and comprehensive, he remained unsatisfied with the Cartesian picture of the relation between body and soul.

Descartes' views of causation are such that there is a *prima facie* contradiction between the thesis that body and soul are (or exemplify) separate substances, and the thesis that there is also interaction between them. Malebranche did not seek to question the Cartesian idea of substance, although his writings are remarkable for containing an extended metaphysics from which that idea could be eliminated without detriment to the system's integrity. Instead, he questioned the theory of causation implicit in Descartes: the theory that the states of a substance must be explained in terms of its essential nature. It seemed to Malebranche that such a theory could explain neither our ability to perceive the material world, nor our ability to act on it. Furthermore (and in this he showed how much he had let the Cartesian conception of material substance fall into the background of his philosophy, replacing it with the more modern idea of the material object), he even regarded it as incompatible with the view that there is causal action between separate bodies, since it seemed to imply that each body, being complete in itself, had nothing to gain from or to impart to its surroundings. Rejecting the view that bodies have an intrinsic 'power' to affect us and each other as a mere superstition, Malebranche adopted the theory, already proposed by the Cartesians du Cordemoy (c. 1605–1684) and Arnold Geulincx (1624–1669), of 'occasionalism', which he defended with great vigour. This theory perhaps the first developed account of the concept of causation in modern philosophy argues that, since the laws of the universe have their origin in God, it is God who produces the events that conform to them. No event produces another of its own nature. Rather, when one thing occurs, then this is the occasion for God's production of that thing which we know as its 'effect'. In this view, there is no special difficulty posed by the relation between mind and body, since to speak of interaction between them can only be a manner of speaking: just as it is only a manner of speaking to refer to interaction between anything.

There is much more to Malebranche's metaphysics than this theory (often wrongly thought to be, not a general philosophy of causation, but rather an *ad hoc* apologetic whereby to reconcile the Cartesian theory of mind with the obvious). In particular Malebranche upheld and developed the Cartesian theory of continuous creation; he supported the view that science must be rooted in *a priori* metaphysical principles; and he reaffirmed the distinction between the rationally conceivable essence and the empirically perceivable properties of things. But his influence in these matters was less great than it might have been. The Cartesian philosophy was already being eclipsed by the more systematic work of Spinoza and Leibniz, and by the powerful attack on rationalism initiated by Hobbes and given magisterial form in Locke's *Essay on the Human Understanding.*

It is impossible to leave the subject of the Cartesian revolution without taking a brief forward glance into that intellectual movement known to the historian of ideas as the 'Enlightenment', and known to philosophers either as the eighteenth century, or as nothing at all. By the end of the seventeenth century, scientific knowledge, and the Cartesian clarity of expression, had become universal properties of the educated class; and a new literature began to arise, encyclopaedic in its aims, anti-authoritarian in its preconceptions and outspoken in its style (see especially Pierre Bayle (1647–1706): *Dictionnaire historique et critique,* 1696). Culminating in the writings of Voltaire, Diderot and d'Alembert, this movement has gained international status in the eyes of the intellectual historian. But it remains decidedly French in its tone and manners. Clear, elegant, haughty and ironical, the '*philosophes*', as they came to be known, stand at the end of a century in which intellectual, political and moral revolutions had upset the authority of Church and State, and humbled in their eyes all mortals whose pretensions to eminence could be backed neither by reason nor by experiment. Most of the *philosophes* had their intellectual roots in Cartesian scepticism; but by now this scepticism, separated from the intellectual accomplishment of the metaphysics which stemmed from it, had become a literary device, a means to sustain a detached attitude of rational unbelief, while treating of matters that could allow neither systematic development nor the easy extraction of a moral.

The *philosophes* and the figures of the literary Enlightenment, authors of literary masterpieces as diverse as Voltaire's *Le Siècle de Louis XIV* and Diderot's *Le Neveu de Rameau,* would not have existed but for the decades of Cartesian metaphysics which cleared the intellectual air for them. Nevertheless, they play an insignificant part in the history of philosophy, neither adding to nor subtracting from the metaphysical ideas which their urbane scepticism made it more agreeable to them to ridicule than to understand. No doubt it is a further tribute to Descartes that his method should transmute itself into so many literary forms. But the history of philosophy proceeded independently, returning to the legacy of Descartes with a spirit which he would have recognised, but which was not his own.

8

Libertarian Challenge in Philosophy

Introduction

Libertarian thinking has also played a role in reshaping the societies of the former Communist world and in laying the foundations for the "new world order" proclaimed by former U.S. president George Bush, a new world order built upon the foundations of free trade and respect for human rights. In addition, libertarian ideas have contributed to institutional changes in the areas of criminal justice and the provision of welfare services, supporting programs that emphasize personal responsibility and retribution for wrongdoing. Libertarianism has also provided support for privatization of public services, public utilities, public schools, and public pension plans. While no reasonable person would claim that these changes in the political currents of the times are directly due to libertarian philosophy, it would be equally unreasonable to suppose that the flowering of libertarian philosophy in the 1970s and 1980s has been without any influence on the course of events. In any case, however much libertarian ideas may have contributed to the political currents of the times, as philosophical ideas, they are worthy of serious attention. Libertarianism offers a relatively clear, coherent, and powerful conception of how societies ought to be organized. Its strong central commitment to individual liberty and individual rights cannot but appeal to us who, living at the end of the twentieth century, know of the horrors of the gulag and the Holocaust. Still, libertarianism is not without its difficulties.

The Metaphysics of Rights

Libertarianism is a rights-based theory. It bases itself on a strong conception of rights that human beings have independent of any consideration of utility or the collective good of the society as a whole. Further, according to the libertarian, these rights are natural in the sense that they do not depend upon any human agency and cannot be taken away by any human agency. This conception of human rights as natural is one libertarians share with Locke and the other great thinkers of the naturallaw and natural-rights tradition. But, as we have seen already, Bentham and the utilitarians subjected the ideas of natural law and natural rights to a withering criticism. According to Bentham, claims about natural rights were metaphysically suspect. Such rights were strange entities, not detectable by the scientific methods of observation and reason based on observation. Because claims to have such rights were untestable and unprovable, they were, on Bentham's view, "nonsense," empty words without meaning or significance. The conservative philosopher Edmund Burke concurred with Bentham in this at least, dismissing the proclamations of rights by American and French revolutionaries as subjective products of human fantasy. How might the libertarian defend the notion of natural rights against such criticisms?

There are a number of lines of argument open to the libertarian here. Actually, Bentham and Burke ignored at least one promising line of defense for claims to natural rights. Natural-rights theorists thought that claims about rights could be derived from observation and reason. By observation we learn that it is in the nature of knives to have sharp edges. By observation we learn that such an edge is conducive to cutting and is damaged by use as a pry bar. By reason we conclude that the right way to use a knife is for cutting and that to use a knife to pry nails is a misuse of it a use contrary to its nature. In the same way we learn by observation that human beings have a capacity for autonomous self-direction, for forming goals and plans to reach those goals. Accordingly, to enslave a person is to misuse him, to use him contrary to his nature. Human beings have a natural right to liberty because liberty conforms to human nature, to the natural capacity humans have to form their own life plans and act accordingly.

But there is a problem with this argument. The argument moves from claims about the nature of a thing to conclusions about how we ought to treat the thing. Because human beings have the capacity for autonomous self-direction, we ought to respect their liberty of action. But there is a logical lacuna here. From claims about what is the case, nothing follows about what should be the case. I might, for example, acknowledge that humans have the capacity for self-direction but hold that this is an evil trait in them that ought to be suppressed. Arguments for natural rights rest upon the suppressed premise that we ought to treat things in accordance with their natures. Given this premise, and the claim that humans have by nature a capacity for autonomous self-direction, it would follow that we ought to treat people in accordance with that capacity, that we ought not enslave them. But how can we prove the premise that we ought to treat things in accordance with their natures?

Locke and many of the natural-law theorists did have an answer here. Locke argued that God made us, that God does nothing in vain, and that accordingly God intends for humans to use their capacity for autonomous self-direction. But if this is so, then God intends for us not to interfere with other people so as to prevent their using this capacity. So far these premises speak only of what is the case. They tell us what human nature is and what God's intentions are. So far nothing has been said about what ought to be the case. But now Locke adds the premise that we ought to do what God wants. With this premise, Locke is able to bridge the gap between the "is" and the "ought." But it is not a premise Bentham or the utilitarians were willing to accept. In their view, the need to have recourse to theology was a sign of the metaphysical and unscientific status of the natural-rights tradition.

The modern libertarian John Hospers offers an alternative grounding of the central libertarian claim for a natural right to liberty. He holds that the right to liberty is a consequence of one's ownership of his own life:

> *The political philosophy that is called libertarianism (from the Latin* libertas, *liberty) is the doctrine that every person is the owner of his own life, and that no one is the owner of anyone else's life; and that consequently every human being has the right to act in accordance with his own choices, unless those actions infringe on the equal liberty of other human beings to act in accordance with* their *choices."*

This argument is clearly inadequate as an attempt to provide a general foundation for a theory of natural rights. In the first place, to say that everyone is the owner of his own life is to attribute a bundle of ownership rights over one's own life to each individual. But clearly this begs the question, assuming the existence of a natural right of ownership when it is the existence of such rights that is at issue. A philosopher such as Bentham, who questioned the whole idea of natural rights, would not be impressed by this argument.

There is also considerable room for doubt about the truth of the presupposed ownership rights, even assuming that some natural rights do exist. After all, it has long been a tenet of several of the world's great religions that our lives belong to God and not to ourselves. Other philosophers have held that our lives belong, at least in part, to our parents and to the community that nurtured us. In Plato's *Crito,* for example, Socrates seems to hold all of these positions, arguing that suicide is wrong because it amounts to stealing from the gods and that we owe a degree of obedience to our parents and the communities that have nurtured us.

Another libertarian strategy for supporting claims about the existence of rights draws on the resources of social-contract theory. Like Rawls, the libertarian asks us to imagine individuals entering into a social contract whereby they agree to live together according to certain fundamental rules. The libertarian argues that it is in the self-interest of each to adopt inviolable rights to life, liberty, and property as fundamental rules governing social life. While by doing so each loses the freedom to act aggressively against the others, each gains security against the aggression of others. Since such security is necessary for just about any course of life a human being might happen to desire, each gains more by entering into this agreement than she loses by doing so. In this way fundamental rights can be grounded in the self-interest of rational individuals.

But here too there are difficulties. While it is true that each individual is better off in a society where everyone respects rights to life, liberty, and property than she would be in a society where no one does so, each is even better off living in a society where everyone else respects those rights and she does not. It is in the self-interest of Lucrezia to promise to respect basic rights and persuade others to do so also. But it may well be in her self-interest, when she is nearly certain she can get away with it, to break the promise she has made and poison her rich uncle. Further, each person who enters into the social contract on the basis of self-interest is in exactly the same position as Lucrezia. It is in the self-interest of each of us to agree to respect basic rights and yet to break this argument when it is to our advantage to do so. For this kind of reason, it is difficult to see how strong rights can be constructed on the basis of individual self-interest. Just as the principle of utility would seem to require the consistent utilitarian to defect from respecting rights in some situations, so rational self-interest would seem to require defection in some cases. Like utilitarianism, self-interest fails to provide a solid foundation for morally inviolable rights.

For the most part, Nozick is not concerned to prove that

rights exist. He simply assumes that individuals have a strong right to liberty and explores the implications of this. However, in a section where Nozick explains his view of the right to liberty as a side constraint against coercive interference, he suggests that such an inviolable right against coercion rests on Kantian moral theory: "Side constraints upon action reflect the underlying Kantian principle that individuals are ends and not merely means; they may not be sacrificed or used for the achieving of other ends without their consent." It is certainly true that the Kantian principle, insofar as it sets constraints on how people may be treated no matter what the end in view may be, seems to provide support for a rights-based political philosophy. But the Kantian principle, at least as developed by Kant, itself rests upon dubious metaphysical foundations.

Kant held that human beings are metaphysically different from mere things. Insofar as we are viewed as parts of the natural universe, everything about us is causally determined. Were this the whole story about us, in Kant's view we would not be morally responsible for our actions and would not have the peculiar quality of rational practical agency that elevates us above other animals and objects, making of us ends that may not be treated as mere means. In short, Kant's defense of rights rests on a metaphysics that rejects naturalism. For him, human beings are contained within the natural order only insofar as we concern ourselves with the phenomenal world of appearances. The true nature of human beings lies hidden in the world of things in themselves. Now it may be that Kant is wrong in thinking that naturalism precludes responsibility and that the Kantian principle is reconcilable with naturalism, but it is not obvious that this is so. In any case, the libertarian who embraces the whole of Kant takes on considerable metaphysical difficulties, and the libertarian who wants to extract the moral principle from its surrounding Kantian metaphysics needs to show that this is possible.

Perhaps in the end the best approach for the libertarian to take is to simply assume that certain rights do exist. Most of us are prepared to follow the libertarian in postulating inviolable or nearly inviolable rights to life and liberty.

However, a much greater controversy surrounds the libertarian view that each individual also has a strong right to property. Let us now turn to consideration of some of the difficulties faced by the libertarian with regard to such a right to property. Does the libertarian have good reason to think that every individual has a right to property? Is the right to property inviolable or nearly so? Is taxation to pay for entitlements claimed by positive rights a violation of individuals' rights? These are some of the questions we will be considering.

Libertarian Property Rights: A Critical Assessment

Libertarians often compare taxation to support welfare safety nets with armed robbery, slavery, and forced-labor camps. Since taxation is backed up by the coercive power of government, it is viewed as morally equivalent in kind to the coercive power of the thief, the slaveholder, and the dictator. Such a view rests upon the assumption that people have strong rights over the property that they own, rights that are somehow essentially connected with the right to liberty, so that taxation and slavery are essentially the same. Do we have such rights? What is the connection between property rights over things and the individual's right to liberty? How do we come to have property rights over things?

The Problem of Original Acquisition

Suppose we were to trace the ownership history of some piece of property, either in land or in some other kind of good. The object will have a history of transfers from one owner to another. These transfers may involve sale, trade, gift, or bequeathment, for example. The history of an object may also involve some process of manufacture, where the manufacturer purchases raw materials and combines them to form a finished product, which is then sold to a customer. All of these transfers involve a change in ownership rights from one person to another. But how did anyone ever first come to own anything? If we trace the ownership of any object backward in time, eventually we must reach a point where land, or ore, or trees, or some other natural product that was not owned by any human being comes to be owned by someone. Strong property rights of the kind envisaged by the libertarian give the owner of the thing complete control over the thing, control that includes the right to prevent others from using the thing without permission of the owner. How can this be? How can some individual come to have exclusive rights over a part of the world that previously was not owned by anyone at all? The idea that individual human beings can somehow acquire ownership rights over parts of the earth has struck many people as strange. Many of the native American peoples believed that the land belonged to the people as a whole for their use. A similar view, that the earth belonged in usufruct to the living, was held by Thomas Jefferson as well.

This problem of original acquisition is important for the libertarian in at least two ways. First, according to Nozick's libertarian theory of justice, the justice of any distribution of goods is a function of the history of that distribution rather than of the pattern exhibited by that distribution. If the distribution was reached by just transfers from justly acquired initial holdings, then and only then is the distribution just. This account needs some theory of justice in original acquisition. Second, libertarian complaints that taxation to support welfare safety nets is slavery requires property rights of a very strong kind, rights that are not in any way encumbered by social obligations. But since transfer can only transfer rights previously acquired, the libertarian is going to need some account of original acquisition that yields strong property rights of the kind presupposed by the criticism of taxation for social welfare programs. Can the libertarian deliver?

Locke argued that by mixing one's own labor with objects in their natural state, one comes to have a property right over the natural object. Some libertarians appear to have endorsed this Lockean account of original acquisition. But other libertarians have rejected Locke's account for the reasons we noted in our discussion of it. Briefly put, it is not clear why one gains a right over the entire object and not just over the portion of the worked object made up of the labor one mixed in.

Ayn Rand has suggested that property rights are derivable from the right to life. She argues that since material goods are necessary to sustain life, we have a right to possess them. However, this suggestion ill serves the libertarian cause. In the first place, it fails to establish the strong kind of property rights necessary for libertarian criticisms of the welfare state, since it grounds rights over property only to the extent that we have need of that property to sustain life. Second, Rand's argument construes the right to life, and the derivative rights to material goods, as positive rights of the kind that libertarians reject. For the libertarian, the right to life, properly understood, is the negative right not to be killed, not the positive right to the material goods necessary to sustain life. Finally, Rand's argument reveals a deep fissure between her own ethical egoism, according to which the highest virtue consists in selfishness, in doing what is good for the self, and libertarianism, which puts respect for the rights of others on a moral par with pursuit of one's self-interest.

Having noted that "many writers seem to think that there is a terrible problem about extending a right of personal freedom to the use of items in the external world," Jan Narveson goes on dismiss the supposed problem: "Just as we can do what we wish with the natural parts of our own person, bodily and psychological, so we may do what we wish with bits of external nature, so long only as we do not thereby damage or impede the uses by others of such objects." But, as stated here, Narveson's view amounts to nothing more than the mere assertion that, "just as" we have a right to liberty, so too we have property rights over bits of the external world. In particular, Narveson does not give us any reason for thinking that property rights over external objects are "extensions" of a right to personal freedom, in the sense of being somehow based on or derivable from the right to personal freedom. We will return to this question concerning the relationship between the right to liberty and property rights below. For now, let us focus on the restrictions on property rights mentioned by Narveson when he says that we may exercise control over bits of external nature "so long as we do not thereby damage or impede the uses by others of such objects."

Suppose you and I are hunter-gatherers living in proximity to one another. Suppose there is a section of woods that is particularly rich in wild fruit, berries, nuts, and small game. Now suppose I claim this woods as my own property and forbid you to forage for food there. But surely in doing so I damage or impede your use of the woods. After all, before I claimed it as my personal property, you were free to use it as you liked. Now, wouldn't this be true of all original acquisitions? Strong private property rights of the kind claimed by libertarians certainly do include the right of the owner to exclude others from use of the thing. So don't all original acquisitions damage or impede the use of the thing acquired by others?

This objection is not entirely fair to Narveson. What he says is that my claiming the woods as my own must not damage or impede your use of "such objects." To be sure, my claim impedes your use of this woods, but so long as there are plenty of other woods readily available to you, you retain access to "such objects." Here Narveson clearly has in mind a proviso that Locke attached to his own account of original acquisition: I am entitled to make a part of nature my own only if there be "enough and as good left in common for others." The idea, then, is that I can make some part of nature my own private property so long as equally good portions of nature remain available for other people to use in common or claim as their own. If I were to claim the only source of water in the area as my own, I would be violating the proviso, while if I claim an acre of land, leaving plenty more available, I would not.

There is a certain reasonableness to the Lockean proviso. Clearly, if I claim the only source of water as my own, I seriously damage your interests in a way that I do not when I claim the single acre as my own, leaving you with ample land for your own use. But can the libertarian go along with Locke, as Narveson appears to do? Prior to any act of original acquisition you were at liberty to cross this piece of land. Now I claim this piece of land as my own. You are no longer at liberty to cross this piece of land. By my own unilateral action I have canceled your right to cross this piece of land. That there is as much and as good left over should not be relevant for the libertarian, for whom the right to liberty is inviolable.

There is also a regress problem that seems to render the Lockean proviso unsatisfiable. Nozick provides a clear formulation of the problem:

> *Consider the first person Z for whom there is not enough and as good left to appropriate. The last person Y to appropriate left Z without his previous liberty to act on an object, and so worsened Z's situation. So Y's appropriation is not allowed under Locke's proviso. Therefore the next to last person X to appropriate left Y in a worse position, for X's act ended permissible appropriation. Therefore X's appropriation wasn't permissible. But then the appropriator two from last, W, ended permissible appropriation and so, since it worsened X's position, W's appropriation wasn't permissible. And so on back to the first person A to appropriate a permanent property right.*

If satisfaction of the Lockean proviso is necessary for just acquisition, and if, as the regress argument seems to show, it cannot have been satisfied in the real world, where enough and as good is clearly not available for future appropriation, then it seems to follow that no actual property rights can be acceptable.

Having eloquently formulated this difficulty, Nozick claims to have found a way around it:

> *Is the situation of persons who are unable to appropriate (there being no more accessible and useful unowned objects) worsened by a system allowing appropriation and permanent property? Here enter the various familiar social considerations favoring private property. These considerations enter a Lockean theory to support the claim that appropriation of private property satisfies the intent behind the "enough and as good left over" proviso, not as a utilitarian justification of property. They enter to rebut the claim that because the proviso is violated no natural right to private property can arise by a Lockean process.*

The social considerations favoring private property Nozick has in mind here, omitted in the passage quoted above, will be considered below. They all have to do with the social benefits of private property, and they appear to provide a utilitarian case for private property. But Nozick insists that this is not their role here. His idea seems to be that since private property does have the kind of consequences claimed by the utilitarian argument, original acquisition does not leave even those for whom nothing is left to appropriate worse off than they would have been had there been no acquisition of private property.

But this interpretation of the Lockean proviso seems to countenance balancing lost liberties against opportunities and welfare gained. This is made especially clear in a footnote where Nozick speaks in terms of providing compensation only for those individuals "for whom the process of civilization was a *net loss*, for whom the benefits of civilization did not counter balance being deprived of these particular liberties." However reasonable, such a balancing seems flatly inconsistent with Nozick's own view of the right to liberty as a side constraint that may not be violated even for greater benefits.

It should also be noted that even if Nozick is successful in disarming the regress argument, what he has achieved in that case would be only to show that original acquisition has not been shown to be impermissible. We still do not have a libertarian account of how original acquisition is possible, and we certainly do not have a libertarian argument showing that private property rights are anything like direct extensions of the right to liberty. In the passage quoted above, Nozick talks about familiar social considerations favoring private property entering a "Lockean theory" to satisfy the restrictions imposed by the proviso, and just below the quoted passage he talks about private property arising by a "Lockean process." But the fact is that there is no "Lockean theory" or "Lockean process" remaining. The heart of the Lockean theory and the Lockean process was the idea of mixing one's labor with natural objects as the foundation for original acquisition. But Nozick himself has, rightly, rejected that idea. We are left, then, with no account of how original acquisition could produce strong property rights and no account of the supposed connection between liberty and property.

On the Supposed Connection between Liberty and Property

Libertarian comparisons of taxation with armed robbery, slavery, and forced labor reinforce the libertarian claim of an intimate connection between property rights and the right to liberty. Narveson makes an even stronger claim, holding that "liberty = property." Narveson supports his claim in this way: "To own something is to have the right to do with it as one pleases: the disposition of that thing is up to you, not someone else." Now, if I have a right to do with something what I please, then I am free to do with that thing what I please. And if the disposition of the thing is entirely up to me and not to anyone else, then I am free to dispose of it as I see fit. And if I am free to do with or dispose of a thing solely as I see fit, then, perhaps, taxation would involve a violation of liberty, a violation of my freedom to dispose of my property as I see fit. But this argument works only if we assume that our property rights do give us the right to use or dispose of our property solely as we see fit. Do we have such strong property rights? Do we have the kinds of moral rights over the things that we own that Narveson claims that we do, or are our property rights in some way encumbered by social responsibilities? If property rights come with built-in social responsibilities, then we are not free to use and dispose of these things solely as we see fit, and taxation may exist without being a violation of our liberty.

Suppose Charlotte has a position as professor of Latin and Greek at Liberty College. Having this position, she has certain rights. She has, for example, the right to decide what books will be read in her classes and the right to say what she thinks about the matters of her expertise. Now, suppose Charlotte decides to sell her position to Harold, a retired fertilizer salesman with no training in classical languages. If the college intervenes to prevent Charlotte from selling the position to Harold, is it thereby violating her liberty to dispose of her property? If Liberty College requires Charlotte and all of its professors to give a final exam in her classes, is this "tax" on the available time for the course a violation of Charlotte's liberty?

Of course, to have a college teaching position does not include the right to sell the position, and college teaching positions usually come with a number of institutional responsibilities attached. But this example does get us to see that "having" something may not be quite the all-or-nothing affair that Narveson's argument presupposes. Property rights are complex. Ownership of a thing typically brings with it a bundle of rights, including the rights to use and dispose of the thing claimed by Narveson. But, traditionally, property rights have also been thought to carry with them some responsibilities, including the responsibility of paying taxes. When I buy a house from you, I acquire the legal right to use the house and the legal right to dispose of it by selling it to someone else. But in buying the house I also acquire the legal responsibility of paying the property tax that has been assessed against that house. There is nothing mysterious about this. It would be decidedly odd for me to complain when the tax bill comes that the government is stealing my house. I knew about the legal encumbrance on the property when I bought it.

So much is obviously true if we consider the matter solely from a legal point of view. Narveson's complaint would be that the law is immoral in this respect. But this complaint rests upon the assumption that individuals hold moral rights over external things that do not carry with them moral responsibilities that may be morally enforced by governmental power, and Narveson has given us no reason for thinking that this assumption is true.

Property as an Adventitious Right

Within the natural-rights tradition, many authors have distinguished between primary or primitive natural rights, which come to human beings directly from the hand of God, and secondary or adventitious natural rights, which depend upon human interpretations or applications of natural law. Among the primary natural rights are the rights to life and liberty that God gives to each individual human being, and the common right to use of the earth and all that it contains that God gave to humankind as a whole. Individual property rights, which assign particular parts of the external world to particular individuals, are understood as secondary or adventitious rights. A system of such rights is one way for human beings to make use of the earth that God gave in common to all human beings. This distinction between the primary natural rights of life and liberty and the adventitious rights of property can be found in the works of Grotius, Pufendorf, and Blackstone, among others, and may well have influenced Thomas Jefferson in his decision not to include the right to property as one of the fundamental human rights listed in the Declaration of Independence.

Let us pursue this framework for regarding property rights a bit further. God has given us human beings the earth and all that it contains for our common use. Each of us needs food, clothing, and shelter to survive in this world, and each of us has wants for more goods than those necessary for mere survival. How shall we make use of our common heritage to satisfy our wants? We could organize ourselves communistically, regarding all natural resources and all that we produce from these resources as belonging not to individuals but to society as a whole. Or we could institute a system of private property, allowing individuals to claim parts of external nature as their own. Either of these approaches is a way in which we humans might share our common God given heritage. Which system should we adopt? While it might appear that communism is closer to what God had in mind for us in giving the earth to us in common, considerations about the lack of individual incentives in communism, and the strong individual incentives associated with private ownership, might persuade reasonable people that a system of private property would be adventitious to us in trying to satisfy as many of our wants as possible. However, recognizing that God gave the earth to us in common, and recognizing the relative weakness of charity in the human soul, we would want to be sure to arrange our system of private property in such a way that individual property rights were linked with individual responsibilities to maintain the common good and to respect the natural right to liberty God gave to every human individual.

Here, then, is a way of understanding how human beings could have come to acquire private property consistent with natural rights to life and liberty. But it is important to note that the individual property rights produced in this way are not the strong property rights presupposed by libertarians.

A Pseudolibertarian Argument

Since the time of Adam Smith, numerous thinkers have stressed the benefits that free markets bring to humankind. Similar arguments can be made for private property. Relevant here are those social considerations on behalf of private property mentioned by Nozick in the passage quoted above. Private property gives each owner an incentive to care for her property and utilize it in the most efficient way possible. Private property encourages experimentation and innovation, which ultimately benefits consumers. Private property allows individuals greater control over the level of risk to which they are exposed. And private property protects individual liberty by providing means of existence that are not controlled by central political powers. These arguments have been powerfully developed by important thinkers such as Ludwig von Mises, Friedrich Hayek, and Milton Friedman. They are arguments deserving of attention, arguments that may well support the desirability of extensive rights to private property. But they are not libertarian arguments. For the most part, they are straightforwardly utilitarian arguments. They justify private property on the grounds that it has optimal consequences for maximizing the satisfaction of human wants. These are not rights-based arguments of the kind needed by libertarian theory. To be sure, there is no contradiction in being a libertarian and thinking that private property maximizes happiness. But one cannot make the supposed consequence of happiness maximization the grounds for a libertarian conception of property rights. Some other argument would be needed for that. Insofar as we make conduciveness to maximizing happiness the justification for private property, we leave room for considerations of distributive justice of the kind advanced by the new liberals—

considerations that libertarian theory seeks to preclude.

Workers' Rights

Libertarians oppose legally enforced collective bargaining, minimum wage laws, government imposed health and safety regulations, legally imposed limits on the working day, and other measures advocated by socialists and new liberals. They oppose these measures on the grounds that they interfere with the rights of private property, and consequently with the right to liberty. But this argument works only if we presuppose that individuals who do own property have complete and morally unencumbered control over the property that they own. A central argument in this chapter has been that libertarians have not succeeded in showing that individuals do have any such strong property rights. If individual property rights are adventitious rights, rights resulting from human-made arrangements for using our common, God given heritage, there is some reason to think that individual property rights would not be so strong. The view of property rights as adventitious understands them as rights that must come encumbered with communally enforceable moral responsibilities. If God gave us the earth as our common heritage, any way we devise to use that common heritage must provide for the good of all and respect the rights of each. The measures adopted by new liberal governments to protect the rights of workers were measures aimed at protecting workers from the pressures of competition and from the bargaining power held by property owners. They aimed at guaranteeing that the advantages of private property would redound to the common good, and that private property would not undermine the liberty of individual workers. Such measures are fully consistent with strong rights of individual liberty and adventitious rights of private property. They are also consistent, or at least possibly consistent, with the utilitarian argument for private property. The libertarian argument against such measures presupposes a view of property rights that is not adequately supported by libertarian theory.

The Role of Free Markets

In *"What Libertarianism Is,"* John Hospers notes that many readers are apt to respond to libertarian proposals to eliminate all welfare safety nets with the rejoinder "But then you'd let people go hungry." Hospers continues:

> *This, the libertarian insists, is precisely what would not happen; with the restrictions removed, the economy would flourish as never before. With the controls taken off business, existing enterprises would expand and new ones would spring into existence satisfying more and more consumer needs; millions more people would be gainfully employed instead of subsisting on welfare, and all kinds of research and production, released from the stranglehold of government, would proliferate, fulfilling man's needs and desires as never before. It has always been so whenever government has permitted men to be free traders on a free market.*

But has it always been so? Didn't laissez-faire capitalism export grain from Ireland while the Irish people starved? Didn't free markets gives us the sordid, dreary world described by Charles Dickens? Didn't capitalism drive the people of Britain off the land, forcing them to abandon farming beneath the open sky and leaving them prisoners in the darkness of the mines and factories? Didn't capitalism crush the bodies and spirits of whole generations of working men and women? Don't free markets bring the insecurity of periodic crises, with massive unemployment and attendant misery? Isn't Hospers's cheery optimism a testament to the power of ideology to ignore the facts?

Thinkers sympathetic to the libertarian outlook have tried to address the issues raised by these questions. In *Capitalism and the Historians*, F.A. Hayek edited a collection of essays devoted to showing that critics of capitalism had romanticized the past and that in fact, on the whole, the standard of living for the working class rose with the advent of capitalism and free trade in the nineteenth century. Hayek also tried to show that the periodic depressions that seem to accompany the operations of free markets are really caused by misguided governmental interventions. This idea was vindicated to some extent by Milton and Rose Friedman, who tried to show that the great depression of the 1930s was not the result of failures of the market, as has commonly been supposed, but rather the result of mistakes by those in charge of the Federal Reserve system in the United States.

These and other studies of their kind are certainly important, but they fall far short of what is needed to sustain the libertarian position with respect to free markets. In the first place, the arguments of Hospers, Hayek, and the Friedmans sketched above all work within the framework of broadly utilitarian defenses of free markets. For the real libertarian, free markets must be preserved even if they have the disastrous consequences attributed to them by the romantic socialist. Beyond this, the arguments, which remain controversial, would not be adequate to support the view that no intervention in the operation of free markets, is desirable even if they were true.

Suppose it is true that working class wages were rising during the nineteenth century. Does it follow that new liberal measures that interfered with the operation of the market were misguided? Not at all. It is enough for the new liberal to argue that measures that interfered with the market could make things better. In an essay concerned with the problem of world hunger, the philosopher Peter Singer formulates a principle concerning avoidable suffering: "If it is in our power to prevent something bad from happening, without thereby sacrificing anything of comparable moral importance, we ought, morally to do it." Now, even if it is true that living standards had improved under free market capitalism, considerable poverty and suffering remained. What if, by interfering somewhat with the market, it was possible to reduce this remaining suffering without sacrificing anything of comparable moral importance? From the consequentialist point of view, to show this would be sufficient to justify market interference, and this is exactly the claim advanced by Hobhouse in making the case for new liberal measures: "The prime justification of this expenditure is that the prevention of suffering is a duty to fulfil. Any common life based on avoidable suffering is a life not of harmony but of discord."

Of course, supporters of free markets are apt to argue that while Hobhouse and the new liberals may have thought they could do better than the free market, in fact they were mistaken, and the kinds of interferences with the market they initiated only ended up making things worse. This is the kind of argument favored by Hayek and the Friedmans, for example. But, in the end, this argument fails to convince.

If one looks at the whole historical record, from the dawn of free market capitalism in the days of Adam Smith to the present, the evidence seems to support the new liberal position. While standards of living may have been rising under free market capitalism, they did even better during the heyday of new liberal regulation, from 1945 to 1975. It is the welfare-state economies of Germany, Japan, and the Scandinavian countries that have, historically, provided the highest standards of living for the widest portion of people over the longest period of time. Further, to the extent that neoliberal policies have attempted to restore free markets in the period after 1975, they appear to have produced social polarization of the kind experienced in the early days of capitalism, with great wealth on one side matched by great poverty on the other. While this conclusion is based on a highly speculative reading of historical experience, an experience contaminated with all kinds of complexities, it seems closer to the mark of truth than the wild optimism of Hospers's own appeal to history.

Libertarianism offers a clear, coherent, and powerful conception of how societies ought to be organized. No doubt these are virtues in a theory. But, in the end, libertarianism illustrates the wisdom of Kant's point that a theory that doesn't work in practice is not good, even in theory. [28] In any case, Kant himself was no libertarian. He saw no contradiction between his prohibition against using people as mere means, and taxation for social welfare. He held that, "Indirectly, i.e. in so far as he takes the duty of the people upon himself, the supreme commander has the right to impose taxes upon the people for their own preservation, e.g. for the *care of the poor*, for *foundling hospitals* and *church activities*, or for what are otherwise known as charitable or pious institutions."

Libertarianism is a political philosophy that focuses on the rights of individuals. It is the core belief in libertarianism that individuals have the right to do whatever they want with their person or possessions, as long as they do not infringe upon the same rights of others. Because of this belief, libertarians feel that groups, simply made up of individuals, have no more power than an individual. Therefore, most libertarians would say that there should be as little government as is practically possible. The main goal of libertarianism is to help individuals assume control of their lives.

Libertarianism should not be confused with liberalism. They were considered the same in the early to mid nineteenth-century, both sharing the same beliefs such as limiting state power and the benefits of a free market. But around the 1870s liberals were gradually moving toward the belief that the government was necessary in guaranteeing social justice. Liberalism developed into a philosophy which wants an increase in government power, taxes, and regulation. Libertarians feel this philosophy is very close to socialism and therefore do not agree with it. Libertarians believe that collecting taxes is another form of robbery.

This is the true origin of libertarian thought, as then the beliefs of liberals were very much the same as today's libertarians. The origins of libertarianism stretch back into the Renaissance with the humanist scholars of that time. Galileo and Erasmus were among the main humanists who began this type of thought about human rights. Galileo, who was tried on suspicion of heresy, was made to recant his scientific ideas which challenged Church doctrine. This whole event is seen as a crucial part in the development of human rights issues.

9

Political Philosophy from Hobbes to Hegel

Introduction

The *Leviathan* bears the mark of a civil war in which Hobbes and his contemporaries had been made aware of the terror and evil-doing which stem from anarchy. The book aims to justify the power and authority of the sovereign and to show that rebellion is seldom if ever justified, not only because of the chaos that it brings, but also because it involves a breach of a deep and self-contracted obligation. Many of Hobbes's arguments are *ad hoc,* part of his own personal response to the tragic conflict which he had witnessed, rather than arguments from first principles. Nevertheless, his wide influence over his contemporaries is due at least in part to his attempt to provide a metaphysical foundation for political institutions, and to rise above the contingencies of history so as to view human community as it must be, in every age. He was a monarchist, but he inspired the republican Spinoza, whose *Tractatus Theologico-Politicus* displays the same realistic view of human nature, and the same lofty disdain for political fashion, that are characteristic of Hobbes. The fact that Hobbes was an empiricist of a crudely formulated but uncompromising kind shows the extent to which empiricism lies at the basis of modern political philosophy, being the generating principle of major theories of the state, even when these issue from the pen of a philosopher like Spinoza, for whom reason is the ultimate court of appeal.

Hobbes's principal concern was with the concept of sovereignty, and with the rights and powers associated therewith. He conceived civil association as a 'commonwealth', arranged in rank and influence around the sovereign power, much as the parts of an organism are arranged around a single active principle of life. The organic analogy was very important to Hobbes, and enabled him both to describe the nature of the sovereign power, and also to separate it intellectually from any particular person, assembly or constitutional process that might be thought in this or that political arrangement to embody it. Hence his ideas about sovereignty were to prove acceptable to many who did not share his conviction that, unless the sovereign power finds concrete expression in a monarch, it neither commands the allegiance of the citizen nor supports the cohesion of the state. Hobbes's extremely crude empiricism led him to a philosophy of mind that gave little persuasive power to that thought, or to the analogy between the life of a commonwealth and the life of an individual. But this analogy was later to be reinstated by Hegel, with all the philosophical benefits that Hobbes had been unable to provide for it. It then certainly did begin to seem persuasive.

For the purposes of this chapter, the single most important thought to be found in Hobbes lies in his assertion that there can be 'no obligation on any man which ariseth not from some act of his own'. The history of political philosophy in the eighteenth century is largely the history of that thought, and the rising conviction either that it is false, or that it serves to conceal something far more important. If the thought is right then it follows that no one is born into the world encumbered by obligations, and that no state has a right to allegiance unless it arises from some act of 'consent' however tacit, unreflecting or spontaneous on the part of the citizen. (It has to be understood that when Hobbes speaks of an 'act' he means an intentional act of a kind that could be seen as bearing within itself the creation and acceptance of an obligation. Promising is a clear example of this; so too is the knowing engagement in business according to the common laws of contract and trade.)

Hobbes finds his paradigm of obligation in contractual or quasi-contractual relations between 'consenting adults' (to use the modern term). This is naturally an odd starting point for the defence of monarchical government, in which the sovereign usually has rights over the citizen that transcend anything the citizen himself can either contract or even understand. Nevertheless, Hobbes believed that in acquiescing in the benefits of government the citizen does thereby accept, and so put himself under an obligation towards, the established order of the commonwealth. The sovereign, who is nothing but the embodied will of that order, therefore acts with the authority of all those who have overtly or covertly sought his protection.

The philosophical basis of Hobbes's quoted remark is important for what follows. Political philosophy has been preoccupied since its origins by an all-important distinction that between rights (which are enforced only in the name of justice) and powers (which are enforced come what may). Plato's *Republic* opens with an argument that purports to reduce the first to the second; Marx's historical materialism regards the first as a mere institutional reflection of the second, and allows *material* reality to powers alone. Hobbes, preoccupied by legitimacy, saw how fragile are our human conceptions of justice when not supported by material power. What therefore makes the exercise of justice possible? It cannot exist in the 'state of nature', in which the life of man is 'nasty, poor, solitary, brutish and short': it is therefore an artifact, made possible by the power of the state. So the sovereign power creates the possibility of a just order. At the same time, Hobbes recognised, we distinguish legitimate from illegitimate sovereign power. Is this merely as the 'vulgar' Marxist would persuade us an ideological illusion? Or does it have some independent basis in reality independent, that is, of the evident motive that we all have, out of greed or cowardice, to believe that where might is, there right is also?

Clearly rights exist only between persons, and a distinguishing mark of persons is that they can engage in voluntary transactions and thereby acquire at least a *sense* of obligation towards one another. It therefore seemed clear to Hobbes that we can make sense of 'rights' if we trace them back, through the complex history that surrounds them, to those acts in which the sense of obligation is first aroused. Rights can be seen as *conferred* by one person on another. They have their objective foundation in a habit of reflection that informs and is indispensable to the friendly commerce between rational beings. Their origin is wholly different from the origin of power, and hence they can stand in judgement on the exercise of power, even when power seeks to overthrow them. The happy commonwealth is clearly the one in which right and might are in consort, so that the sense of obligation confers its authority upon those *de facto* powers which seek its allegiance. Such thoughts raise enormous philosophical questions about the nature of rational agency, and about the relation between fact and value. But they serve in part to explain why so many moral and political philosophers have concentrated on the act of promising as a starting-point for their investigations. They also show the philosophical basis of a doctrine which was to develop through Locke and Rousseau to become one of the most influential of all political ideas, the doctrine of the social contract (or 'compact' as Locke called it).

In the state of nature, Hobbes believed, rights cannot be enforced: instead there is a war of all against all, which can be brought to an end only by some agreement to cease fighting. This agreement is rational, to the extent that each person benefits from it. What form would such an agreement take? Surely, Hobbes argued, people would contract together to establish, first of all, a sovereign power supreme over every citizen, and capable of enforcing the law and maintaining the peace. The sovereign so established lies outside the contract which creates him, and therefore is not bound by its terms. Hence rebellion can never be sanctioned by the contract, unless the sovereign acts in such a way as to undermine the whole basis of the civil order, and so to bring the contract to an end.

John Locke's *Two Treatises of Civil Government* (1689–1690) were written, like the *Leviathan,* in defence of political forces which were active in the England of his time. Locke wrote in defence, not of absolute monarchy, but of a constitutional settlement, such as was established in 1688, in which a compromise of social forces dictated the structure of government institutions. Locke believed that Parliamentary rule had been threatened by the Stuart court, and he followed his patron, the first Earl of Shaftesbury, into exile during the difficult years of King James II. His first treatise was a polemic against the doctrine of the divine right of kings, upon which the Stuart kings had depended for their legitimacy, and which had been vigorously defended by Sir Robert Filmer. This somewhat parochial work is irrelevant to our concerns, except in so far as it shows that the dispute which animated Locke was the very same that had animated Hobbes the dispute over the nature and ground of legitimate government. In the second *Treatise* Locke gave what is perhaps the first extended account of the logic of the social contract.

Locke had a less bleak vision of the state of nature than Hobbes. Even in a state of nature, he argued, there is a law which all people recognise, and which they would uphold if their interests did not conflict with it. This law is implanted in us by reason (which is in turn the medium through which God's will is manifest to us). This 'law of nature' generates the 'natural rights' which are commonly recognised by all rational beings, whatever the particular political constitution which might have been imposed upon them. In subscribing to the existence of these 'rights' Locke showed the influence of the ecclesiastical philosopher Richard Hooker (1553–1600), who in his turn had adopted and reworked the mediaeval idea of 'natural law' in order to endow the Church with an authority which could transcend, regulate, and also take part in the practice of government. The theory of 'natural rights' variously stated and defended still has its following. It is characterised by its 'international' character; it specifies rights which are supposed to be independent of, and antecedent to, the rights generated by any particular political arrangement. It can therefore provide a court of appeal against the particular laws which provide a grievance to the citizen. It is for this reason that the notion of 'human rights' (the latest form of the theory) has seemed to provide American liberalism, which has its constitutional foundation in the philosophy of Locke, with an international creed to rival the ideals of socialism.

The question, 'How can there be natural rights?' appears throughout the history of philosophy in many forms and disguises, but Locke deserves credit for his clear formulation of the question and his uncompromising answer to it. It seemed to him that we are compelled by reason to acknowledge the existence of rights independently of any convention, agreement or contract which might have served to create them. To use an ancient distinction: there are rights which stem from nature and not from convention. There are, for example, natural rights to life and limb, and to the freedom which is presupposed in the exercise of choice. There is also a natural right to property, in defence of which Locke offers interesting and influential arguments. By 'mixing' his labour with an object, as when he cultivates a field, or transforms a raw material, a worker makes it his own. Thereby he transforms a relation of power into a relation of right. Nobody else can now make exclusive use of the object in question without denying this right. Yet the right arose quite naturally. It involved the intercession of no agreement or conventional usage which might have served as its 'ground'. It is given to reason to see that this 'mixing of labour' generates ownership. A person owns the fields that he has tilled as much as he owns the parts of his body. However, as Locke recognised, rights of this kind will be open to qualification. Two people may till the same field; or I may owe the opportunity to 'mix my labour' with an object to you, who have already, through your own labour, placed me, or it, in the appropriate relation.

Furthermore, I have the rights to the fruits of my labour only if I leave 'enough and as good' for others. Nevertheless, Locke thinks, such qualifications and provisos do not destroy the reality of private property as a natural right.

How persuasive is Locke's argument? Its historical importance can hardly be denied. Not only does it give clear application to the mediaeval ideas of natural law; it also provides a vivid terminology with which to describe the essence of material property. This terminology brings the concept of abstract human labour perhaps for the first time, though, certainly not for the last, into the centre of political thinking. Moreover it implies a connection between a person's freedom and his control over the product of his labour. This was later to occupy the attention of political philosophers of every persuasion.

Despite this historical importance, however, it is extremely difficult to accept either Locke's exposition of the doctrine of a natural right, or the particular examples that he gives of it. Just what is it about human reason that enables it to perceive natural rights? Does Locke suppose that there are *a priori* laws of practical reason like the categorical imperative of Kant? Or does he suppose that there is some notion of justice which can be given a clear exposition without reference to the particular political conflicts in which it is permanently embroiled? Locke provides no answer other than a theological one. Nor does he say what it is about the 'mixing of labour' that enables us to pass from a mere fact of nature (that people do things) to a law of right (that people own things). All the same, there is an intuitive power in the conception which called philosophers back to it again and again.

Even if there are natural rights, it is not to be supposed that all people in a state of nature will observe them. Hence society and its institutions are necessary, and these institutions will demand forms of obedience and create forms of obligation which surpass what can be regarded as merely 'natural'. The question therefore arises: what criterion of right and legitimacy will operate outside the realm of 'natural law'? Locke's answer recalls that of Hobbes. The criterion of legitimacy is mutual consent, and the resulting civil constitution is to be construed in contractual terms: it arises from an 'original compact'. The reason for this is as follows: all social order requires the restriction in untold ways of the freedom which a rational being enjoys in a 'state of nature'. By what title, then, can a rational being be deprived of his freedoms? The only title must be that he himself has, through whatever impression of the advantage which accrues to him, contracted not to enjoy them. In return, therefore, the civil order has a benefit which it is obliged to confer on him the benefit for which he contracted. This benefit is difficult to describe, but we know at least that it includes a measure of security in matters of life, limb, and property, together with such other comforts of human society and material well-being as the efficient order of a commonwealth might bring. The 'original compact' is not, however, made with a sovereign power, since the existence of such a power is, conceptually speaking, the end result and not the foundation of the compact. This compact is made between free beings in a state of nature, as they mutually relinquish their freedom and join forces for the common good.

In normal cases, a contract may involve a surrender not merely of freedoms, but of rights in exchange for rights of another kind. It is therefore open to someone to argue that the citizens of Locke's community have bargained away many of their rights in exchange for civil protection perhaps even the rights to life, limb and property. Locke wished to avoid such a result for he believed that natural rights *set limits* to government, thereby giving grounds for rebellion should they be violated. He argued, therefore, on grounds that are none too clear, that natural rights are *inalienable*: even if you seek to bargain them away, you cannot succeed, since they are not the kind of thing that can be bargained.

There is another difficulty for social contract theories of Locke's variety. On what grounds do we infer the existence of a social contract in any given society? Certainly there is seldom, if ever, an *explicit* contract; and how can we infer an *implicit* contract in so complex a case? Locke's answer is that a civil society, when legitimate, is made so by the 'tacit consent' of its citizens, a consent which could be represented, for clarity's sake, in the form of an explicit 'compact' defining the rights and duties of the parties in the manner of a contract at law. Unfortunately, as Hume pointed out in an essay on the 'Original Contract', the metaphor begins to look precarious. For what is the criterion of tacit consent? Locke was prepared to say that a traveller who passes through a country tacitly consents to the civil order there prevailing otherwise how could he be bound by its laws? This seems counter-intuitive. Even more counter-intuitive, Hume argued, is the suggestion that ordinary people, born into a situation from which they lack the means to escape, have tacitly consented to all the burdens which they inherit.

Locke found less difficulty than we might in postulating a means (namely migration to a 'vacant place') whereby a citizen's consent to the arrangement which surrounds him might, on becoming conscious, also be withdrawn. We now know that there are very few 'vacant places', and hence that there is a great problem in describing what it would be for a single citizen to withdraw his consent from the arrangement which surrounds and (if he is lucky) protects him. But then, *pari passu,* there must be precisely the same problem about making sense of what it is not just to *live* in a political order, but also to consent to it.

Locke introduced into political thought another highly influential conception, that of the separation of powers. Hobbes's sovereign is the single autonomous fount from which all the actions of the commonwealth take their origin. His powers are legislative, military and domestic at once. Locke argued that, even if such powers are, in practice, exercised together or by a single authority, they are separable in theory, and can be both exercised and justified independently. He went further, arguing that these powers were in fact already separated at least to some extent—in the constitution of England, and that they *ought* to be separated if that constitution were to command the consent of its subjects. He proposed that the powers which sometimes are, and always ought to be, so separated are the following: the legislative (involving the creation of laws), the executive (involving the execution of those laws and the business of government), and the 'federative' (involving the making of treaties and the waging of war).

The theory of the separation of powers is familiar from the American Constitution, which explicitly acknowledges it as one of its foundations. It was adopted and refined by the eighteenth century political theorist Charles Baron de Montesquieu (1689–1755), in his *Esprit des lois* (1748), a vivid celebration of principles which he thought to be enacted in the English constitution and which he recommended as the only certain salvation for a society adapted to the complex pursuits of contemporary man. Such a society must combine the strongest possible safeguards of liberty with the greatest internal cohesion, and it was through the separation of powers, Montesquieu argued, that this could be achieved. Such a separation (in Montesquieu's theory, between the executive, the legislative, and the judiciary) guarantees the individual liberty, by ensuring that each power can be curtailed by the others. It also ensures cohesion, through the internal relations between the powers, which make it impossible that any one of them should be exercised without the elaborate co-operation of the other two. Discussion of this intriguing conception has continued unabated to the present day, so much so that it is now very difficult to separate the basic philosophical ideas from the manifold prejudices which have woven themselves into them. Nevertheless it is another of the achievements of Locke's varied genius that he should have discovered the way in which to decompose, so to speak, the Hobbesian conception of sovereignty, and to give to it at least the semblance of a reasoned basis.

The theory of the 'social contract' is perhaps most familiarly associated with the great eccentric Jean-Jacques Rousseau (1712–1778), who threw to the winds the common sense and political sagacity which motivated Hobbes and Locke. He found in the contractual theory of politics, not only a philosophical basis for legitimacy, but also a pretext for his admiration of the 'noble savage' and a political elaboration of his grossly sentimental vision of human nature. Rousseau believed that man is good by nature and made bad only by institutions. Rousseau extracted from this prejudice an influential philosophy of education (*Émile,* 1762), and a beautiful celebration of romantic love (*La Nouvelle Héloise,* 1761). He wrote the famous *Social Contract* (1762) under its influence. In this work the contractual basis of society is offered as the only possible excuse for it, and an extreme democracy (as opposed to mere representative government) is advocated as the best way of making sense of Locke's theory of 'tacit consent'. But the book also shows, and to some extent confronts, the paradoxes of extreme democracy. For the theory of the social contract compels Rousseau to favour what many individual participants in it could only regard as tyranny.

In Rousseau's version the contract's terms are very explicit. It involves 'the total alienation of each associate, together with all his rights, to the whole community'. The reason for this is that nobody may, under the terms of such a contract, obtain a personal advantage, so that the only interest in assenting to it must be an interest in the common good. Hence in Rousseau's version the contract creates an association with almost absolute rights over its members. The association thereby created is called, when passive, the 'State' and, when active, the 'Sovereign'. In its active manifestation it has both personality and will. Rousseau calls this will the 'general will'. The details of Rousseau's theory need not here detain us although we should note the idea, famous in his day, and murderous in the aftermath of revolution which Rousseau's thinking did not a little to precipitate, that he whose will conflicts with the general will must be constrained by the general will, since his own participation in the social contract ensures that thereby he will merely be 'forced to be free'. What is important from the philosophical point of view is the assertion that the general will is not to be thought of as the sum of individual wills. As Rousseau puts it, there is a distinction between the 'general will' and the 'will of all'. The original contract does not merely aggregate the wills of those who subscribe to it: it brings into existence a new order of volition. This 'general will' is a separate entity, attached to the sovereign power, which is itself conceived in personal terms. It was this part of Rousseau's analysis that was to inspire Hegel.

Why should one speak of the state as a person? Hegel in *The Philosophy of Right* (1821) confronts this question directly, and tries to reconcile it with intuitions concerning legitimacy which while he pays lip-service to the theory of the social contract are fundamentally anti-contractual. Kant had presented a picture of personality which involved the following features. A person is an agent; he is autonomous; he has will and reason. He also has rights, obligations, and duties, and it is of his nature to be treated as end and not as means, any other treatment being simply a way of denying his personhood. Whether or not he is also of necessity an organism was a question which Kant obscured, by replacing the distinction between animal and rational being by the more obscure (although in the context equally suggestive) distinction between the empirical and the transcendental self. Now it is clear that Hobbes's 'commonwealth' *is* a kind of organism. It is born, it flourishes, it dies. It can be injured and healed, and its parts bear a relation to the whole which could fairly be called organic. (Admittedly, the concept of 'organism' is a deep and difficult one, subject of much philosophical debate from Aristotle to the present day. It would be too distracting at this juncture to do anything more than assume that we intuitively understand it.) What then can be meant by asserting that the commonwealth is also a person?

The Hegelian answer is this: first, the commonwealth has a will of its own, which is shown by the fact that there are acts of state, such as the declaration of war or the passing of a statute, which are the acts of no other person. Secondly, the state has reason. It acts for reasons, and can be persuaded and dissuaded through constitutional processes—into doing this or that. Thirdly, the state has rights (against its citizens, and against other states). It also has obligations (for example, to provide for the well-being of its members). Fourthly, the state is to be treated not as means only, but as end. Its rights are to be respected, and it is to be regarded with those interpersonal attitudes, ranging from love to resentment, which we reserve for beings which have the nature of ends in themselves.

Note that I have introduced a new conception that of the state. One of the most important advances in Hegel's political philosophy lies in his distinction between state and civil society and in his attempt to demonstrate that it makes sense to speak of the latter, but not of the former, in contractual terms. In making the distinction Hegel was to some extent influenced by Roman law, which distinguishes the true legal 'person', who has legal rights and obligations, from the various forms of association which arise out of voluntary contractual or quasi-contractual bonds between their members, but achieve no legal personality thereby. But the basis of the distinction is much deeper than jurisprudence reveals. I will therefore try to reconstruct it in different terms.

Hegel's politics have their roots in his conception of the individual self. It is a presupposition of all contractarian theories of the state that the rational being in a state of nature has autonomous choice. How else can he enter into a bargain of such a momentous kind? Hegel denied this autonomy, not because of its historical impossibility, but because of its logical impossibility. He regarded autonomy as a kind of artifact. It is not, and cannot be, given to the subject in a state of nature, but is, rather, acquired by him through that process of dialectical interaction with his kind, a part of which we have already seen in the parable of the master and the slave. In the state of nature the subject exists as pure subject. He has will of a kind, but neither self-consciousness nor the freedom which expresses it. He emerges from this darkness at the end of a struggle (and since the contractarian allows himself an historical myth, so much the more can Hegel, who regarded history as 'the unfolding of the concept'). Only then, in the light of mutuality, when he recognises himself as a social being, bound by a moral law which constrains him to recognise the selfhood of others, and to see them as ends and not as means, does the individual acquire his freedom.

By then society already exists. Society could not, therefore, have been based in any contract, since the individual autonomy, without which no contract can be made, presupposes the society which is supposedly formed through it.

The objection is a profound one. It makes clear that political philosophy cannot proceed independently of the philosophy of mind, and that the notion of individual autonomy which is assumed in social contract theory (and which still has its advocates in modern liberalism) may in fact beg all the political questions that it is supposed to answer. But if we accept the Hegelian conception of the subject, what can we say about the concept of legitimacy? Again in Roman spirit, Hegel draws our attention to the concept of piety (*pietas*). This is the ability to recognise and act on obligations which are not the product of individual choice. Such obligations surround the individual at birth, forming his self-consciousness, and invading his freedom, even before he has fully acquired either. These obligations are those of the household. Disloyalty to the household is disloyalty to self, since it involves the rejection of the force without which freedom, will and reason would be empty gestures in a moral void. Hence it is an essential part of rationality to recognise obligations which are not self-imposed, or 'contracted'. All the arguments for thinking that a rational being must recognise a legitimacy in contractual rights are therefore arguments for saying that he must also recognise legitimacy in something else. It is this 'something else' which it is the business of political philosophy to describe.

Having introduced a concept of legitimacy which transcends individual contract, the way is open for Hegel to expound and defend the conception of the state as an entity, the authority of which transcends anything that might have been conferred on it by 'tacit consent', much as its historical reality transcends the life of any individual subject. This great 'person' clearly has rights that no small person could have (for example, the right to demand the death of an individual citizen). Hegel has reversed, in one stroke, the whole doctrine of the 'natural right', and replaced it by one of 'artificial obligation'. The individual has no natural rights which transcend his obligation to be ruled by the state which has determined his autonomy. This thought may be attacked as a tyrant's charter: Hegel thought that it was not, and he based his rejection of the charge in an account of the nature of individual freedom.

The individual finds his freedom only in the process of self-discovery. This process implicates every institution by which the individual is surrounded. The first of these institutions (both historically and conceptually) is the family. It is one of the important advances of Hegel's political thought that he recognised, what until then had so seldom been acknowledged, that the political being derives his social sense from an arrangement which is private. It is private in the sense of depending on obligations of piety, and these could never have been contracted. The family and its obligations are therefore deeply implicated in the individual's initial rise to freedom. But his freedom cannot be completed in these relations of 'natural piety'. The individual requires a sphere of free action in which he can try out his will against others and achieve a resolution in just relations. This sphere is the sphere of consent, and hence of contract. Hegel calls it 'civil society': it is the nexus of unformed association which surrounds and gives identity to the family. This unformed association can be described in contractual terms, since it has its essence in the mutual recognition of obligations arising out of individual choice.

However, no social contract can fulfil the freedom which it generates. It will always remain vulnerable to the tyranny of individual will, and so can break down at any moment. It adds to the agent only an imperfect sense of the *objective* reality of social order. It is an association of subjects, but not yet an independent objective being. The individual rises to full self-consciousness only in confronting the social object. Only then does he have a conception of the limits of his action. When he perceives these limits, he will see how to express his freedom within them. In short, civil society stands in need of institutions which protect and foster it, and which enshrine the objective reality of the body politic. The sum of these institutions is the state, and if the state is to have the objective reality which individual freedom requires, it must have the status of a person, with rights, obligations, reason and will. Hence the full flourishing of individual freedom is only possible if the individual can 'realise' himself in institutions which circumscribe his rights. What seemed like tyranny is nothing but freedom in its highest, most self-knowing, form. But it is perhaps worth mentioning the fact that they are not the sum of Hegel's political thought, but rather the framework within which he conducts arguments of great interest and complexity, all designed to overthrow the simplifications of Enlightenment politics. Hegel replaced the theories of 'natural right' and 'social contract' with something more plausible as a description of political reality, less murderous as an ideology, and above all more able to take account of the fact that man is an historical being, who creates himself and his institutions through a continuous process, the legitimacies associated with which can be fully understood only in historical terms.

Among Hegel's arguments there is a complex defence of private property as an indispensable instrument of freedom. The right to property is indeed a genuine right. It is created by institutions which, as it were, instil the world with the relations of ownership, and so make objects into the focal points of rights and obligations. Ownership humanises the world. It makes it intelligible, by imprinting on it the distinctive features of personality. It is a part of the stage-setting for that individual autonomy which is the end of politics. Hegel showed some disposition to be moved by Locke's conception of the 'mixing of labour'. However, this process creates, not property rights, but a kind of self-image in the labourer (a '*Bildung*'), and a self-striving of which property is the natural fulfilment. The institution of property thereby becomes integral to the process of politics, even though there may be no 'natural right' to its benefits.

The *Philosophy of Right,* perhaps the most succinct work of political philosophy ever written, contains many such arguments, and succeeds, if not in answering, at least in asking almost all the important questions of modern political philosophy. It therefore set the stage for the flowering of political interest among philosophers which was to reach early expression in the writings of Karl Marx.

The 17th Century English philosopher Thomas Hobbes is now widely regarded as one of a handful of truly great political philosophers, whose masterwork Leviathan rivals in significance the political writings of Plato, Aristotle, Locke, Rousseau, Kant, and Rawls. Hobbes is famous for his early and elaborate development of what has come to be known as "social contract theory", the method of justifying political principles or arrangements by appeal to the agreement that would be made among suitably situated rational, free, and equal persons. He is infamous for having used the social contract method to arrive at the astonishing conclusion that we ought to submit to the authority of an absolute undivided and unlimited sovereign power. While his methodological innovation had a profound constructive impact on subsequent work in political philosophy, his substantive conclusions have served mostly as a foil for the development of more palatable philosophical positions. Hobbes's moral philosophy has been less influential than his political philosophy, in part because that theory is too ambiguous to have garnered any general consensus as to its content. The formerly dominant view that Hobbes espoused psychological egoism as the foundation of his moral theory is currently widely rejected, and there has been to date no fully systematic study of Hobbes's moral psychology.

Apart from his philosophical works on history, society, and the state, Hegel wrote several political tracts most of which were not published in his lifetime but which are significant enough in connection to the theoretical writings to deserve some mention.

Hegel's very first political work was on "On the Recent Domestic Affairs of Wurtemberg" which was neither completed nor published. In it Hegel expresses the view that the constitutional structure of Wurtemberg requires fundamental reform. He condemns the absolutist rule of Duke Ferdinand along with the narrow traditionalism and legal positivism of his officials and welcomes the convening of the Estates Assembly, while disagreeing with the method of election in the Diet. In contrast to the existing system of oligarchic privilege, Hegel argues that the Diet needs to be based on popular election through local town councils, although this should not be done by granting suffrage to an uneducated multitude. The essay ends inconclusively on the appropriate method of political representation.

10

Hegel and its Influence in Philosophy

Introduction

Hegel's lectures, published after his death, contain influential works on aesthetics and the philosophy of history; while the *Encyclopedia* adumbrates an entire system in which science, logic, mind, art, morality and religion are given their respective situations, and in which the whole of the world, as it appears to reason, is blessed, as it were, by an act of philosophical recognition. There are three specific works which will concern us, all published in Hegel's lifetime: *The Phenomenology of Spirit* (1807), *The Science of Logic* (1812–1816) and *The Philosophy of Right* (1821), which will be considered in chapter 14. The first two are notorious for their difficulty, in despite of which they have spawned interpretations and rival philosophies by the thousand. To many of Hegel's contemporaries it did indeed seem true that the key to the mysteries of the universe had been found, and that Hegel's implicit claim to utter the ultimate truth about everything should be upheld. Since his death the course of philosophy has been, to put it roughly, a process of steady disillusionment with Hegel, culminating in the vigorous rejection of his thought and method by analytical philosophers in the early years of the twentieth century. But even in our century his influence is felt. His philosophy of 'being' survives in amended form in the writings of Heidegger, and his theory of self-knowledge is present, in some version or other, in most of the major works of phenomenology, and in most theories of art. In this chapter I shall try to sketch certain central Hegelian themes in order to show why Hegel must still be seen as a towering presence in modern philosophy.

In one sense it was unfortunate that Hegel sought to found his philosophy in a general theory of logic, and particularly unfortunate that he should have advanced the theory of the 'dialectic' as containing the whole of metaphysics, thus illustrating, in Bertrand Russell's words, 'an important truth, namely, that the worse your logic, the more interesting the consequences to which it gives rise'. Hegel imagined himself to be replacing the empty formalism of the neo-Aristotelian logic with a new science, which has both form and content, and from which the nature of metaphysical truth can be derived. He therefore invented a new starting, point for logic, which was to deal, not with the formal structure of argument, but with the nature of Being itself. Logic deals with truth, not merely in the formal sense of telling us which arguments *preserve* truth, but in the substantive sense of telling us what truth is, and hence what is true (the 'is' here being an 'is' of identity).

That ambitious project is apt to look eccentric in the light of the development of modern logic. This logic has removed from its subject matter not only the metaphysics of Hegel, but also the particular brand of formalism advanced by Aristotle. It is therefore now necessary to read Hegel with more attention to detail, and less respect for system, than he himself would have countenanced. The surprising thing, however, is that his 'dialectical' philosophy still seems both important and often acceptable.

The term 'dialectic' was used by Plato to describe the method of Socrates, who sought philosophical truth through disputation. Kant had given a far more precise meaning to the term, and it was this meaning which Hegel adopted, to make use of it in a manner wholly antipathetic to the Critical philosophy. The second negative part of Kant's *Critique of Pure Reason* had been devoted to exploring the fallacies which attend the attempt to pass from the circumscribed realm of the 'understanding' into the limitless space of 'pure reason'. In its desire for absolute truth, human reason commits itself only to the absolute falsehood of self-contradiction. Kant's diagnosis of the fallacies of pure reason contained a section called the 'Antinomy of Pure Reason'. Here Kant had tried to describe certain contradictions into which reason strays in its ambition to pass from the circumscribed viewpoint of empirical knowledge to the realm of absolute cosmology, in which the 'whole' of things is grasped as it is in itself, independently of the limitations imposed by our perceptual capacities. I have already referred to an ambiguity in Kant's conclusions: it is not entirely clear whether he is saying that the limits of human understanding and the limits of truth are one and the same, or whether, on the contrary, he is gesturing towards a world of 'things-in-themselves' about which we can at least know that we do not know them. Because of this ambiguity it was possible for Hegel to interpret Kant's 'critique' of pure reason as heralding its eventual celebration. The Kantian contradictions, Hegel thought, were only contradictions from the limited point of view of the understanding. They therefore provided a kind of logical impetus to transcend that point of view into the world of pure reason itself, from the perspective of which these and many other contradictions could be resolved.

Thus while Kant had used the word 'dialectic' to refer to the propensity to fall into contradictions, Hegel used it to mean the propensity to transcend them. This process of transcendence is the true course of logic, and 'dialectic' is the name for the intellectual pursuit whose endpoint is not limited or partial, but on the contrary, absolute truth itself. 'A deeper insight into the antinomies or, rather, into the dialectic nature of Reason shows us that *every* concept is a unity of opposite moments, which could therefore be asserted in the shape of an antinomy.'

What then is the structure of reason's dialectic? It should be recognised that the terms of Hegel's logic are not propositions or judgements, but rather concepts: and it is *concepts,* in his view, that are true or false. Falsehood is a form of limitation or incompleteness, whereas truth is a form of wholeness, a transcendence of all limitation. (Here and elsewhere we see the influence of Spinoza.) Dialectic is the method of progression among concepts, whereby a 'more true' (or, as Spinoza might say, 'more adequate') concept is generated from inadequate beginnings, through overcoming the oppositions intrinsic to them.

The dialectical process is, then, as follows: a concept is posited as a starting-point. It is offered as a potential description of reality. It is found at once that, from the standpoint of logic, this concept must bring its own negation with it: to the concept, its negative is added automatically, and a 'struggle' ensues between the two. The struggle is resolved by an ascent to the higher plane from which it can be comprehended and reconciled: this ascent is the process of 'diremption' (*Aufhebung*), which generates a new concept out of the ruins of the last. This new concept generates its own negation, and so the process continues, until, by successive applications of the dialectic, the whole of reality has been laid bare.

The metaphor is attractive, but how do we interpret it? Hegel's logic is in stark contrast with traditional theories, which see logical relations as timeless, determined not by content but by structure. A thought does not need time, one feels, in which to generate its consequences: indeed it is the essence of a *logical* consequence that it is inseparable from the thought itself: a logical consequence can be neither lost nor acquired. Yet Hegel thinks of concepts as *moving towards* a greater grasp of reality, and he speaks of the 'working through' of the dialectic as being necessary both to the truth and to the meaning of the result. He refers to the successive stages as 'moments', which have to be 'overcome', in the act of 'diremption' whereby a new concept is born.

These temporal similes would be less puzzling if it were not also the case that Hegel thought of historical processes in dialectical terms—as the successive generation and overcoming of contradictions. And it is this aspect of Hegel, put forward overtly in the lectures on the philosophy of history, but covertly elsewhere, that has been the most influential, perhaps because the most intelligible, of his theories. It often seems that the whole of Hegelian metaphysics points towards a logical and historical interpretation at once. To some extent this reflects a confusion on Hegel's part, between logic conceived as a science of the relations among ideas, and logic conceived as the intellectual operation whereby those relations are discovered. Clearly, if it is true that we must undergo some dialectical process in order to know logical relations, this is a fact about *us,* and not about logic. But even this confusion can be glimpsed only obscurely, since Hegel writes at a level of abstraction so great as to attribute the process of thinking not to any particular subject, but rather to a *general* subject of thought. Logic becomes, in the end, the history, or perhaps the anatomy, of an eternal, impersonal 'concept'.

This notion becomes a little clearer if we examine the beginning and the end of the dialectical process, and say something about the course between them. The starting-point of logic is, for Hegel, not arbitrary. Modern conceptions of logic have tended to the view that logic is an instrument whereby the consequences of some premise are derived. Logic is powerless to give knowledge until the premise is determined. This was emphatically not Hegel's view, who thought that the premise of logic is determined by logic itself. The premise of logic is 'pure indeterminate being' conceived without any of the particular determinations through which it makes itself manifest to the understanding. Being is the single great *a priori* concept, from reflecting on the nature of which we arrive at an *a priori* theory of reality. (The modern logician will be reluctant, as we shall see, to admit that there is any such concept as that of pure being: this only shows that Hegel's metaphysics can no longer be so easily disguised as a logic, with all the incontestability which that label implies.

Logic begins, then, from 'being', and advances towards its conclusion, which is the 'absolute idea or truth itself'. This absolute idea is thought and reality at once: it is like the God of Spinoza, who comprehends the whole of things and, being identical with that whole, exists thinking Himself. Each concept in the dialectical process that leads to this supreme conception is obtained from that of being by a sequence of dialectical transformations.

Imagine a kind of impersonal dialectical 'thought', or thinker, attempting to understand the world. It has nothing available to it but thought and so must put forward, as its sole instrument of knowledge, the 'concepts' which enlighten it. Of necessity it begins from the single most indeterminate concept that which is contained in all concepts and yet which is logically precedent to them, the concept of being. But what is being, considered as 'unmediated' by reflection, and as free from extraneous determinations? It is, surely, nothing, or (as the English translators of Hegel prefer to write it) Nothing. Hence the concept of being contains within itself its own negation nothing and the dialectical opposition between these two concepts is resolved only in the passage to a new concept. This concept is 'becoming', which captures the truth contained in that previous opposition, the truth of the *passage* of being into nothing and nothing into being. To our impersonal thinker the world now appears as becoming rather than as being, and this perception is 'truer' than the preceding one, although as yet far short of that absolute truth in which all such oppositions will be resolved.

Becoming seems to be a specifically 'temporal' characteristic, but we cannot assume at this stage that the 'temporal' character of Hegel's logic is anything more than a metaphor. From the point of view of logic 'becoming' suffers from the same defects as 'being'; it generates its own contradiction out of 'the equipoise of arising and passing away'. So it gives way to a higher truth, which is that of 'determinate being', in which being and nothing are finally reconciled. Determinate being is that more familiar, less abstract, form of existence of which our world presents us with examples: being becomes determinate by being limited and so, as it were, incarnate in a certain identity. From this 'limitation' further oppositions arise and the process continues, until our 'thinker' is brought by a seemingly ineluctable process to the absolute idea itself, so perceiving the whole of reality as 'coming forth' from that indispensable concept from which all thinking must begin.

It would not be unfair to say that Hegel's metaphysics consists of an ontological proof of the existence of everything. The character of this, as of any ontological proof, is that it proceeds from concept to reality, arguing moreover that the discovery of reality and the 'unfolding' of a concept are one and the same. In Hegel's metaphysics this aspect is to some extent concealed by his reluctance to specify the nature of the abstract 'thinker' for whom the dialectical succession of concepts unfolds. His genius for abstractions leads us always away from the subject of thought, to thought itself. And the nature of the resulting metaphysics is such as to abolish the distinction between thought and reality altogether, thus displaying the principal characteristic of idealism.

It is not to be expected that such a logic can readily be made intelligible, or that a philosophy which is able cold-bloodedly to announce (for example) that 'Limit is the mediation through which Something and Other is and also is not' should be altogether different from arrant nonsense. Nevertheless, a *picture* of the dialectic is not hard to form, and this picture is important to bear in mind as we turn to that part of Hegel's philosophy the philosophy of mind and of politics which seems now to be most worthy of study and most likely to contribute to the pursuit of knowledge. The picture I have in mind is one that can be seen at its clearest in Leibniz's theory of time. According to Leibniz, ours could be the best possible world only if it were also the richest—the richest in the number and variety of monads that it contains. For this to be possible some monads must contain predicates which cannot from our limited point of view co-exist. For example, a thing cannot be both red and green at once: these two attributes seem to contradict each other. But it *can* be red and green successively. So that, in the order of phenomena, the dimension of time enables monads (whose reality is timeless), as it were, to display their abundance of predicates in succession. In perceiving the world under the aspect of time we thereby reconcile what might otherwise have seemed to be contradictions pertaining within it. As Leibniz put it (*Réponse aux réflections de Bayle*): 'Time is the order of possibilities which are inconsistent, but which nevertheless have some connexion.' In some such way it is the dialectic of contradiction which squeezes the Hegelian concept out of its logical changelessness into the order of succession, replacing being by becoming, and logical stasis by ontological evolution.

The constant slide between logical and temporal relations is of the very essence of Hegel's philosophy and preceded the official formulation of his doctrine of logic, exemplified in what is probably the greatest, and certainly the most intricately suggestive of his works, *The Phenomenology of Spirit.* This was written in 1806 and completed in Jena on the eve of the Napoleonic battle outside that town. The complexity and range of the *Phenomenology* defy description: it covers all subjects from art to theology, from science to history, and contains some of the most suggestive examples and intellectual parables in the whole of literature and philosophy. I shall content myself with a resume of what I take to be its central argument.

It will be remembered that Kant's positive philosophy in the *Critique of Pure Reason* was delivered by the 'Transcendental Deduction'. According to this, the pure 'subject' of Descartes and the empiricists is capable of knowing itself as subject only because it also knows the world as object, disciplining its experience in accordance with the *a priori* categories of the understanding. From the epistemological point of view Hegel did not so much advance beyond as dance around this master thought of Kant's, but he danced in a fascinating way. In the Hegelian whirlwind epistemology melts into ethics, metaphysics into the philosophy of mind, and theoretical understanding into practical reason. This amalgamation of practical and theoretical reason partly explains the temporal emphasis of

Hegel's logic. For it is of the essence of practical reason to *advance* towards *decisions,* and not to be detachable from the circumstances of the reasoner. Conclusion and argument are here inseparable, yet neither can be represented in the wholly a-temporal manner demanded by traditional theoretical logic.

Let us allow ourselves, then, as Hegel allows himself, full use of the temporal metaphor. We explore the relation between subject and object in the manner laid down in Fichte's primeval drama. We show how the pure subject *advances towards* self-consciousness through successive postulations of the objectivity of his world. Now Hegel's 'pure subjectivity' is an abstraction, and he goes on to argue, both in the *Phenomenology* and elsewhere, against any view of the 'I' that does not grant universal status to its subject matter. Nevertheless, we can without distortion regard him as referring also, and primarily, to the individual subject, and laying down, in parabolical, quasi-historical terms, the conditions which must be fulfilled if that subject is to rise to the self-consciousness that fulfils his nature.

Like Kant, Hegel recognised that the existence of the self in any form brings with it a peculiar immediacy the immediacy of Kant's Transcendental Unity of Apperception. And Hegel took over from Kant one of the major conclusions of the *Critique of Pure Reason* (established in that part of the Dialectic called the Paralogisms, where the rationalist theory of the soul is demolished). This is that the 'immediacy' with which our mental states are presented to us can provide no clue as to the nature of those states. It is the mere surface glow of knowledge, wholly without depth. The immediacy of the pure subject is, as Hegel would put it, undifferentiated, indeterminate and so devoid of content.

It follows that the pure subject we have imagined can gain no knowledge of what he is, and still less any knowledge of the world which he inhabits. Nevertheless, as Kant saw, his existence presupposes a *unity,* and that unity requires a principle of unity, something that holds consciousness together as one thing. Spinoza had spoken in this regard of the *conatus,* or striving, that constitutes the identity of organic beings. Hegel has recourse to a similar notion, the Aristotelian *orexis,* or appetite. Through this, the subject is launched forth in a manner which is void of knowledge and uninformed by the prospect of success. Consciousness exists only as the primitive 'I want' of the infant, the contumacious screeching of the fledgling in the nest.

But desire cannot exist without being desire *for* something. As Hegel puts it, adopting Fichte's jargon, desire *posits* its object as independent of itself: our primitive subject has already made a step towards the conception of another, and hence towards a conception of itself as differentiated from the other. Its 'absolute simplicity' is on the point of being sundered. But consciousness is not yet an *agent*: it has no conception of the nature of itself, or of the value of its primitive desire. It remains the slave of appetite and impulse. This is, roughly, the state of animal consciousness, which explores the world purely as an object of appetite, and which, being nothing *for* itself, is without genuine will. At this stage the object of desire is conceived only as a lack (*Mangel*), and desire itself destroys or consumes the thing desired.

There follows a peculiar 'moment' in the consciousness of the primitive subjectivity. This is the moment of opposition. The world is not merely passively uncooperative with the demands of appetite: it also actively resists them. The otherness of my world forms itself into opposition. It seems to remove the object of my desire, to compete for it, to seek my abolition as a rival.

The self has now 'met its match', and there follows what Hegel poetically calls the 'life and death struggle with the other', in which the self begins to know itself as will, as power, confronted with other wills and other powers. Full self-consciousness is not the result of this for the struggle is one that arises from appetite, and brings no conception of the value of what is desired. Hence it does not create the consciousness of the self as standing in definite relation to the world, fulfilled by some things, denied by others. As Hegel would put it, it does not generate the concept of the self *in its freedom.* On the contrary, the outcome of this struggle is the mastery of one party over the other. Conflict is resolved only in the unstable relation of master and slave.

This new 'moment' of self-consciousness is the most interesting, and Hegel's account of it was destined to exert a profound influence on nineteenth century ethical and political philosophy. One of the parties has enslaved the other, and therefore has achieved the power to extort the other's labour. By means of this labour he can satisfy his appetites without the expenditure of will and so achieve leisure. With leisure, however, comes the atrophy of the will; the world ceases to be understood as a resistant object, against which the subject must act and in terms of which he must labour to define himself. Leisure collapses into lassitude; the otherness of the world becomes veiled, and the self—which defines itself in contrast to it becomes lost in mystery. It sinks back into inertia, and its newly acquired 'freedom' turns into a kind of drunken hallucination. True freedom requires self-consciousness, without which there can be no conception of how one is bettered by an action, and therefore no conception of its value. But the self-consciousness of the master is fatally impaired. He can acquire no sense of the value of what he desires through observing the activities of his slave. For the slave, in his master's eyes, is merely a means; he does not appear to pursue an end of his own. On the contrary, he is absorbed into the undifferentiated mechanism of nature, and endows his petty tasks with no significance that would enable the master to envisage the value of pursuing them.

But now let us look at things through the eyes of the slave. Although his will is chained, it is not removed. He remains active towards the world, even in his submission, and while acting at the behest of a master, he nevertheless bestows his labour on objects, and imprints his identity upon them. He makes the world in his own image, even if not for his own use. Hence he differentiates himself from its otherness, and discovers his identity in the act of labour. His self-consciousness grows, and although he is treated as a means, he unavoidably acquires both the sense of an end to his activity and the will to make that end his own. His inner freedom intensifies in proportion with his master's lassitude, until such time as he rises up and enslaves the master, only himself to 'go under' in the passivity that attends the state of leisure.

Master and slave each possess a half of freedom: one the scope to exercise it, the other the self-image to see its value. But neither has the whole, and in this toing and froing of power between them each is restless and unfulfilled. The 'dialectic' of their relation awaits its resolution, and its resolution occurs only when each treats the other not as means, but as end: which is to say, when each renounces the life and death struggle that had enslaved him, and respects the reality of the other's will. In doing so they accept the categorical imperative of justice to treat others as ends and not as means. They are forced then to see themselves as they see others. Each man sees himself as an object to be respected, standing outside nature, bound to a community by reciprocal demands upheld by a common moral law. This law is, in Kant's words, the law of freedom. And at this 'moment' the self has acquired a conception of its agency; it is autonomous yet law-governed, partaking of a common nature and enacting universal values. Self-consciousness has become *universal* self-consciousness.

But the progress of our undifferentiated subject is not complete. Hegel explores the development, from the primitive conception of right so far established, to the religious world-view (the 'unhappy consciousness') in which the exercise of self-discovery oversteps the limit of personal autonomy. The unhappy (or alienated) consciousness endows the objective world with the power that belongs to itself alone, and so becomes forlorn, guilt-ridden and anxious for redemption. Hegel describes the overcoming of this religious consciousness, and the growth of the ethical life (or *Sittlichkeit*), the ultimate end of which is the development of the free citizen in the protective state.

First of all what are we to make of the story-like form which the *Phenomenology* takes? Although Hegel expressly says that the *Logic* simply lays out the general principles of the *Phenomenology*, it is fairly clear that a temporal interpretation is, in the latter case, far more plausible and could be attempted by someone for whom the method of the 'dialectic' was strictly nonsense. It is interesting to note that there are *two* temporal interpretations of the 'moments' of consciousness. The *Phenomenology* contains a parable of the subject, launched with its infantile 'I want' into a world that it gradually reduces into possession, so giving both itself and the world objective form. It also contains a covert history of the human race. Such was the astonishing intellectual effrontery of Hegel, that he made no efforts to deny that mankind *as a whole* must evolve in accordance with the pattern of the *Phenomenology.* We have already shown the episodes corresponding to the pre-historical state of nature, to the undifferentiated 'species' being of the animal, to the episode of primitive combat among tribes, to the Roman *imperium,* with its need for slavery and autocratic rule. (We are also led to understand, furthermore, that the states of mind described in the passage referring to the master and slave are those of the emperor Marcus Aurelius, and of his intellectual master, the stoic slave Epictetus.) Not surprisingly we find that the later stages of the evolution of consciousness fall one by one into the successive periods of history, and by a miracle of predestination, self-consciousness reaches its apogee in that free, protestant, Germanic *Wissenschaft* of which Hegel was both prophet and exegete.

But these historical interpretations are both fanciful and misleading. There is a deeper, logical point that emerges from the argument. To discover it we need to interpret the 'moment' of consciousness not as a stage on the way to self-consciousness, but rather as a state contained within self-consciousness. In saying that the religious consciousness is somehow higher than the primitive recognition of a moral law, Hegel could be taken to refer not to a temporal but rather to a conceptual priority. But this conceptual priority in fact reverses the 'temporal' ordering, in the following way.

Just as Kant had argued that my knowledge of myself as subject presupposes knowledge of an objective world, so Hegel seems to argue that the 'earlier' moments of consciousness presuppose at least the possibility of the latter. The immediate knowledge of self (the Cartesian premise) presupposes the activity that constitutes the self, and this presupposes desire, and hence the knowledge of objects. This in turn presupposes the struggle with the other and the reciprocal dealing which stems from that. Eventually we are driven to the conclusion that the 'self' or 'subject' is not possible except in the context of the political organism which 'realises' it.

The process of 'self-realisation' may admit of degrees, but these degrees do not mark 'stages on the way'. However fragmentary my self-consciousness, it exists only because I participate in that collective self-transcending activity which constitutes the full elaboration of the human mind. I may participate in it only waywardly or spasmodically; to that extent will my self-understanding and freedom be shattered or impaired. But if I am even to *exist* as a subjectivity (as a being that knows itself immediately) I must acknowledge and participate in the claims of the objective arrangements which transcend me.

Construed in this way, as an analytic rather than a genetic theory of rational self-consciousness, the thesis of the *Phenomenology* can be seen as an extension of the Transcendental Deduction. Hegel tries to show that knowledge of self as subject presupposes not just knowledge of objects, but knowledge of a public social world, in which there is moral order and civic trust. Moreover he tries to show from whence arises the *a priori* claim of that most contentful and contentious of the Kantian imperatives the imperative to treat rational beings as ends and not as means. Whether the argument is valid is not in point: what we should notice is the extent to which it transcends in ambition anything envisaged by Kant. For it aims to defeat epistemological and moral scepticism simultaneously. It also abolishes the distinction between practical and theoretical reason (since the constraint on the subject to acknowledge the existence of the other stems always from the exercise of activity and will). It thus gives cogency to that peculiar logic, the workings of which we have already discussed, which treats reasoning in dynamic terms.

Having offered that interpretation of the *Phenomenology*,

however, I must now express a hesitation. For the self-realisation described in the *Phenomenology* is not, despite what I have implied, a realisation of the individual. The individual 'I' is, for Hegel, only a metaphor. No philosophical argument can proceed from the cognisance of an individual, for in that very act of cognisance the individual becomes universal. Every thought is the subsumption under a concept. It is for this reason that Hegel put forward, in the *Logic,* the view that the true subject matter of thought is the concept itself. I may think, in my own case, that I am directly acquainted with some individual thing, but, just as soon as I begin to utter this thought to myself, I must designate that thing I must employ the concept 'I'. And 'I', like any concept, is a universal. Hence Hegel feels quite justified in abstracting so far from the first-person viewpoint of Descartes and the empiricists as no longer to regard their puzzles as intelligible. The real subject matter of the *Phenomenology* is not the concrete, sceptical, solipsistic self, but the universal, affirmative spirit (*Geist*), whose progress towards realisation in an objective world is something in which you or I may participate, but which transcends every merely local manifestation of its implacable movement.

Much of Hegel's metaphysics thus develops independently of any epistemological basis. He avoids the first-person standpoint of Descartes not through any rival theory of knowledge, but by a process of abstraction which, because it abolishes the individual, leaves no evident room for the theory of knowledge at all. This makes Hegel's metaphysics so vulnerable to sceptical attack that it is often thought to have little to bequeath to us but its poetry.

The dialectic of reason advances from pure, immediate being, through all the determinations of being which in sum constitute reality, so as to consummate itself in the absolute idea. As I have said, this absolute idea is the whole of reality, the truth of the world, and God Himself. Nothing exists in actuality that is not some determinant of pure being, and whose existence is not derived from the dialectical working out of that concept. Reason, because it generates everything, comprehends everything; hence, in a famous phrase, 'the real is rational and the rational is real'. Everything which exists, exists of necessity; but it exists not in virtue of some eternal essence, but in virtue of the struggle of reason to constrain its successive concepts to give birth to their ever more detailed progeny. Hegel calls this struggle the 'labour of the negative'. And the world thus generated, being the product of reason, shows 'the cunning of reason' it reveals itself to reason, so that the apparently contingent can be seen to be really necessary, and the arbitrary and diffuse as directed and whole.

For Kant, the thing-in-itself was an 'infinite resistance principle' it stood proxy for the idea that our knowledge has a limit. For Hegel, the thing-in-itself is actual and knowable, being nothing but the absolute idea and its successive revelations. There cannot be more than one such transcendent thing: but nor can there be less than one. The absolute idea is the single immortal substance of Spinoza. It has, in Hegel's view, only one nature, and that nature is revealed to us in consciousness. In our advance towards it, we 'posit' the world of nature (seeing the idea as 'force' and hence as 'matter', the locus of force) and the world of 'spirit'. These are modes of realisation, which the absolute undergoes in us, but in which it does not exhaust itself. How, then, do we know the absolute? Hegel's nearest approach to an answer to this lies in his theory of the concrete universal, according to which the world as *given* is both known (because it is universal) and also sensuously known (because it is concrete). Hence, in moments of pure observation we see it as it eternally is, while seeing it transfixed in time, beleaguered by all its determinations, clothed in attributes, specified to a comprehensible point of being. Philosophy shows the world thus, but philosophy is a lingering occupation: art shows it more immediately, since art is the sensuous *shining* of the idea.

From the obscure but tantalising theory of 'the concrete universal' (a theory which, announcing itself in blatant contradiction, drew a prolonged breath of admiration from the intellectual world) grew the idealist philosophies of art, of history and of the state. All these have been profoundly influential, and their outline is sufficiently known. The poetic appeal of the doctrine that the real is rational and the rational real, combined as it was with a theory of history that represented events as proceeding with whatever inevitability had seemed proper to the proofs of logic (history being nothing more than the 'march of reason in the world'), has had consequences so disastrous in politics, in history and in the criticism of art, that it is not surprising if Hegel has recently been execrated as the greatest intellectual disaster in the history of mankind. Rightly understood, however, he was the true philosopher of the modern consciousness, and those who, like Russell, see only the pretentious exterior of his thinking, show themselves to be blind to the profound spiritual crisis that Hegel was striving to describe the crisis of a civilisation that has discovered the God upon whom it depended to be also its own creation.

There are several overall themes that reoccur in these political writings and that connect with some of the main lines of thought in Hegel's theoretical works. First, there is the contrast between the attitude of legal positivism and the appeal to the law of reason. Hegel consistently displays a "political rationalism" which attacks old concepts and attitudes that no longer apply to the modern world. Old constitutions stemming from the Feudal era are a confused mixture of customary laws and special privileges that must give way to the constitutional reforms of the new social and political world that has arrived in the aftermath of the French Revolution. Second, reforms of old constitutions must be thorough and radical, but also cautious and gradual. This might sound somewhat inconsistent, but for Hegel a reform is radical due to a fundamental change in direction, not the speed of such change. Hegel suggests that customary institutions not be abolished too quickly for there must be some congruence and continuity with the existing social conditions. Hegel rejects violent popular action and sees the principal force for reform in governments and the estates assemblies, and he thinks reforms should always stress legal equality and the public welfare. Third, Hegel emphasizes the need for a strong central government, albeit without complete centralized control of public administration and social relations. Hegel here anticipates his later conception of civil society, the social realm of individual autonomy where there is significant local self-governance. The task of government is not to thoroughly bureaucratize civil society but rather to provide oversight, regulation, and when necessary intervention. Fourth, Hegel claims that representation of the people must be popular but not atomistic. The democratic element in a state is not its sole feature and it must be institutionalized in a rational manner. Hegel rejects universal suffrage as irrational because it provides no means of mediation between the individual and the state as a whole. Hegel believed that the masses lacked the experience and political education to be directly involved in national elections and policy matters and that direct suffrage leads to electoral indifference and apathy. Fifth, while acknowledging the importance of a division of powers in the public authority, Hegel does not appeal to a conception of separation and balance of powers. He views the estates assemblies, which safeguard freedom, as essentially related to the monarch and also stresses the role of civil servants and members of the professions, both in ministerial positions and in the assemblies. The monarchy, however, is the central supporting element in the constitutional structure because the monarch is invested with the sovereignty of the state. However, the power of the monarch is not despotically for he exercises authority through universal laws and statutes and is advised and assisted by a ministry and civil service, all members of which must meet educational requirements.

11

Deeper Sense of Politics and Philosophy

Introduction

The recent work in political philosophy has deepened our understanding of what is political. Traditional political philosophy has taken for granted a distinction between the public and the private. The public sphere is the sphere of government. The private sphere is the sphere of business, voluntary non-governmental organizations, family, and individual life. Traditional political philosophy has concerned itself with the public sphere and with the proper boundary between the public and private. It has left the private sphere outside the scope of its concern. Recent political philosophy has challenged this limitation of the discipline's scope. It has called attention to the extent to which even the private sphere is shaped by philosophical assumptions, assumptions that assign specific roles to individual persons and that define these roles, at least in part, in terms of relationships of power and subordination that are highly political in nature. In earlier chapters we have already explored the extent to which the "private" sphere of business and economic life involves issues of justice that must be addressed by any adequate political philosophy. In this chapter we will explore how political ideas penetrate even deeper into the private realm, influencing our very conception of ourselves as individual human beings. As a way of getting at the kinds of issues involved, we will focus on matters of gender and race, but it should be noted that similar issues arise in considering, for example, how class, ethnicity, religion, and sexual orientation enter into our sense of who we are.

Political Philosophy of Patriarchy

As a way of getting at how political philosophy enters into the deepest recesses of the private sphere, let us consider briefly how philosophical ideas have shaped traditional ideas about women and the proper role of women in social life. For thousands of years, in Western societies at least, women have been assigned roles that make them subordinate to men. In the family, the church, the state, and all the important institutions of society, with some notable individual exceptions, men have held the positions of power. Women's rights have been restricted often severely restricted. Women have been denied education, the right to own or control property, and the right to express their opinions or to participate in public life. They have been denied a say in how their children should be raised. They have even been denied control over their own bodies and their own sexual life. They have been controlled by the decisions of fathers, brothers, and husbands. Sometimes this control has been exercised with gentleness and respect; at other times it has been exercised with brutality and contempt.

This system of male domination, patriarchy, has been a central feature of human social existence for thousands of years. It has been so pervasive that until very recently most men and women have assumed that it reflected the natural order of things. But, in fact, this is not so. Patriarchy is a historical creation, made by human beings. Archaeological research points to the existence of societies in the Neolithic and the Bronze Age in which women played a more equal role. In much of the world early conceptions of God were of a female figure—a mother who gave birth to the natural universe and all living things and who continued to rule over it. Violent suppression of the religion of the mother God was a part of the historical process by which patriarchy came to be.

While undoubtedly violence played a role in the creation of patriarchy, patriarchal institutions also received support from ways of thinking that depicted them as good, just, wise, divinely ordained, or natural. Religions were developed, Judaism, Christianity, and Islam among them, that centered around a father God and gave privileged positions to men. Art and literature told stories of the heroic actions of the mythic males who supposedly founded the ancient nations and gave them their laws. In these representations of history and social life, women were depicted as lesser beings, rightly assigned to subordinate and supporting roles. In this way, the belief that patriarchal institutions were good seeped into the thinking of women as well as men.

Western philosophy emerged after the establishment of patriarchal institutions. While some philosophers, such as Plato, questioned the view that women were rightly subordinate to men, it is not surprising that most philosophers were unable to escape the prevailing patriarchal prejudices that shaped the consciousness of their times. Aristotle, who came after Plato, reaffirmed the superiority of males over females and defended slavery, arguing that some men were by nature masters and others by nature slaves. Following Aristotle, almost all philosophers, these (male) lovers of wisdom, decided that male domination was natural and good. For two thousand years Western philosophers have been finding "reasons" to show that this was so.

Denied education, unable to read or write, most women had no opportunity to participate in the discussions of the philosophers. There were some exceptions. Hypatia, the daughter of a mathematician, was well educated in both mathematics and philosophy. She lectured on mathematics and philosophy in Alexandria, Egypt, becoming one of the world's leading geometers and heading the Neoplatonist school of philosophy there. Angered at her pagan religion and "the freedom of her ways," a mob, instigated by the Christian bishop of Alexandria, brutally murdered her in A.D. 415. This suppression of the female voice has been with us for thousands of years. We can only speculate on what might have been said had women been given the opportunity to speak and write. In the absence of that voice, our collective consciousness of who women are, and what their role in society should be, has been largely shaped without the participation of women themselves.

It is only in the recent past that this has begun to change. The American and French Revolutions called into question age-old beliefs. They proclaimed the rights of men and advocated radical changes in the way society should be governed. In 1792 Mary Wollstonecraft published *A Vindication of the Rights of Women*, a work that applied the revolutionary philosophy of natural rights to the cause of emancipating women from the domination of men. It was not long before African-American slaves in the United States were appealing to the same revolutionary philosophy to demand their own emancipation. Though still incomplete, these struggles have initiated profound changes in our social existence and have forced a redefinition of the boundaries of political philosophy.

Natural Rights and Human Nature

The theory of natural rights is embedded in the broader theory of natural law. According to that theory, the right way to use a thing was to use it in accordance with its nature. Aristotle took it as obvious that human beings differed in important ways in their natures. Of particular importance for Aristotle was whether or not human beings had a capacity for rational self-direction. Those men who had this capacity were rightly masters; those who lacked this capacity were rightly slaves. Aristotle thought of the having or not having of this capacity as a matter not of education or training but of nature: "From the hour of their birth, some are marked out for subjection, others for rule." Of course there were some cases in which a man who had this capacity was enslaved, but in this case the man was being treated contrary to his nature and the enslavement was unjust. Similarly, there were cases where a man who lacked this capacity was in a position of mastery over others. This too, in Aristotle's view, was contrary to nature, and so unjust. However, where a man who had this capacity ruled over a man who lacked it, there was no injustice. Aristotle thought of women as having this capacity to some extent, but to a lesser extent than men, who were by nature masters. Thus, on Aristotle's view, in the well-ordered household, the husband ruled over his wife and over his slaves as well. In roughly this form, this view that men rightly should rule over women prevailed among almost all thinkers, including even such champions of the Enlightenment as Jean-Jacques Rousseau and Immanuel Kant.

Wollstonecraft *A Vindication of the Rights of Women* directly challenged this way of thinking. Agreeing with the fundamental ideas of natural law and natural rights, she questioned the assumption that women lacked the power of rational self-direction, an assumption crucial to justification of the subordinate status of women and the denial of their equal rights:

> *But if women are to be excluded, without having a voice, from a participation of the natural rights of mankind, prove first, to ward off the charge of injustice and inconsistency, that they want reason, else this flaw in your NEW CONSTITUTION will ever show that man must, in some shape, act like a tyrant, and tyranny, in whatever part of society it rears its brazen front, will ever undermine morality.*

Wollstonecraft directly criticized the popular ideas of Rousseau, according to whom women were creatures of feeling rather than reason and according to whom "woman is made to please and to be dominated." Like Aristotle and the other philosophers before him, Rousseau based his case regarding the proper role for women on observations of women around him. Admitting that many women were preoccupied with dress, appearance, and pleasing men, Wollstonecraft argued that this fact was a product of social conditioning rather than innate disposition. She also pointed out that this conditioning of women is but the obverse of a coin that includes the conditioning of men to lives of unreasoning brutishness. Throughout her book Wollstonecraft drives these points home, affirming the rational capacity of women, appealing to women to live up to their human nature, and appealing to men to cease oppressing women.

Wollstonecraft's opposition to the subordination of women to men worked within the framework of natural-law theory made popular, in some quarters at least, by the American and French Revolutions. Opposition to the enslavement of Africans in the Americas followed a similar pattern of argument. Although the enslavement of Africans by Europeans lacked the historical depth of the subordination of women to men, Europeans were quick to relegate Africans to Aristotle's category of natural slaves. Accordingly, the defense of slavery rested on the widely held assumption that Africans were inferior to Europeans, a view also endorsed by Kant and by the great Enlightenment naturalist Linnaeus, who classified Africans as the lowest of the four races of man and as properly to be "governed by the arbitrary will of his masters." But like the view that women were incapable of rational self-direction, so too the view that Africans lacked this capacity was vulnerable to the refutation of experience. In his speech "What to the Slave Is the Fourth of July," delivered in 1852, when slavery was still widely accepted in the United States, Frederick Douglass effectively challenged this presupposition of African inferiority:

For the present, it is enough to affirm the equal manhood of the Negro race. Is it not astonishing that, while we are ploughing, planting, and reaping, using all kinds of mechanical tools, erecting houses, constructing bridges, building ships, working in metals of brass, iron, copper, silver and gold; that, while we are reading, writing and ciphering, acting as clerks, merchants and secretaries, having among us lawyers, doctors, ministers, poets, authors, editors, orators and teachers; that, while we are engaged in all manner of enterprises common to other men, digging gold in California, capturing the whale in the Pacific, feeding sheep and cattle on the hill-side, living, moving, acting, thinking, planning, living in families as husbands, wives and children, and above all, confessing and worshipping the Christian's God, and looking hopefully for life and immortality beyond the grave, we are called upon to prove that we are men?

Like Wollstonecraft, Douglass spoke on behalf of an "other" banished from the family of humankind by the prejudices of the dominant group of males of northern European descent. And, like Wollstonecraft, by the very eloquence and power of his argument, he undermined the justification of that banishment.

Sadly, discrimination against women and African-Americans continued long after the arguments of Wollstonecraft and Douglass had been heard. Indeed, in the late nineteenth and early twentieth centuries, views that women and Africans were inferior to European males in their capacity for rational self-direction were reinforced by the pronouncements of modern "science."

Having won legal equality in the early twentieth century, by midcentury women faced the hostile pronouncements of Freudian psychology, according to which a woman's interest in work outside the home was viewed as a sign of an unsuccessful navigation of the path to normal adult development. Although now widely viewed as pseudoscience, Freud's theory haunted the lives of a whole generation of women, relegating them to the traditional roles of mother and supportive wife.

African-Americans also faced a scientific establishment that pronounced them inferior to whites. By the turn of the century, theories that classified humankind into a variety of different races and ranked them as higher or lower in terms of intellectual and moral capacities were widely accepted by both the intellectual establishment and popular consciousness in northern Europe and North America. Not surprisingly, these theories placed people of northern European extraction at the top of the hierarchy of races and, reflecting the racist heritage of the era of the slave trade, put people of African extraction at the bottom of the hierarchy.

Though the theories were irredeemably flawed pseudoscience, they were widely accepted and had a significant influence on both public consciousness and public policy. Like women, African-Americans faced a long struggle before their equal humanity came to be acknowledged, a struggle fought as much on the terrain of science as on the terrain of ethics. By now the natural equality of all human beings is widely, though not universally, accepted. Still, important differences remain about how current public policy should reflect this equality.

Formal and Fair Equality of Opportunity

The laws of the United States and the laws of the various states discriminated against women and African-Americans. Neither was permitted to vote or to hold office, for example. Formal equality of opportunity involves doing away with such explicit legal discrimination. Formal equality is also often understood to involve the elimination of discriminatory private rules and practices that, while they lack the status of law, nonetheless function to explicitly exclude people of certain categories from certain opportunities. For example, in the nineteenth century many universities, law schools, and medical schools explicitly denied admission to women. Formal equality of opportunity involves the elimination of all such explicitly discriminatory rules, laws, and regulations. In the United States, despite some notable exceptions in private educational institutions and social clubs, women had largely won formal equality of opportunity by the 1920s.

African-Americans were less fortunate. Despite some gains in the direction of formal equality in the Thirteenth, Fourteenth, and Fifteenth Amendments to the Constitution, the Compromise of 1876 allowed the states to re-establish extensive systems of legal discrimination. These "Jim Crow" laws remained in effect until finally overcome by the civil rights movement in the 1960s.

While formal equality was a major step forward for women and for African-Americans, significant disadvantages remained. A medical school may drop its explicit rule against admitting black students, but without an education, the formal right to be considered equally with white applicants from privileged backgrounds is an empty one. Fair equality of opportunity involves, in addition to formal equality, the social guarantee of the resources necessary to make formal equality more than an empty right. It is fair equality of opportunity that is required by Rawls's principles of justice. In the United States, the commitment to fair equality of opportunity has been most significantly expressed in the commitment to public education, to the provision of the educational resources necessary for fair as opposed to merely formal equality of opportunity. In fact, however, there are rather severe limits to the achievement of fair equality of opportunity. In the United States, funding for public schools remains based largely on property taxes. The effect of this is to give far more educational resources to students from wealthy suburbs than is available to students from poorer inner-city and rural areas. Children from wealthier homes are also apt to have available opportunities for private lessons in music, sports, and the arts, and to have opportunities for travel, opportunities that better prepare the child to compete for positions. In addition to these limits to fair opportunity, there are also limits of a different kind, limits that have been addressed by policies of affirmative action. In the next section we will examine the idea of affirmative action and some of the issues connected with that idea.

Affirmative Action

Let us suppose a society in which formal and fair equality of opportunity have been achieved. There are no rules or laws banning groups from certain positions, and individuals in all groups have access to sufficient resources to allow them to compete for positions. Suppose, however, that there remain widespread prejudices that stigmatize members of a certain group as intellectually or morally inferior. Being subject to these prejudices, admissions officers and prospective employers are going to be apt to pass over applications from members of the stigmatized group. They are also apt to feel less comfortable, more suspicious, and more critical while interviewing members of the stigmatized group. For these reasons, given a choice between two more or less equally qualified applicants, decision makers are apt to prefer the individual they are comfortable with over the individual from the stigmatized group. Given the widespread nature of the prejudice against members of the group, even with formal and fair equality of opportunity, members of the group are likely to be systematically excluded from attractive and rewarding positions in the social structure.

Though fair equality of opportunity was also missing in the period just after the final demise of formal discrimination against them, African-Americans in the United States faced widespread prejudices of just this kind. To a certain extent, women too found themselves in such a situation. It was not at all uncommon in the late 1960s for women applicants to medical school or law school to be passed over for financial aid because administrators believed they would marry and drop out of school, thereby wasting the aid that was given them. It was also not at all uncommon for a woman or African-American to be passed over because the prejudices of the relevant decision maker were so strong that he could not accept an apparent equality of credentials as real.

Affirmative action aimed at rectifying the injustices persisting because of such prejudices. A series of federal and state mandates were issued requiring institutions receiving government money to take affirmative steps to find, recruit, hire, or appoint qualified applicants from groups that were victims of prejudices that worked to unfairly exclude them. Proponents of affirmative action justified such measures on two grounds: that it was just restitution to victims of past wrongdoing, and that it would produce a better society in the future, a society that was both happier and more just.

From the beginning, affirmative action was sharply criticized. For restitution to be just, it was said, it needs to compensate the actual victims of wrongdoing. But affirmative action awarded benefits to individuals who may not themselves have been victims of wrongdoing. Further, critics argued, women and racial minorities are not the only victims of past wrongdoing. The Irish, for example, were victimized by prejudice and discrimination for several generations. In selecting women and racial minorities for current restitution, affirmative action unfairly privileges some victims over others. Critics also argued that affirmative action constitutes "reverse discrimination," substituting discrimination against white males for discrimination against women and racial minorities, thereby creating more victims of wrongdoing. Justice, the critics held, requires that positions go to those most qualified to fill them. It was wrong to consider gender or race in the past, and it is wrong to consider them now.

Defenders of affirmative action replied that we commonly provide restitution to the descendants of those who have been wronged, as, for example, when we require that property belonging to Jews who perished in the Holocaust be returned to their descendants or to other victims of the Holocaust when no such descendants can be found. They also argued that while other groups and other individuals did suffer discrimination, racial minorities and women have suffered more persistent and damaging discrimination, and that, in any case, more justice is better than less even if it is not perfect.

Defenders of affirmative action also pointed out that it is questionable whether justice requires that positions go solely to those most qualified for them. We have long accepted consideration of geographic distribution as one criterion for admission to educational institutions. Why is consideration of racial distribution an injustice if consideration of geography is not? In any case, defenders of affirmative action have argued that we need to do something to create a happier and more just society in the future. Affirmative action is necessary to achieve this end.

Opponents of affirmative action have argued that the future-regarding case for affirmative action is just as weak as the case based on restitution for past wrongdoing. It is to the good of society as a whole if positions are filled by those best qualified to hold them. Each of us want the best doctor and the best mechanic. In making race and gender count, affirmative action undermines the principle of merit, which best serves the interests of society as a whole. Further, critics of affirmative action argue, affirmative action actually ends up reinforcing prejudices and injuring the very people it seeks to help. The black person who does happen to be the best-qualified person for a job will be widely viewed as having gotten the position not because of qualifications but because of race. To this skepticism and distrust of blacks in positions of importance will be added a dose of resentment from white males who will feel that they have been unfairly overlooked. In such a climate, racial prejudices are likely to deepen, not subside. The only correct policy, the critics argue, is a color-blind policy that does not consider race or gender at all.

Defenders of affirmative action reply that race and gender should count only in selecting from among qualified applicants. Further, they argue, while the public may face black holders of positions with some degree of skepticism and distrust, experience in dealing with the many qualified blacks who do come to hold positions will erode that skepticism and distrust, experience that the majority population would likely never have without some form of affirmative action. Finally, supporters of affirmative action are likely to point out that the "color blind" policy recommended by opponents of affirmative action is a fantasy. In the United States at least, color consciousness and prejudice based on color consciousness are too deeply ingrained to make any truly color-blind decision making possible. It is an indication of the depth of the problem, and something of a grotesque irony as well, that Charles Murray, who has publicly argued for color-blind repeal of affirmative action policies on the ground that the old racial prejudices have been largely overcome, is himself coauthor of a book purporting to show that blacks are genetically determined to have lower IQs than whites, a book that made the best-seller lists in the United States. It is surely unrealistic to think that a society in which such a book makes the best-seller list is a society that can ignore race.

The Personal and the Political

Traditionally, political philosophy has focused on the institutions of government and their relationship to individual citizens. But thinking about the role of women and racial minorities in the history of the United States has led us to see how aspects of our lives, such as gender and race, that we tend to think of as personal and outside the realm of concern of political philosophy are in fact highly politicized. These politicized conceptions of gender and race are reflected in the roles traditionally assigned to particular individuals. Affirmative action policies try to subvert these politicized roles by opening doors for qualified individuals from traditionally oppressed groups to enter desirable positions. But such efforts cannot address the full range of constraints affecting the lives of people from such groups.

Consider, for example, the "personal" difficulties facing women today. Though most women have sometimes worked outside the home, and many women have worked a great deal outside the home, the traditional woman's role has required a substantial amount of domestic labor and primary responsibility for child care. With these demands upon their time, many women have found it necessary to forgo career opportunities outside the home, even when such opportunities arise. Consequently, women are dependent upon their husbands for the income necessary to sustain the home. But this dependence brings with it a certain degree of risk. Being dependent upon her husband for the support of herself and her children, the supple wife is vulnerable to spousal abuse. Such abuse, whether physical or psychological, has, unhappily, been far from uncommon. In a famous letter to her husband, John Adams, written just a few months before the signing of the Declaration of

Independence, Abigail Adams makes reference to the abuses suffered by women at the hands of men:

> *That your Sex are Naturally Tyrannical is a Truth so thoroughly established as to admit of no dispute, but such of you as wish to be happy willingly give up the harsh title of Master for the more tender and endearing one of Friend. Why then, not put it out of the power of the vicious and the Lawless to use us with cruelty and indignity with impunity? Men of Sense in all Ages abhor those customs which treat us only as the vassals of your Sex.*

What this letter clearly reveals is a hidden political dimension to the relations between husband and wife. Custom gave to men power over their wives. What Abigail Adams sought was political action that would limit men's power. Sadly, though he was undoubtedly among those men who aspire to be friends rather than masters, John Adams was unwilling to interfere in these matters, leaving in place those ancient customs that left women subject to the cruelties and indignities of their husbands. It is only now, under the impetus of modern feminism, that some efforts are being made to address these issues. But even now, with laws against spousal abuse, and with shelters for battered women, her condition of economic dependence makes it difficult for a woman to escape an abusive husband. What will she do? If she takes a job, what will become of her children? Affordable child care is simply not available for all who need it.

The state of dependency forced upon a woman by the responsibilities of home and children also makes her vulnerable to economic ruin. In California, men increase their standard of living by 42 percent following divorce, while women's standard of living declines by 73 percent. Women are faced with a choice: between marriage and children, on one hand, and an upwardly mobile career path, on the other. In agreeing to marriage, and in taking on the responsibilities of home and child care, women are forced to give less time to their careers. Consequently, their earning power, even if they eventually return to full-time work, is likely to be far less than that of a man who made a primary commitment to his career. Having made the commitment to marriage, the woman now finds herself in desperate economic straits when the marriage collapses. Now, where formal and fair equality of opportunity obtain, it is possible for a woman to avoid economic dependency provided she is willing to give up home and family or provided she is lucky enough to find a man willing to run the risks traditionally run by women. But for the vast majority of women, home and family life remain highly valuable, and the vast majority of women end up with the primary responsibility for home and children. The problem of dependence and its risks remains a serious matter for very many women.

These aspects of the choices faced by women are by now commonplace. The feminization of poverty has become well known. The point here is just that these now familiar facts highlight some very difficult problems that have not been addressed by traditional political theory. Formal equality, fair equality, and affirmative action, even if perfectly applied, would not suffice to liberate women so long as women carry their traditional responsibilities. How can we reconcile the needs of home and children with free-market economics and free-market labor markets? What business can remain competitive when it alone allows a woman to take substantial time off from her job? What business can remain competitive when it alone offers good-paying jobs to women whose skills have been eroded by years away from their profession?

Perhaps even deeper than this is the simple matter of the direct relationship between the sexes. Men and women alike carry in their heads prejudices that tend to value men's lives more than women's lives. These prejudices are relics of past ideologies, of the ideas of Aristotle and the other philosophers who relegated women to subordinate roles. In this sense, political philosophy enters not just into the framework of the institutions we inhabit, but into the soul itself. Despite all of the attention that the effects of advertising, pornography, and the acculturation of children have received, it remains true that many men and women continue to see women in much the same way as women were seen in the days of Mary Wollstonecraft, as ornaments, playthings, and servants of men. At its most basic level, perhaps, the problem is that because women and men alike are deluded by false conceptions of women, women are not treated with the respect due them as human beings. From this point of view, one of the central tasks of political philosophy must be to bring this false consciousness to light. But there remains also another task as well: that of trying to conceive how society could be remade so as to free women from the difficult choices and traps forced upon them by the weight of tradition and the way society is now organized. The true liberation of women will require both a change in the consciousness of human beings and a change in the social structures within which we live our lives.

Emancipatory Consciousness

In *The Wretched of the Earth*, the psychologist Frantz Fanon describes the destructive consequences of racism on the lives of Algerians before the time of Algerian independence. Fanon emphasizes the extent to which racism poisons the consciousness of those who are stigmatized by it. Racism is internalized. It turns a people against themselves. Violence against one's own people, suicide, destructive patterns of behavior, derision of oneself and others—these are all symptoms of internalized racism. Like the idea that women are rightly subordinate to men, racist ideas enter into the consciousness of individuals on both sides of racial divides, sustaining illusions of superiority and inferiority and undermining the sense of mutual respect necessary for just relationships. Just as political philosophy must bring to light and expose the illusions of sexism, so too it must bring to light and expose the illusions of racism.

This conception of philosophy as devoted to criticizing false consciousness and thereby making possible the emancipation of human beings from the oppressive social relationships sustained by that false consciousness is known as critical theory. It is a view of philosophy that reaches back to the middle of the nineteenth century and finds its exemplar in the work of Karl Marx. Marx conceived of his task as a critique of political economy. He aimed at unmasking the claims of his contemporaries that the laws of the market were, like the laws of chemistry, natural and consequently unavoidable. Marx labored to show that free-market capitalism was the historical product of human making and therefore subject to revision or replacement by other forms of life. In the same way, contemporary feminist philosophers and philosophers concerned with race seek to find the hidden assumptions that enter into our sense of who we are and what are our relationships with others, and to expose these assumptions to the light of critical examination, aiming thereby at the emancipation of those who are oppressed by relationships and institutions based upon such assumptions.

The German philosopher Jürgen Habermas is an important current representative of critical theory. While many feminist and African-American philosophers would not consider themselves Habermasians, nonetheless, Habermas's ideas have had a strong influence on feminist philosophy and upon philosophies of liberation in all parts of the world. While Habermas's philosophy is complex and difficult, we can get a sense of some of his basic ideas by seeing how the framework he developed can be applied to problems of racial and sexual oppression.

When I make any kind of claim in philosophy, my making that claim carries with it an implicit commitment to reason. If I say that members of one group should be treated differently than members of another group, I open myself up to the question as to why this should be so. But the reason that I offer is itself open to further questioning; for example, Wollstonecraft and Douglass questioned the reasons offered in support of discrimination against women and Africans. Habermas conceives of philosophy as an open-ended dialogue in which every statement carries with it an implicit commitment to reply to any and all questions that might be raised by serious and fair interlocutors. Attempts to exclude questions or persons, or attempts to close the dialogue before all questions and views have been heard, involve arbitrary interventions that violate the commitment to reason implicit in the very first attempt to say something about the world. Such arbitrary interventions are, in this sense, a betrayal of reason, and it is one of the tasks of philosophy to protest against such betrayals. For Habermas, the correct answer is the one that would emerge at the end of such an open-ended dialogue where every individual is given the opportunity to speak and question until no further questions remain. Of course, no actual dialogue can satisfy this ideal, but the ideal provides the basis for a critique of actual political discourse. Habermas's work draws our attention to the moral and political significance of excluded voices, the voices of women, of racial, religious, and ethnic minorities, of homosexuals, and of the poor. Unlike natural-law theory and utilitarianism, which are essentially "monological," deriving claims about the rightness of certain political and social arrangements by logical inference from abstract principles, Habermas's approach rests on "dialogical" foundations, which require the genuine participation of these excluded voices. While there is considerable theoretical controversy about Habermas's claim that commitment to certain moral principles is inherent in the use of language, Habermas's framework provides a model for understanding much of the work that philosophers have done in critically examining racial and sexual oppression.

There are, however, a number of philosophers who feel that an adequate philosophical understanding of emancipatory consciousness forces us to step outside the boundaries of critical theory as it was understood by Marx and is understood by Habermas. These philosophers believe that a philosophically adequate understanding of emancipatory consciousness must incorporate some of the ideas of the poststructuralist or postmodernist philosophies developed by Michel Foucault, Jacques Derrida, Gilles Deleuze, Julia Kristeva, Luce Irigaray, and a number of other French thinkers in the 1970s and 1980s. While we cannot do justice to any of these thinkers here and while important difference exist between them, nevertheless we can sketch some ideas that have emerged from this body of work that some philosophers have found important for understanding emancipatory consciousness.

Like the critical theorists, the postmodernists emphasize that our consciousness of ourselves, other people, and the world around us is a historically constructed system of ideas. Like the critical theorists, the postmodernists view us as, so to speak, prisoners of these constructed ideologies. Thus, for example, women grow up thinking of themselves as inferior or subordinate to men because they internalize the historically constructed ideology of patriarchy. Critical theory aims at dispelling the power of this ideology by showing that it is false. But to show that something is false, it is necessary to shine the light of truth upon it. In this respect, critical theory might be said to agree with the biblical idea that knowledge of the truth will set us free. But this, the postmodernists say, is to assume a dichotomy of truth and falsehood that cannot itself withstand critical reflection.

According to the postmodernists, it is not only the systems of beliefs about the world and our place in it but also our methods of reasoning and standards of evaluation that are historically constructed. We believe that there are "true" and "false" representations of the world, and that there are standards of logic and good reasoning that will allow us to discern which is which. But in fact, the postmodernist argues, all we humans can ever reach with our thought is our own constructed image. Insofar as the world is for us at all, it is as an image constructed by our own consciousness of it. Further, the postmodernist argues, this imagemaking thought that is for us inescapable is always historically situated. It is the thought of a man or a woman, a European or an African, a worker or a capitalist. The critical theorist is in a sense insufficiently critical, forgetting that the subject of thought and the very canons of rationality that that subject embraces are in reality parts of a complex, particular, constructed subjectivity.

The postmodernist says that despite its talk of dialogue, critical theory imagines that all of us share some purely logical consciousness, unsullied by prejudices growing out of a particular situation in life. Critical theory addresses itself to this pure consciousness, a consciousness that, because it has been purified of all particularity and all prejudice, is universal, standing for the consciousness of each and every one of us. It is this pure consciousness that makes possible the kind of dialogue imagined by the critical theorist, a dialogue that reaches some agreement. But, not surprisingly, being themselves not pure consciousness but particular, embodied, and usually male consciousnesses, critical theorists mistake their own masculine, white, European, bourgeois consciousness for the universal consciousness of everyone engaged in the dialogue. Behind the emancipatory mask of critical theory stands the prison of a particular way of thought passing itself off for the one, true, universally valid way of thought.

Guarding against this error, postmodernist understandings of emancipatory consciousness stress the importance of recognizing the validity of the consciousness of particular women and particular people of color. They resist attempts to validate one voice and discredit another, arguing that any such judgments rest on unsustainable claims to universality and objectivity. But beyond this they also reject the assumption underlying critical theory that there is some universal logic guaranteeing that different points of view can, eventually, come to agreement about what is right and true. For the postmodernist, genuine respect for others must rest content with the irredeemable otherness of others and the existence of multiple "truths"; the tyranny of objective truth must give way to the tolerance of subjective opinion.

Though on the surface well suited to support the expression of views by oppressed and marginalized peoples, in the end the postmodernist perspective seems untenable. While it is undoubtedly true that prejudices often have paraded behind the mask of objective truth, the very unmasking of such claims seems to presuppose the possibility of valid judgments between conflicting truth claims.

Consider, for example, the struggle to overcome legal discrimination against women and African-Americans. In the early years of the American republic, it was thought that there were important differences, with respect to the capacity for rational self-direction, between males of northern European descent and males of African descent, as well as important differences in this same respect between males and females. But whether or not Africans or women have this capacity is a question of fact, at least to a significant degree. Scientific racism claimed to provide factual evidence to support its conclusions about Africans. But this evidence did not stand up. Nor did the widely accepted view that women were incapable of rationally governing their own lives stand up to the critical challenge raised by Wollstonecraft and others. When the evidence points against the belief necessary to justify discriminatory practices, those discriminatory practices become difficult to defend. This point shows the inadequacy of the view that political commitments are subjective, that in politics there are only opinions and that no opinion is better than any other. In fact, political commitments are entangled with questions of fact, questions that are at least in principle answerable. In its criticism of objectivity and the canons of scientific rationality as themselves merely subjective points of view, postmodernist philosophy appears to be mistaken. Our brief examination of the real histories of debates over gender and race seems to show not a confrontation between incommensurable standpoints but a dialogue between "others" who, despite their differences, can communicate with one another and work toward a shared resolution of their differences.

Structures

Political ideas enter into our sense of who we are and what our relationships with other people should be. In this chapter we have focused on how such political ideas have functioned to sustain sexism and racism and how philosophy can attempt to emancipate women and individuals belonging to racial minorities from the oppressive power of those ideas. But, as we saw in considering the real structural constraints imposed on women by the conflicting claims of career and family, emancipation cannot be entirely a matter of consciousness raising. Emancipation may require, as well, changes in the institutional structures of the society within which we live. In the next chapter we will examine some such institutional structures. In particular, we will focus on how global markets provide an institutional structure that shapes the world we inhabit. We will examine some issues relevant to political philosophy that arise out of the way this structure works. If in this chapter we have examined how politics penetrates our very soul, in the next chapter we will examine how politics is present in relationship with faraway places and peoples.

12

Political Philosophy and its Global Trends

Introduction

We will focus on some issues raised by the role of global markets in shaping the international order. At this point in time the global market functions as the primary institution integrating the separate nation-states and separate peoples of the world into one international order. Political institutions such as the United Nations do certainly play a role, but, at least at this point in time, these institutions are weak, having little power to control events. The global market, on the other hand, already appears sufficiently powerful to threaten the very sovereignty of nation-states. It serves as the dominant institution of the new world order. It provides the structure within which every nation and every individual must live. In this chapter we will consider some issues raised by the structure the global market imposes on the emerging international order.

Imperialism

We looked at racism, with a focus on African Americans and racial minorities within the United States. But racism, of course, is not confined to the borders of the United States. The hierarchy of the races established by the pseudoscientific theories of race popular in the late nineteenth and early twentieth centuries cast a shadow that covered the entire globe. Those racial theories provided the supposed moral justification for European and North American imperialism, which in the late nineteenth and early twentieth centuries carved up the globe, assigning each part of it to the dominion of one of the imperial powers. The relatively brief period of imperial domination established the institutional foundation upon which the present is built, and it inflicted wounds on the colonized peoples of the world that have not yet healed. Any adequate political philosophy must address a range of current issues rooted in the experience of imperialism. Writing in the early hours of this century, W.E.B. DuBois clearly stated the problem. "The problem of the twentieth century," he said, "is the problem of the color-line, the relation of the darker to the lighter races of men in Asia and Africa, in America and the islands of the sea."

Classic colonialism took the form of direct political control of the colonized region, though that control often employed a bureaucracy and police force made up, at least at the lower levels, of indigenous peoples. Such direct political control, involving if necessary the coercive use of the military forces of the imperial power, clashed with at least some versions of natural-law theory. In proclaiming the decision of the people of the American colonies to become independent of Great Britain, the American Declaration of Independence refers to "the separate and equal station to which the Laws of Nature and of Nature's God entitle them." Such a right to self-determination seems flatly inconsistent with colonialism. If a people has a natural right to a separate and equal station among the nations of the world, then no foreign power may rightly rule over them, at least not without their consent.

Taking the brave words of the American Declaration of Independence as their philosophical creed, and the anticolonial struggle of the American Revolution as their model, colonized people around the world struggled to gain national independence from their colonial rulers. One by one the colonized regions of the world gained their independence, becoming equals among the sovereign powers of the world.

The right to self-determination claimed by the Americans and by other anticolonialists is not without its difficulties. In the first place, despite the words of the American Declaration, it is hard to see how such a right could be a natural right, like the rights to liberty and life. The right to liberty and the right to life belong to individual human beings, beings that are natural objects. Nations, on the other hand, are very different kinds of things. They are collections of people. But collections are, in a sense, not natural. They are products of human history and human making. How can such artificial entities have natural rights?

It might seem that this difficulty could be circumvented by making the national right to self-determination a right derived from the individual right of liberty possessed by each individual. If each individual Filipino desires freedom from American colonial rule, then for the United States to maintain that rule is for it to violate the right of liberty of the various individual people who constitute the Filipino nation. But this line of thinking seems to have dangerous implications. If I and three of my friends decide to form an independent country, do we have a natural right to do so?

Typically, at least, the right to self-determination is construed as a collective right distinct from the right to liberty of individual human beings. Julius Nyerere, for example, identifies three basic kinds of rights: the national right of self-determination, the individual right to liberty, and an individual right to freedom from hunger, poverty, and disease. Here the right to self-determination attaches itself to a nation constituted by the shared history and traditions of a group of people. This leaves us then with the problem of how such a historically constituted entity can have a natural right. There are also problems about what distinguishes a group having the right to self-determination from a group that lacks that right. Do all people having a shared history and tradition constitute a nation? Do all such nations have a right to form independent sovereign states? In the American Civil War, Southerners claimed distinct nationhood on the basis of shared history and traditions. Did the Southern states then have a right to secede from the union? Do the Bosnian Serbs, who undeniably have a shared history and shared traditions, have a right to self-determination? There seems to be no theoretically satisfactory way to answer these questions.

In any case, in the aftermath of World War II, the formerly colonized nations of the world claimed their independence. But the independence they gained was only formal. In many ways, and to greater or lesser degrees, these newly independent nations remained under the control of their former colonizers. In some cases the former imperial powers maintained control through puppet regimes that, though they claimed to represent the peoples of the new nation, in fact served the interests of the former colonial power. In other cases the institutions created in the colonial era made it difficult or impossible for the newly independent country to control its fate. Of particular importance in this regard is the role of international markets. During the colonial era, vast regions of Asia and Africa were integrated into the structure of global capitalism. Most often, the colonies served as sources of raw materials and as markets for manufactured goods. With the end of direct colonial rule, newly independent governments found their options severely limited by the constraints imposed upon them by their nation's role in the global capitalist system. The locus of control had shifted from foreign governments to foreign banks, but control remained outside the formally independent nation. Classical colonialism, involving the direct control of external political power, had come to be replaced by neocolonialism, involving the indirect control of the world market and the financial institutions of the developed capitalist world, such as the World Bank and the International Monetary Fund. Capitalism had become a world system marked by a division between developed and underdeveloped countries, with the formerly colonized regions of the world falling among the underdeveloped countries.

In the decades after World War II, as the division between developed and underdeveloped parts of the world became clear, there was a revival of interest in Marxist theories of imperialism. While Marx's own scientific work focused on the theory of capitalism as a self-contained and isolated system, the generation of Marxists who came after Marx attempted to extend the Marxist theory of capitalism to include the interaction between capitalist economies and precapitalist economies that occurred in the era of imperialism. Incorporating the theory of imperialism developed by J.A. Hobson, who was not a Marxist, the Marxist thinkers Rudolf Hilferding, Rosa Luxemburg, Nikolai Bukharin, and V.I. Lenin attempted to work out an understanding of imperialism as the necessary outcome of capitalism. Despite important differences, these thinkers all agreed in seeing imperialism as a safety valve for capitalism. According to Marxist theory, as capitalism developed, it encountered increasingly deep and frequent crises, resulting in business failures, deep cuts in production, and unemployment. Expansion overseas relieved some of this pressure by providing new markets for the glut of products produced and by providing higher returns on investment. Nonetheless, according to these classical Marxist theories, capitalism contained within it a system of incentives that would lead to increasingly rapid development. This being so, the export of capitalism to other parts of the world should eventually result in the development of those other parts of the world. From the viewpoint of classical Marxism, one would expect that eventually the entire world would be more or less evenly developed into a single capitalist system of the kind analyzed by Marx.

By the 1960s and 1970s, with the division between developed and undeveloped parts of the world appearing largely unchanged since World War II, new "structural" theories of imperialism appeared. André Gunder Frank and Immanuel Wallerstein developed an account of the world capitalist system that saw the appearance of a developed center and a permanently underdeveloped periphery as inevitable structural features of capitalist economies. In this respect their theories broke radically with the traditional view that capitalism would inevitably lead to universal development. But Frank and Wallerstein retained a link with classical Marxism in their idea of the importance of exploitation as a feature of capitalism. According to their theories, exploitation of the underdeveloped periphery by the developed center was also a necessary feature of the world capitalist system. On this view, so long as the former colonies remained dependent upon the world capitalist system, they would be locked into underdevelopment, with all of the surplus wealth necessary for development being exported to the centers of the system. Indeed, according to these structural theories, the pattern of "underdevelopment" found in countries on the periphery of world capitalism was not simply an extension of a precapitalist past, but rather something produced by capitalism. Accordingly, development could come only by breaking with the world capitalist system, a conclusion that was also reached by Samir Amin in his refinements of the theory and by the independent account of imperialism, stressing unequal terms of trade within the world capitalist system, developed by Arghiri Emmanuel.

Despite their significant contributions to understanding capitalism as a world system, because of internal difficulties and because of evidence of development in some of the underdeveloped parts of the world, none of these theories appears to be ultimately successful. The view that capitalism necessarily produces a developed center accompanied by an underdeveloped periphery has given way to the view that eventually capitalism will produce a more or less uniform worldwide state of development, with classical Marxists and champions of freemarket capitalism agreeing in blaming the protracted phenomenon of underdevelopment on mistakes made within the former colonized regions of the world.

Nonetheless, enormous disparities exist between the standard of living that prevails in developed countries and that in the underdeveloped parts of the world, a division that often coincides with the color line pointed out by DuBois. In much of the underdeveloped world life is hard and short. Must we fold our hands and tell the poor of the world that eventually things will get better? Have we an obligation to provide them aid?

Lifeboat Ethics

In the 1970s, with episodes of widespread starvation breaking out in different parts of the world, proposals were made to establish a world food bank that would store supplies of grain for distribution when emergency situations produced the need for it. In a much-discussed article Garrett Hardin, a professor of biology and student of population growth, argued against this proposal. He compared the nations of the world to lifeboats and the plight of starving people to the plight of people who had fallen overboard.

Approximately two-thirds of the world is desperately poor, and only one-third is comparatively rich. The people in poor countries have an average per capital GNP (Gross National Product) of about $200 per year; the rich, of about $3,000. (For the United States it is nearly $5,000 per year.) Metaphorically, each rich nation amounts to a lifeboat full of comparatively rich people. The poor of the world are in other, much more crowded lifeboats. Continuously, so to speak, the poor fall out of their lifeboats and swim for a while in the water outside, hoping to be admitted to a rich lifeboat, or in some other way to benefit from the "goodies" on board. What should the passengers on a rich lifeboat do? This is the central problem of "the ethics of a lifeboat."

No doubt each of us feels sympathy for the plight of those who are about to drown. Our natural impulse would be to pull from the sea into our lifeboat as many as we possibly could. But of course, each lifeboat has a limited carrying capacity. If we give free rein to our feelings of sympathy, we will pull too many people aboard, the lifeboat will be swamped, and we will all drown. Difficult as it may be, we must hold our sympathy in check.

But what does this lifeboat ethics have to do with aid to starving people? An important element in Hardin's argument has to do with what he calls "the tragedy of the commons."

> The fundamental error of the sharing ethics is that it leads to the tragedy of the commons. Under a system of private property the man (or group of men) who own property recognize their responsibility to care for it, for if they don't they will eventually suffer. A farmer, for instance, if he is intelligent, will allow no more cattle in a pasture than its carrying capacity justifies. If he overloads the pasture, weeds take over, erosion sets in, and the owner loses in the long run. But if a pasture is run as a commons open to all, the right of each to use it is not matched by an operational responsibility to take care of it. It is no use asking independent herdsmen in a commons to act responsibly, for they dare not. The considerate herdsman who refrains from overloading the commons suffers more than a selfish one who says his needs are greater. Christian-Marxian idealism is counter-productive.

Hardin argues that a world food bank would function like a common pasture. Its resources would be open to all who want to use them, with no corresponding responsibility for protecting the resource. But this undermines any incentive to behave in a responsible way. In particular, Hardin thinks the existence of a world food bank would undermine incentives for underdeveloped countries to control human birth rates. Requiring each country to feed its own people forces each country to protect the resources necessary to grow or purchase food and forces each country to limit its population to what it can afford to feed. If a country could turn to a world food bank whenever the needs of its population outstripped its own resources, its already too large population would be fed, would reproduce, and would create even greater demands upon the world food bank in future years. Eventually such unchecked population growth would produce a demand not even the world food bank could meet. Like the overloaded lifeboat, planet earth would be swamped by a population that exceeds its carrying capacity. Hardin concludes that rich countries should give food aid to poor countries only in emergency situations, and only then if the poor country has acted responsibly to husband its resources and limit its population.

Hardin's argument has been criticized because of the many morally relevant features of the real world omitted by his metaphor of the lifeboat. Why do some people, overwhelmingly people of color from Asia and Africa, just happen to find themselves in overcrowded lifeboats? According to at least one authority, Bangladesh, among the poorest and most overcrowded of "lifeboats," once had a prosperous economy, an economy that was reduced to poverty by British imperialism. To the extent that current patterns of development and underdevelopment were produced by the actions of the imperial powers, surely those powers have some duties of restitution. Hardin ignores this history, taking the overcrowding in some lifeboats for granted.

Also missing from Hardin's analogy is any characterization of the amount of room occupied by the rich who luckily find themselves in one of the less crowded lifeboats. The average American uses up to thirty times as much of the earth's resources as the average Asian or African. Hardin focuses on birth rates in the underdeveloped world, which undoubtedly do increase pressure on world resources, but ignores consumption rates in the developed world, which put much greater per capita stress on the carrying capacity of the planet.

Related to this point is another facet of the real world obscured by Hardin's argument. Guatemala is one of those countries Hardin would describe as an overcrowded lifeboat. Many of its people, mostly people of Indian extraction, suffer from malnutrition. Diarrhea caused by malnutrition is one of the leading causes of death there. Yet Guatemala has rich agricultural lands that are not being used to feed its people. Why is this so? Because the good land is being used to grow coffee and bananas for export to the developed countries of Europe and North America. Guatemalan coffee and bananas are not the only food products making their way from the underdeveloped to the developed world. There is in fact a net transfer of protein from the developing nations to the developed countries. Then why don't the governments of Guatemala and other underdeveloped nations use their resources to feed their people? This has been tried. For example, in 1954 in Guatemala the democratically elected government of Jacob Arbenz attempted to redistribute some good land to poor farmers. The land redistribution was blocked by a military coup, a coup supported by the government of the United States. American support for the coup was arranged by the Central Intelligence Agency (CIA) during a time when the CIA was headed by Allen Dulles, brother of U.S. Secretary of State John Foster Dulles and member of the board of directors of United Fruit Company, an American company that owned land in Guatemala. Such features of the neocolonial order are surely morally relevant, but they are completely obscured by Hardin's lifeboat analogy.

Public Goods and Collective Action

Despite the serious flaws in Hardin's argument, it turns on a theoretically interesting problem involving the relationship between individual action and what are called public goods, a problem that has ominous implications for the future of life on planet Earth. Consider the pasture shared by independent herders. Suppose I have one cow grazing on the pasture and I sell her milk at the end of each day. It occurs to me that I could double my income by adding more cows to my herd. Since the pasture costs me nothing, there is no additional cost. But presumably you and all the other herders who share the commons will be in the same position. So we all increase our herds. But now we have far too many cattle for the available forage. Though the incomes for each of us rise dramatically in the short run, eventually the pasture is overgrazed, we cannot feed our cattle, and we all lose. This is Hardin's "tragedy of the commons."

In this case, every individual's pursuit of self-interest combined to produce an outcome contrary to the self-interest of each. Suppose you see this. Should you then decide not to increase your herd? Not necessarily. Suppose enough of the other herders do decide to voluntarily restrict their herds. Then your increasing your herd will not cause overgrazing. So, in this case, you should add to your herd. Suppose, on the other hand, that most of the others do not curb the size of their herds. What should you do? If you don't increase the size of your herd, you will miss out on those short-term profits and suffer the disaster of overgrazing as well. As Durocher said, nice guys finish last. So you might as well add to your herd and at least reap your share of the short-term profits. Thus it appears that, even if you realize the possible disaster of everyone doing likewise, the individually rational thing for you to do is to increase the size of your herd. But clearly everyone else can reason in the same way. We seem, then, to have reached an impasse whereby each person acting rationally in his or her own self-interest is led to act in ways that produce a collective outcome contrary to the self-interest of each. What we have here is a problem of collective action.

Problems of this kind are not at all uncommon. Suppose there is a beautiful plot of grass between your school and your favorite coffee shop. Should you walk across it? If enough people do, you will kill some of the grass and create an ugly muddy path. Still, you alone will make no difference. You alone walking across will not kill the grass. So if others don't, your doing so will cause no harm. But if others do, your not doing so will not cause any good. So you might as well. But then all others can reason likewise.

You work in a plant where labor is badly treated. There is talk of forming a union and going out on strike. If enough people join, the strike will be won and conditions will improve. Should you join? If you do and enough others don't, you will gain nothing and you risk being fired. If enough others do and you don't, you risk nothing and you share in the improved conditions. But if everyone thinks this way, you all lose the opportunity to improve working conditions.

Each of these cases can be seen as involving the provision of a collective good, a good such that if it is provided to one member of a group, it is necessarily provided to all members of the group as well. A union contract sets wages and working conditions for all who work in the plant. The green grassy area, if it is there at all, is there for the enjoyment of all who pass by. A lush common pasture, if it is there for any of us, is there for all of us. Such collective goods are different from private goods such as candy bars or shoes. If I consume the candy, no one else can do so. If I wear the shoes, no one else can do so without my giving them up. Collective goods are often called public goods because there are a number of such goods that have traditionally been provided by governmental agencies. Consider defense against foreign invasion and the provision of courts and police to maintain law and order. If such goods are provided at all, we all benefit from them. However, it should be noted that a thing can be a collective good without being something provided by government to the public as a whole, as for example the common pasture or the union contract. On the other hand, there are some goods typically provided by public agencies that are not really collective goods. Public schools provide educational instruction without a direct charge to the consumer, but it is possible to provide education as a private good paid for by the consumer and not the public.

Public Goods, Markets, and Externalities

Since the time of Adam Smith, economists have recognized that public goods will not be provided by free markets. Suppose Dr. Strangelove invents a missile defense system that will shoot down enemy missiles with near-complete success. Unfortunately, the system is very expensive. Farther, suppose the system will function as a public good. That is, if the system is set up, it will protect everyone within the borders of the country and not just those who pay for it. Suppose, for example, that it is prohibitively costly to arrange it so that it will shoot down only those missiles that threaten, homes of those who have paid for the system. Now suppose Strangelove opens a Web site and offers the missile defense system for sale. Because of the expense, no individual or small group of individuals can afford it. Its purchase, then, will depend upon payment from a large number of individuals. Even though it is in the interest of each of us to have the system, each of us can reason that it is in our individual best interest not to pay for it, for if enough others pay we benefit anyway. Rational self-interest would lead each of us to act as a "free rider," enjoying the benefit of the public good but escaping our share of the cost. But since each of us can reason in this way, the system is likely to go unpurchased. The traditional solution to this sort of problem is for the government to buy the system and use its coercive power of taxation to force each of us who benefit to pay our fair share of the expense.

Because markets are unable to supply a public good, even though everyone in a society would prefer the good and would be willing to pay for it, the problem of public goods is often referred to as a market failure. Externalities also involve market failures. Negative externalities are costs incurred in the production of a good that do not appear in the market price of the good. Pollution is a classic example. Acid rain caused by coal-fired power plants may damage hardwood forests hundreds of miles away. A cost is incurred. Because the hardwood forest is damaged, the supply of hardwood is decreased, and the cost of hardwood is increased. But of course this cost is paid by consumers of hardwood, not by consumers of energy. In the free market, energy produced by coal-fired plants may be cheaper than energy produced by solar or wind power, though if the externalized costs were included in the reckoning, solar might be cheaper than coal. Because markets respond to market prices, not true costs including externalities, markets can inefficiently distribute scarce resources.

The classic solution to this kind of difficulty is to internalize the externalized cost, perhaps by requiring air scrubbers on smokestacks in coal-fired power plants and making the market cost correspond to the real cost of the energy produced. But, like public-goods problems, this too is likely to require the coercive intervention of government. Because internalization imposes costs on producers, and because competitive markets force producers to keep costs of production as low as possible, only coercive regulations requiring all producers to bear the costs are likely to succeed.

In the last few decades this classic solution has been modified somewhat, with governmental agencies setting clean air standards and then granting saleable permits to pollute above these standards. This method allows for the use of market incentives to reduce pollution and reduces inefficiencies resulting from small gains purchased at heavy costs. However, this particular scheme still involves coercive governmental regulation.

Planet Earth as a Public Good

We are now in a position to see the importance of the problems of collective action, public goods, and market externalities discussed above. A livable planet Earth is in the interest of every individual. Yet we live in a system of global capitalism based on free markets. We know that such a system is capable of producing negative externalities. We also know that such a system is not well designed for providing public goods.

Now consider the phenomena of global warming and depletion of the ozone layer. Both of these involve costs imposed on humankind and all other living things as well. They involve costs because they impose unwanted risks, conceivably including even the risk of the destruction of all human life. Global warming and depletion of the ozone layer are caused by substances released into the atmosphere as by-products of the production and consumption of goods sold on the open market. The costs they impose are not reflected in the market prices of those goods. They are thus market externalities. Internalization of these costs is likely to greatly increase the market prices of some commodities and is not likely to occur, as we have seen, without coercive regulation. At the same time, measures to clean the air and repair damage to the ozone, both public goods, are likely to be very expensive and likewise unprovided without coercive regulation.

All of this, however, leaves us with a very interesting difficulty. Briefly put, we live in a global capitalist system that relies on free markets to determine how resources will be utilized. Because of known market failures, free markets are likely to produce pollution and unlikely to produce public goods such as a livable planet Earth. The traditional solution to such problems involves coercive governmental interference with the market. But at present there is no governmental agency capable of imposing such controls on the global capitalist system. We appear to be heading for disaster.

The Globalization Thesis

As the twentieth century draws to a close, one of the topics that has been much discussed concerns the phenomenon of globalization. The last few decades have seen a number of agreements to reduce or eliminate the remaining barriers to international trade and investment. Technological advancement in computers, computer networks, and communications have made it much easier to conduct business on a global scale. Responding to the ever-present competitive pressures of free markets and the ever-present rewards for cutting costs, corporations have taken advantage of the opportunities opened to them by the new international agreements and the new technologies. Increasingly, labor-intensive production processes have been transferred from developed countries, where the total costs of wages and benefits are high, to underdeveloped countries, where the total costs of wages and benefits are low. Such transfers also tend to reduce costs because of reduced environmental regulation in underdeveloped countries.

A number of critics have argued that this globalization of capitalism has undermined the ability of nation-states to control their economic fate. In a world of global competition, regulations and taxes imposed upon business by one nation to maintain high wages, limits to the working day, strong social safety nets, and high environmental standards raise costs of production within that nation, making indigenous firms less competitive on the world market. Challenged by overseas competitors with lower costs of production, firms have incentives to transfer their operations to other nations with less onerous regulations. The regulative strategies at the heart of new liberalism and the welfare state, strategies that turned on the use of governmental regulation and governmental power of redistributive taxation, appear to be ineffective in a world of global competition. In short, globalization appears to render the nation-state obsolete. In doing so, it also appears to have undercut the ability of a people to democratically control their fate. A nation whose people persist in voting for politicians who support traditional welfare-state commitments will find itself losing out in international competition and paying the price of increasing unemployment.

Notice that the problem threatening here has structural similarities to the problems of collective action and collective goods discussed above. It may well be that no producer wants to lower the standard of living of workers, but each is forced to act in ways that produce that effect out of rational self-interest. The softhearted employer who insists on paying a living wage and controlling pollution will find himself driven out of business by his more ruthless competitors. Knowing that others are likely to act to reduce costs, the rational producer has no choice but to do likewise.

As we saw in our discussion of the problems of collective action, the traditional solution to such difficulties involves coercive regulation by governmental agencies. Minimum-wage laws, legal limits on the working day, health and safety regulations, and regulations requiring anti-pollution technologies all force each competitor to meet these standards. In effect, the regulations raise the costs of production for all producers, thereby preventing downward competition, whereby the ruthless competitor drags the good-hearted employer to his level.

The problem is that, just as there is no power able to impose global environmental regulations, so too there is no power able to impose regulations aimed at protecting wages, hours, and working conditions. In effect, global markets pit nation against nation in a struggle of downward competition. The nation that can promise companies the lowest taxes, lowest labor costs, and least costly environmental regulations wins the prospective industrial development. The nation that is more finicky in these matters loses out. Competing against one another to attract investment from global capitalism, nations are trapped in a downward competition, a race to the bottom, that threatens both workers' standards of living and environmental conditions.

A Kantian Argument

Recognizing the potential for downward competition in free trade agreements, organized labor and environmental groups have sought to introduce regulation of working conditions and environmental regulations into international agreements to expand free trade. These proposals make eminent sense in light of the regulatory history of dealing with such problems within the confines of nation-state politics. So far such attempts have largely failed, with the small steps toward regulatory action actually taken producing only language that is vague and without effective enforcement mechanisms. Effective regulation has met with strong opposition from nation-states in the underdeveloped world, which see such regulation as interference with national sovereignty, and with opposition by powerful corporations, which view such regulation as unwarranted intrusion into the operation of the free market. There are some additional problems as well. Given the striking divide between the developed world and the underdeveloped world inherited from the age of imperialism, any imposition of uniform global standards regarding wages and benefits for workers and environmental regulations would almost surely work to stifle investment in the underdeveloped world. Globalization offers the promise of eventually overcoming the chasm that separates developed countries from underdeveloped ones. The trick is to see to it that globalization brings the underdeveloped world up rather than bringing the developed world down. Just how this trick can be done is quite another matter.

There is, however, yet another difficulty that must be faced. In the *Groundwork of the Metaphysic of Morals*, Immanuel

Kant offered several distinct versions of what he took to be the underlying principle of all morality. One of those versions is formulated this way: "I ought never act except in such a way that I can also will that my maxim should become a universal law." Though most philosophers reject Kant's own view that this principle provides a sufficient foundation for answering all moral questions, most philosophers do regard Kant's principle as a necessary condition for any morally acceptable action. That is, for it to be morally permissible for me to do X under circumstances Y, it must also be permissible for everyone else to do X under circumstances Y. My action must be "universalizable" if it is to be morally permissible. The force of this consideration is clear even to the child who is confronted with the question "What if everybody did that?"

But now consider this. In the countries of the developed world we have a way of life that is, despite some minor differences, more or less the same from one developed country to another. It is this way of life to which much of the underdeveloped world aspires, and it is this way of life we had in mind in saying that the trick is to lift the underdeveloped world up rather than pull the developed world down. In short, we aim at universalizing the way of life achieved in the advanced industrial world. But is this possible? Remember that the average citizen of the United States consumes thirty times as much of the earth's resources as the average person of Bangladesh. There are good reasons for thinking that this high-consumption way of life cannot be universalized without bringing ecological disaster to planet Earth. The conclusion implied by these premises, and the Kantian principle of universalizability, is that the way of life we all enjoy in the developed world is not morally acceptable and that therefore we ought to make major changes in it.

On the other hand, there is another widely accepted principle of ethics that says that "ought implies can." We cannot be obligated to do something that is impossible for us to do. Many philosophers have interpreted "impossible" in terms of what is unreasonably demanding. On this "morality lite" understanding of the principle, we cannot be obligated to make the changes in our way of life apparently demanded by the Kantian principle since those changes make unreasonable demands upon us.

Political philosophy is the study of such topics as liberty, justice, property, rights, law, and the enforcement of a legal code by authority: what they are, why (or even if) they are needed, what makes a government legitimate, what rights and freedoms it should protect and why, what form it should take and why, what the law is, and what duties citizens owe to a legitimate government, if any, and when it may be legitimately overthrown. In a vernacular sense, the term "political philosophy" often refers to a general view, or specific ethic, political belief or attitude, about politics that does not necessarily belong to the technical discipline of philosophy. Political philosophy can also be understood by analysing it through the perspectives of metaphysics, epistemology and axiology thereby unearthing the ultimate reality side, the knowledge or methodical side and the value aspects of politics. Three central concerns of political philosophy have been the political economy by which property rights are defined and access to capital is regulated, the demands of justice in distribution and punishment, and the rules of truth and evidence that determine judgments in the law.

Western Philosophy: As an academic discipline, Western political philosophy has its origins in ancient Greek times and society, when city-states were experimenting with various forms of political organization including monarchy, tyranny, aristocracy, oligarchy, and democracy. One of the first, extremely important classical works of political philosophy is Plato's The Republic, which was followed by Aristotle's Politics and Nichomachean Ethics. Roman political philosophy was influenced by the Stoics, and the Roman statesman Cicero wrote on political philosophy, expressing clearly and to the point the main Stoic thesis.

Far East Philosophy: Independently, Confucius, Mencius, Mozi and the Legalist school in China, and the Laws of Manu and Chanakya in India, all sought to find means of restoring political unity and political stability; in the case of the former three through the cultivation of virtue, in the last by imposition of discipline. In India, Chanakya, in his Arthashastra, developed a viewpoint which recalls both the Legalists and Niccolò Machiavelli. Ancient Chinese civilization and Indian civilization resembled Greek civilization in that there was a unified culture divided into rival states. In the case of China, philosophers found themselves obliged to confront social and political breakdown, and seek solutions to the crisis that confronted their entire civilization. The Confucian School always deals with political problems on the basis of ethics while the other schools of political thought, of which there are about twelve in China, do not necessarily include ethics in their discussion of political philosophy. In spite of the existence of these different schools of political philosophy, there are still some Western scholars who refuse to admit there is such a thing as Chinese political philosophy. The Chinese people would eventually accept the Confucian philosophy as the guardian spirit of politics.

13

Phenomenology and Existentialism in Philosophy

Introduction

The best way to describe this phenomenon of intentionality is to make a distinction, again relying on scholastic terminology, between the 'material' and the 'intentional' object of a mental state. When I see as a ghost what is in fact a piece of fluttering cloth, then the intentional object of my seeing is a ghost, while the material object is a piece of cloth. The intentional object is that which is 'present to consciousness', and it may not correspond to any material reality. This possibility of non-correspondence explains the peculiarity of the intentional object. Intentional objects are of many logical types: they can be propositions (the objects of belief), ideas (the objects of thought), individuals (the objects of love and hate). They can be indeterminate (a lion), or determinate (the lion before me). In every case they have no existence independent of the mental state that 'refers to' or is 'directed onto' them. There is no 'real relation' between fear, say, and its intentional object, since the two cannot be thought of as existing separately. This is one of the few genuine cases where one might wish to speak, in Bradleyan terms, of an 'internal' relation.

Brentano believed that this property of intentionality is peculiar to mental phenomena and common to all of them. It therefore formed, for him, a distinguishing mark of the mental. The property has, however, an intricate logic, and presents rather more difficulties in the description than my brief summary conveys. It has therefore proved difficult to substantiate this particular aspect of Brentano's thought, or fully to understand its implications. In particular a confusion, sometimes accidental, sometimes deliberate, between intentionality and a lack of what logicians call extensionality has made discussions of this topic in recent years peculiarly vertiginous. It must be said of the phenomenologists, however, that their knowledge of modern logic has not, in general, been sufficient to permit these confusions. It is the *phenomenon* of intentionality that has been of interest to them, and not the search for some general differentiating characteristic of the mental.

The first important phenomenologist was Brentano's pupil Edmund Husserl (1859–1938), who began his philosophical career with a book on the foundations of arithmetic that is now chiefly remembered for Frege's devastating critique of it. Among Husserl's many writings, those that have attracted the most attention are the *Logical Investigations* (1900–1), *Ideas for a Pure Phenomenology* (1913) and *Cartesian Meditations* (1929, first published 1950). The first of these is of great interest, announcing the theme for which Husserl is known, that of a 'pure phenomenology'. This theme is further elaborated in the second of his major works. In these works he begins the description of what he was to call the 'method' of phenomenological reduction. Husserl's thought rests on two master-premises. First, he reaffirms the essence of the Cartesian position, that the immediate knowledge that I have of my own conscious mental states is the one sure foundation for an understanding of their nature, provided only that I can isolate what is *intrinsic* to the mental state, and separate it from all that is extraneous. Secondly, the intentionality of the mental makes 'meaning' or 'reference' essential to every mental act. To focus on the revealed nature of mentality is therefore also to understand the fundamental operation of 'meaning', whereby the world is made intelligible. In virtue of these two premises Husserl was able to construct a philosophy which, like that of Descartes, aimed to produce a complete metaphysical vision from reflection on the peculiarities of consciousness.

But study of the first-person case is blind if it is impossible to isolate what is contained in it. Just as Descartes sought to separate the 'clear and distinct' idea from the mental states with which it is mingled, so did Husserl propose a method whereby to isolate the pure deliverances of consciousness from the encumbrances which impede our understanding of them. This method is that of 'phenomenological reduction', or 'bracketing' (*epoché,* from the Greek). All reference to what is susceptible to doubt or mediated by reflection must be excluded from the description of every mental state, leaving the remnant of pure immediacy alone. Let us consider the case of fear. I must not suppose that the object of fear exists independently of my fear. Fear does not guarantee the existence of its object, but only of its own 'direction' towards an object. We should therefore 'bracket' the material object in examining the nature of fear. But the intentional object remains: we cannot eliminate from fear the *idea* of an object, since this is contained in the mental state and immediately present to the consciousness of the one who fears.

What else remains, after the process of bracketing? Husserl spoke of a 'mental act', the process of direction itself, which in some way constitutes the essence of fear. The peculiar method of phenomenology is that it takes this mental act as its datum. Nothing else can be described which is either more fundamental to knowledge, or more able to reveal the essence of what is known. Is not the phenomenologist burdened, then, with the old Cartesian question, of how to advance beyond the first-person case to knowledge of an independent world? The title of Husserl's later, impenetrable work *Cartesian Meditations* suggests, as does its content, that his 'method' has indeed cast him into the pit of scepticism.

But the major object of this scepticism is, historically speaking, somewhat surprising. It is not the objective world but the observing subject himself. The person (or self) exists for Husserl only in the performance of intentional acts. But he is not identical with any of these intentional acts. Nor can he be the object of such an act since, if he were, then there would have to be some other subject performing the act of which 'he' is the object. But who is this subject if not himself? The 'I', as Ryle expressed it in another context, is systematically elusive. In what sense, then, can we know that it exists? The 'I' exists, Husserl thought, only as the subject and never as the object of consciousness. It must therefore be 'transcendental' in something like the sense of Kant's 'transcendental self'. Many of Husserl's voluminous writings are spent in the pursuit of this creature which he declared to be unknowable, and it is not surprising that they have seemed to many, in consequence, to be unreadable.

It is unclear from what I have said that there is any special 'method' of phenomenology. How, for example, is it distinguished from the psychology of introspection? In the *Logical Investigations* Husserl expressly rejects 'psychologism' the view that logic is a very general science of the mind. In setting up phenomenology in its place, he claimed to be enunciating a method that is free from, and indeed presupposed by, every empirical enquiry, (His view about the status of his theory was therefore the opposite of Brentano's; which of them was right is not a matter that I feel able to decide.) Phenomenology is the necessary preliminary to any science of the mind, since it locates prior to any description, classification or explanation the individual mental acts which psychology must investigate. Moreover, it is the sole access to meaning. Meaning is created by mental acts, and the world becomes present to consciousness only through those acts. Hence our understanding determines the essences of things, by fixing the manner in which they are known. Phenomenology therefore yields a knowledge not of facts, but of essences. It is consequently (so it is argued) an *a priori* science.

Husserl was aware of the impasse into which he had been driven by his Cartesian method, and in his last unfinished work *Transcendental Phenomenology and the Crisis of the European Sciences,* published posthumously in 1954 he attempted to overcome the subjective emphasis of phenomenology by means of a theory of the social world. The focus shifts from 'I' to 'we', albeit a 'transcendental "we"'. This plural subject is something like the implied community of language users, who together construct the common-sense world in which they are situated. Husserl calls this common-sense world the *Lebenswelt,* or 'life-world': it is a world constituted by our social interaction, and endowed with the 'meanings' that inhabit our communicative acts. We reach the transcendental 'we' by an imaginative self-projection, from the 'here' of first-person awareness to the 'there' of the generalised other. What is given in this process is not the elusive residue of some phenomenological reduction, but the *Lebenswelt* itself.

The concept of the *Lebenswelt* enabled Husserl to revive a project of post-Kantian idealism: the project of distinguishing the human realm (the realm of meaning) from the realm of nature (the realm of science and explanation). Inspired by Kant's division between understanding and practical reason, the romantic theologian F. D. E. Schleiermacher (1768–1834) had argued that the interpretation of human actions can never be accomplished by the methods employed in the natural sciences. The human act must be understood as the act of a free being, motivated by reason, and understood through dialogue. The same is true of texts, which can be interpreted only through an imaginative dialogue with their author. 'Hermeneutics' the art of interpretation involves the search for reasons rather than causes, and the attempt to understand a text as an expression of rational activity the very activity that is manifest in me.

A later Kantian philosopher, Wilhelm Dilthey (1833–1911), extended Schleiermacher's hermeneutical method to the entire human world. Our attitude to other people, he argued, is fundamentally distinct from and even opposed to the scientific attitude. We seek to understand their actions not by explaining them in terms of external causes, but 'from within', by an act of rational self-projection that

Dilthey calls *Verstehen.* In understanding human life and action I must find the agent's reasons for what he does. This means conceptualising the world as he does, seeing the connections and unities that he sees. For example, I understand your fear of speaking in a certain place, once I conceptualise it as you do, as somewhere 'sacred'.

Our every-day ways of conceptualising the world do not, as a rule, follow the direction required by scientific explanation. Rather, Dilthey suggests, they represent the world as 'ready for action'. I see the world under the aspect of my own freedom, and describe and respond to it accordingly. This before me is not a member of the species *Homo sapiens* but a *person,* who looks at me and smiles; that beside her is not a piece of bent organic tissue but a *chair* on which I may sit; this on the wall is not a collection of tinted chemicals but a *picture,* in which the face of a saint appears; and so on. In short, we are not merely in dialogue with each other; we are in dialogue with the world itself, moulding the natural order through concepts, so as to align it with our aims. Our categories do not *explain* the world, so much as endow it with *meaning.*

Husserl took this idea a stage further, by suggesting that the pre-scientific vision of the world expresses not merely our identity as rational beings, but our *life.* The world appears to us in the guise of a 'lived environment': a place in which we situate ourselves as acting and suffering organisms. We understand objects as 'friendly' or 'hostile', 'comfortable' or 'uncomfortable', 'useful' or 'useless', and in a thousand ways divide the world according to our interests. Our classifications form no part of the enterprise of scientific explanation, and have an authority that no science could remove. The new task of phenomenology is to awaken us to the *Lebenswelt,* and to vindicate those 'we'-thoughts in which the meaning of objects is created and made public.

Dilthey was the first to attempt a systematic distinction between the *Geisteswissenschaften* (humanities) and the natural sciences, suggesting that the first are really extended and transhistorical exercises in *Verstehen.* Husserl recognised, however, that these 'human sciences' had entered a condition of crisis during our century, precisely because natural science had presumptiously invaded their territory, and so prompted people to throw away, as useless remnants of a vanished world-view, the concepts through which the *Lebenswelt* is understood and organised. The crisis is not only intellectual; it is also moral, indeed, a crisis of civilisation itself. For the *Lebenswelt* falls apart when not sustained by reflection. The result is a loss of meaning, a moral vacuum, into which we are led whenever we surrender to the false gods of science.

No philosopher in our time has been more acutely aware of this moral vacuum than Martin Heidegger (1889–1976), a pupil of Husserl's, who can fairly claim to be the most important thinker, and the darkest, of the existentialist school. Husserl had delivered, during his middle years, two series of lectures, later published as *The Phenomenology of Internal Time Consciousness,* in which he claimed to rediscover, on the level of phenomenological analysis, the age-old metaphysical problem of time. Inspired by this and other later Husserlian writings, Heidegger composed his *Being and Time* (1927), which is the most complex of the many works inspired, directly or indirectly, by Kant's theory of time as the 'form of inner sense'.

It is impossible to summarise Heidegger's work, which no one has claimed to understand completely. In the next chapter I shall give reasons for thinking that it may be unintelligible, from the very nature of the phenomenological 'method' which it employs. Its language, like that of the later Husserl, is metaphorical and contorted to the point almost of incomprehensibility; the reader has the impression that never before have so many words been invented and tormented in the attempt to express the inexpressible.

Heidegger claims that his method is phenomenological, and that its essence is captured in the slogan, 'To the things themselves!' Philosophy is the study of phenomena, where 'phenomena' is taken in its original Greek sense as referring to whatever 'shows itself'. Phenomena are not mere appearances, but those things which *show themselves* to consciousness. Hence the priority of phenomenology over any physical or psychological science. Phenomenology is also the fundamental form of 'ontology' the study of what is. Despite its Cartesian beginnings, phenomenology in the work of Heidegger breaks loose from epistemology and launches itself, with a daring unprecedented since Hegel, onto the sea of speculation, with only one question as its guide. This question is that of 'the meaning of being', a question which, we are invited to suppose, was the subject-matter of all those ancient philosophies, Socratic and pre-Socratic, which the Cartesian method submerged.

Being (*Sein*) must be distinguished from *Dasein. Dasein* is the kind of being that characterises human self-consciousness. It is the 'thing which understands being'. It would be convenient if we could give the term '*Dasein*' its normal translation of 'existence'. Unfortunately, Heidegger, who can certainly be thought to multiply terms to the limit of possibility, whether or not beyond necessity, has forestalled us. He introduces a third term, *Existenz,* which denotes 'that kind of Being towards which *Dasein* can comport itself in one way or another, and always does comport itself somehow'. *Dasein,* by contrast, has its being '*for its own*'. *Dasein* is what Sartre later described as *être four-soi,* and what Hegel had already described as being-for-self (*Fürsichsein*).

As we shall see, both Heidegger and Sartre owe far more to Hegel than their vocabulary. All these are more or less pompous ways of distinguishing things from persons. What then is the argument, or, failing that, the thesis, of *Being and Time*? I am not sure, but perhaps the following represents a part of it. First, while Heidegger rejects the use of such terms as 'subject' and 'object', preferring technicalities of his own, he is clearly concerned with the modern problem of self-knowledge. What is self-knowledge, what is its object and what does it yield by way of insight into the objective world? He begins, therefore, from the first-person case, saying that 'the assertion that it is I who in each case Dasein is, is ontically obvious'. But ontical obviousness is one thing, content another. We must answer the 'problem of being'. This poses itself initially as the question: 'Who (what) am I?' As Kant showed in the Paralogisms, no amount of study of the immediate knowledge characteristic of the first person will answer this question. Heidegger notices and applauds the result, but does not, as he perhaps should, feel threatened by it. Now, we can know from phenomenological analysis that the essence of *Dasein* lies in its existence: it *at least* has existence, and it has existence *essentially.* This ontological argument for the existence of the subject should not be taken too seriously. For if we know nothing else about this *Dasein* than that it exists, we have hardly advanced even so far as the first Cartesian question.

Heidegger precedes his theory of being (which is in fact a theory of self-consciousness) with a fascinating, but maddeningly abstract, description of the world of phenomena. Since all being is being in the world, then the essence of the world as phenomenon must be explored if being is to be understood. We learn that the world contains things, but that thinghood must be construed not in its modern, scientific sense, but in its ancient meaning the meaning of the Greek term *pragmata.* Objects are 'to be used', or 'ready to hand'. Hence we can understand them as 'signs'; that is, we interpret them as bearing an immediate relation to ourselves. (Here we again encounter the influence of Dilthey.) The world first comes into consciousness as a sign, as *logos.* It is that which 'bears a meaning for us'. This explains *Dasein*'s 'fascination with the world'. Seemingly independent objects can be constantly appropriated for *Dasein*'s own uses, made into expressions, and assigned a meaning. This is the 'abolition of distance' (*Entfernen*) between objects and ourselves. We are led to understand that this abolition of distance also provides the first 'phenomenon' of space it is this which leads to my sense of having spatial position in my world.

But this peaceful union of *Dasein* and its world is broken, as ever, by the appearance of the Other. In relation to this existence of others my own existence is put in question. I become aware of what Heidegger calls my 'thrown-ness' (*Geworfenheit*), which is the lack of any reason for my existence in the world; the fact that I am simply there. It is this which appears in the phenomenon of fear, and which precipitates that great turning away from the world which others have called alienation, but which Heidegger prefers to call 'the Fall'. *Dasein* 'falls', not into sin or Hell, but into 'inauthenticity'. Confronted with the absolute enigma of my own being I flee from myself. I lose myself in anxiety, and in order to escape that anxiety I try to cease to be myself and instead become one of 'them'. I become an object, part of that world which first shattered my composure by showing my arbitrariness, and which now tempts me to deny myself, by melting into the impersonal 'they' of role, form and 'idle talk'.

However, this inauthenticity brings with it a sense of the absurd. This is the sense that objects are *without* meaning. They had a meaning for *Dasein,* but have no meaning for the consciousness which identifies itself only impersonally, as a part of 'them'. This sense of absurdity translates itself into anxiety, and in anxiety the first answer to the question of being is formed. 'Who am I? answer: myself.' Whatever else I am, I am that. Anxiety, as Heidegger puts it, 'individualises'. Precisely because it has no object, because its intentionality is universal, undifferentiated, without focus, it can only be grasped as mine. In the experience of anxiety I am cut off from them, and thrown back into my individuality, my existence, as the ultimate fact.

This sense of individuality has, as its principal manifestation (one might almost say 'moment'), the exercise of a peculiar mental capacity which Heidegger calls 'care' (*Sorge*). The attitude of the anxious self to the world is one of care: apprehension for itself and for others, and the attempt to understand the world as an object of knowledge and activity. This care brings with it the separation of subject and object, and the idea of objective truth. As Heidegger puts it, care 'uncovers the world', and so finds what is objective in relation to itself.

The 'caring' self has a new kind of being a wholeness which Heidegger also describes as a being-towards-death. For anxiety brings with it the apprehension of finiteness and vulnerability; and 'care' is simply understanding the world as the locus of finite and vulnerable existence. In being-towards-death I recognise my predicament as a creature conditioned by time, and see that only *in* time is my redemption possible, so that care becomes the 'call of conscience'. I have to make myself responsible for my acts and my existence: this is the single answer that I have to undifferentiated anxiety, and it is my first glimpse of authenticity. I am more fully myself in recognising the call of something that is both integral to me, and yet which also points beyond me. I have been summoned out of the lostness of 'they' and called upon to announce myself in resolution.

But resolution requires what Heidegger calls an 'anticipatory resoluteness'. I must see the future in a certain way—as at least partially closed to me if I am to have this attitude. I can decide to do something only in so far as I do not regard the question whether or not I shall do it as already settled. The future must therefore have a special status for me. It must be the object of different attitudes from those that I direct towards the present and past. It follows that I can only become authentic if I realise that my being is in time, not just in the sense that all things are in time, but in the deeper sense that time must form and determine all my outlook on the world, separating the future, which is the object of resoluteness, from the past, which is the object of guilt and responsibility. It can do that, Heidegger says, only if I see my freedom and my temporality as one and the same thing. This is 'being free for death'. The final answer to the riddle of existence is this: I am a being who is extended in time, and whose redemption lies in that freedom which time alone provides, the freedom to make of my life what I choose it to be, and thereby to change from thrown-ness to resolution. In that change lies the realisation, and acceptance, of mortality.

There is a certain poetry in Heidegger's vision, and moments of true philosophical insight. But how much of it is really philosophy, and how much an embroidered description of a private spiritual journey? Such questions take us into the heart of philosophical method. One thing is clear, which is that Heidegger's conclusions, where intelligible, are clearly intended as universal truths, not merely about the human condition, but about the world as such. Their status is synthetic and *a priori*; they could be neither proved nor disproved by any form of science. It is tempting sometimes to interpret them in a scientific or pseudo-scientific way, as gestures towards a psychology of self-consciousness. But that interpretation can hardly account for the generality and abstractness of what is put forward, besides suggesting (what is clearly false) that these theories could be measured against empirical evidence and so refuted or confirmed. On the other hand, Heidegger does not give any arguments for the truth of what he says. Most of *Being and Time* consists of compounded assertions, with hardly a 'thus', 'therefore', 'possibly', or 'it might follow that', to indicate the relations which are supposed to hold between them. The crucial thesis that idealism does not need a refutation, since its falsehood is *given* in *Dasein*'s quest for self-knowledge, is supported, not by argument, but by etymology, and the etymology of a Greek word to boot. Even if the whole of Heidegger's philosophy is both meaningful and true, therefore, we have yet to be given a reason to accept it. Looked at critically, Heidegger's ideas seem like spectral visions in the realm of thought; vast, intangible shadows cast by language. Perhaps, if there were no distinction in grammar between *Sein* and *Dasein,* no abstract nouns of the kind exemplified by '*Geworfenheit*', these shadows would dissolve, and nothing come to replace them. This sort of philosophy shows, in Wittgenstein's words, 'the bewitchment of the intelligence by means of language'.

This lack of argument persists in the writings of Jean-Paul Sartre (1905–1980), the French pupil of Husserl and of Heidegger who has done the most to propagate existentialism as a moral and metaphysical doctrine peculiarly suited to the demands of the modern conscience. But it is to some extent compensated for by literary graces, and by an art of persuasion that has made Sartre into one of the most influential writers of our time. In plays, novels and essays he has repeatedly expressed, modified and resurrected the existentialist vision; transforming it from abstract theory to imaginative experience. In his philosophical works the same imaginative methods persist. Faced with the question, 'Is this philosophy or is it psychology?' he would no doubt answer, 'Neither and both'. I shall try to present a philosophy which I believe to be Sartre's. Those parts that might seem to be psychological in nature are so evidently derived from Hegel, that it will need no apology to discuss them as though they were integral to the philosophical history of our time.

Sartre's early work on *The Psychology of the Imagination* (1940) (*The Imaginary,* as its title should have been translated), shows the influence of Husserl very strongly, and, while the English title (and French subtitle) suggest a reluctance to accept that phenomenology and psychology are distinct, the content makes it clear that Sartre is able to argue persuasively for conclusions about the nature of the human mind which are by any standards philosophical. These conclusions reappear, transmuted from their phenomenological form, in Sartre's famous lecture *L'Existentialisme est un humanisme.* This was delivered in 1945, after war-time experiences which had so transformed every aspect of Sartre's intelligence that it is usual to ignore the (in my view) more original and more important work which preceded them. I shall follow the usual practice, and regard this lecture, together with the vast and rambling reflections of *Being and Nothingness* (1943) as containing the fundamentals of Sartre's existentialism.

The premise of Sartre's philosophy is expressed in surprisingly mediaeval terms, as the proposition that 'existence precedes essence'. There is no human nature, since there is no God to have a conception of it. Essences, as intellectual constructions, vanish with the mind that would conceive them. For us, therefore, our existence which is to say, that unconceptualised individuality which was celebrated (but not described) by Kierkegaard is the premise of all enquiry. This existence is determined by no universal idea, and has no prefigured destiny such as might be contained in a vision of human nature. Man must make his own essence, and even his existence is, in a sense, an achievement. He exists fully only when he is what he purposes to be. (Here, as elsewhere, Sartre's philosophy echoes that of Heidegger.)

The premise of philosophy is still, therefore, the premise of Descartes, the 'cogito'; but it is the cogito transformed by

Husserlian phenomenology. All consciousness is intentional it posits an object in which it sees itself as in a mirror. Object and subject arise together and are conceived in radically different ways. Because they are so familiar to us, these ways defy description in the language of common sense. Hence the need for technicalities in order to describe the fundamental difference between the knower and the known (the '*pour-soi*' and the '*en-soi*', as Sartre calls them).

In setting itself up as subject in relation to a possibly unknowable object, the self creates (or posits) a separation in its world, a kind of crevasse which no amount of experience can fill. This crevasse is called '*néant*', or nothingness, which 'lies coiled in the heart of being, like a worm'. That characteristic phrase is part of an evocative description designed to persuade us that the separation of primeval being into subject and object generates a third thing (or rather nothing). It is this third thing that enters the world of self-consciousness in persecutory disguises.

A. J. Ayer accused Sartre of a logical mistake in introducing 'nothingness' as though it were an entity: the logical mistake of the king in *Through the Looking Glass* who takes 'Nobody' as a proper name. But perhaps such criticism, tempting though it is, misses the phenomenological point of Sartre's coinage. Sartre is attempting to describe what is *given to consciousness* in the very act of conceiving itself as related to an objective world, and he perforce must strain language in order to express an experience which is so immediate as to precede every attempt at description.

The experience of nothingness is always with us and hence is elusive, as the ego is elusive. To persuade us of its actuality, Sartre provides various vivid examples, expectation and its disappointment being prominent among them. When I enter a cafe in search of Pierre, and he is not there, he is no more not there because of my expectation than he is not there when I had not thought of him. Yet my experience is changed by my expectation. The cafe reflects back to me, in all its particulars, the absence of Pierre. Pierre's absence becomes a pervasive quality of the consciousness through which these particulars are perceived. The cafe presents a kind of narrative of Pierre's non-existence, which could not be read in any locality where I had not expected him. This idea is certainly fanciful, but it is also typical of Sartrean phenomenology, being at once observant and uncanny. Like Socrates, Sartre attempts to introduce '*aporia*', or intellectual anguish, as a prelude to the introduction of a metaphysical idea which will console the bewildered intelligence.

Only self-consciousness can bring *néant* or nothingness into the world: for the merely sentient being the fracture between subject and object has not opened. But with the sense of nothingness comes anguish. The question arises, 'How shall I fill this void—between myself and the world?', or, to put it in a way which, for Sartre, seems to be equivalent: 'How shall I make myself *part* of the world?' This is the phenomenological meaning of the question 'What shall I do?' It is the present sense of the future, and of the individual's responsibility for that future. Anguish is the proof of freedom. There can be nothing more certain to a person than that he is free, since nothing is more certain than the existential choice which compels the recognition of futurity, and of our responsibility towards it.

What is the outcome of anguish? Initially it manifests itself, Sartre says, as the sense that objects are not properly distinct from each other. They are undifferentiated, passive, awaiting agency. Our sense of the gap between subject and object translates itself into a feeling of nausea at the dissolution of things. The world becomes slime. In reaction I may run away from the future, hide myself in some predetermined role, contorting myself to fit a costume that is already made for me, so leaping across the chasm that divides me from objects only in order to become an object myself. This happens when I adopt a morality, a religion, a social role that has been devised by others and which has significance for me only in so far as I am objectified in it. The result is what Sartre calls 'bad faith', indistinguishable I think from Heidegger's inauthenticity, and once again owing what content we can ascribe to it to the 'alienation' of nineteenth century Hegelian thought.

This false simulation of the in-itself by the for-itself (of the object by the subject) is to be contrasted with the authentic individual gesture. This, the reader will not be surprised to learn, cannot be described in its generality, but can only be seen in its individuality, in the free act whereby the individual creates both himself and his world together, by casting the one into the other. Don't ask *how* this is done. Its end point is what matters, and this Sartre describes as 'commitment'.

Sartre here introduces his well-known defence of ethical subjectivism, arguing that any adoption of a system of values which is represented as 'objective' constitutes an attempt to transfer my freedom into the world of objects, and so to lose it. The desire for an objective moral order is an exhibition of bad faith, and a loss of the freedom without which no moral order of any kind would be conceivable. In what sense Sartre is able to *recommend* the authenticity which consists in the purely self-made morality is unclear. He does recommend it, but, by his own argument, his recommendation can have no objective force. He is therefore more apt to use the language of 'must' than of 'ought':

> *I emerge alone and in dread in the face of the unique and first project which constitutes my being; all the barriers, all the railings, collapse, annihilated by the consciousness of my liberty; I have not, nor can I have, recourse to any value against the fact that it is I who maintain values in being; nothing can assure me against myself; cut off from the world and my essence by the nothing that I* am, *I have to realise the meaning of the world and of my essence: I decide it, alone, unjustifiable, and without excuse.*

In such a way Sartre tries to preserve Kant's ethic of moral 'autonomy', while divesting it of the commitment to a moral law. So far, as I said, there is not much to distinguish Sartre's philosophy from Heidegger's, except for a greater ease and clarity of expression, and a taste for vivid examples. But Sartre picks up another part of the Hegelian legacy. He gives his own version of the master and slave argument, this time under the guise of an examination of love. He attempts to show that all love, and indeed all human relation, is founded in contradiction. He introduces the notion of 'being-for-others' in order to describe the peculiar position in which a self-conscious being can find himself, of being at once a free subject in his own eyes, and a determined object in the eyes of others. (Compare Kant's distinction between the transcendental and the empirical self.) When another self-conscious being looks at me, I know that he searches in me not just for the object, but also for the subject. The gaze of a self-conscious creature has a peculiar capacity to penetrate, to create a demand. This is the demand that I, as free subjectivity, reveal myself in the world.

Taking his cue from 'the life and death struggle' of the *Phenomenology of Spirit,* Sartre now proceeds to describe all human relations in terms of struggle. If I love a woman then this is never simply a matter of lusting to gratify myself on her body: if it were just that, then any object, even a simulacrum of a human body, would do just as well. What I want is *her:* that is, the individual who is only real in her freedom, and who is falsified by every attempt to represent her as an object. As Sartre puts it: love wants the freedom of another, in order to make that freedom its own. But of course, the peculiarity of freedom is that it cannot be borrowed, shared or stolen. It is mine and mine alone. The lover, who wants to possess the body of another only as, and only in so far as, the other possesses it himself, is tied by a contradiction. His desire will fulfil itself only by frustrating itself, leaving him with the freedom of the other yet further removed. In the act of love, the other *becomes* his body, and so loses in the eyes of the lover the subjectivity which defines him. The most evident case of this, Sartre suggests, is sadomasochism, of which he gives a detailed and fascinating analysis.

Sartre's cheerless account of human affection perhaps contains some of his most lasting contributions to thought. Philosophically it is not original, owing what strength it has to the deeper discussions of Hegel. 'Love', wrote Hegel, 'is the most tremendous contradiction; the understanding cannot resolve it'. But contradictions worried Hegel less than they worry others: they were there to be transcended, through the dialectical movement which belongs, not to understanding, but to reason, whether in its pure or in its practical form. Sartre's account stops short of any such metaphysical solution. Nevertheless, it remains in some ways more acute, and more terrifyingly persuasive, than the Hegelian arguments which it borrows. It is in this area—that of the observation of the human world that latter-day phenomenology has been most influential. Sartre's studies of love, of 'the gaze', of hesitation, guilt and anguish, have been matched by other contributions of equal eloquence and power. Perhaps the most important among these have been those of Maurice Merleau-Ponty (1908–1961) in *The Phenomenology of Perception* (1945) and *Signs* (1960). The result has been a mass of phenomenological lore. I call it lore, not out of disrespect, but because of the impossibility of ascertaining its intellectual status. The results of phenomenology can seem both true to experience and yet irritatingly paradoxical, both in their style and in their philosophical presuppositions. Some reasons for this air of paradox will emerge in the chapter which follows.

14

Techniques and Dialectic Method in Philosophy

Introduction

Controversial, since I shall argue that methodology and epistemology are not always quite what they seem, not always just the conscientious analysis of such issues as the roles of hypothesis or definition or observation and reason themselves—though they can be that, to be sure but also, in addition or indeed instead, the basis of self-justificatory polemic. But it will be for subsequent research to investigate how far the suggestions I offer on the basis of the text I consider may, or may not, apply more generally to other material.

It is essential to define the scope of my inquiry here. First, as to chronological limits: very broadly speaking, I am concerned with the period before Christian influence begins to be dominant in the Graeco-Roman world, and before Buddhist influence began to be in China (i.e. around the third century AD). In both cases, however, my principal texts fall within a narrower span, on the Chinese side to the Han (second century BC to second century AD), on the Greek to the classical and early Hellenistic periods (fifth to third centuries BC), though I will take into consideration some much later works.

Secondly, as to subject areas: I shall concentrate here on mathematics and medicine. The choice is, to some extent, arbitrary; but in both cases we have extensive corpora of primary texts which we can use as the basis of our investigation. Within those corpora, I shall be concerned mainly, on the Greek side, with Euclid, Archimedes, and the commentary tradition on Euclid, and with certain Hippocratic treatises, notably *On Ancient Medicine*, together with evidence for Hellenistic medicine in, for example, Celsus and Galen, and then with Galen himself. On the Chinese side, I shall take a little longer to detail the primary texts, since they are no doubt unfamiliar to most Greek scholars. The key mathematical works, the first two substantial mathematical treatises extant from China, are the *Zhoubi Suanjing* (the Arithmetic Classic of the Zhou Gnomon) assembled at some time between the middle of the first century BC and the end of the first century AD and the *Jiuzhang Suanshu* (Nine Chapters of the Mathematical Art) compiled in the first century AD. Neither of these two works is a clearly defined unity, and the *Zhoubi* in particular evidently consists of several very divergent strata. In addition, there is an important commentary tradition on both works, and I shall need to refer especially to the commentary on the Nine Chapters composed by the brilliant mathematician Liu Hui some time between 260 and 280 AD.

For Chinese medicine, our main extant early sources, apart from the silk rolls found at Mawangdui and elsewhere, are the various recensions of the *Huangdi Neijing (the Inner Canon of the Yellow Emperor)*: namely, the *Taisu (Grand Basis)*, the *Suwen (Basic Questions)*, and the *Lingshu (Divine Pivot)*. Again, we are dealing with composite works, dating in the main from the first century BC. In addition, we have important evidence in the *Canggongzhuan, the biography of the doctor Chunyu Yi in Chapter 105 of Sima Qian's Shi Ji (Historical Annals). Sima Qian wrote around 90 BC, and Chunyu Yi himself was active around 170-150 BC.*

The works I shall be considering are, of course, nothing like the only extensive extant texts from Greek and Chinese mathematics and medicine that a comprehensive study would need to take into account, and we must bear in mind that we have indirect evidence for important traditions, in both East and West, that are not represented by substantial extant texts. Indeed, some of these other practitioners, in both cases, do not belong to the circles of the literate élite. Just as the Greeks had their itinerant purifiers, their drug-sellers, and root-cutters, and many types of women healers, very few of whom attempted, or were in a position, to compose treatises on their styles of medicine; so too Chinese medicine is not just a matter of what we read about in the Yellow Emperor.

So such suggestions as I have to offer must be understood as relating merely to parts—certainly not to the whole—of classical Greek and Chinese mathematics and medicine. A fortiori, they are not proposed for use as the basis for generalizations about classical Greek, or classical Chinese, philosophy and science as a whole. As I have repeatedly insisted, each different subject area has to be studied on its own merits, in relation to its own complex institutions, manner of transmission, problem situation, and aims. Actually, one outcome of my limited study, here, of my selected texts will be to underline how difficult it is to see definite patterns even in this restricted sample.

My final preliminary point concerns the distinction between implicit and explicit methodology and epistemology. Both terms can be used in looser or stricter senses. 'Epistemology' can be taken to refer to whatever may be thought to imply a claim to know, or whatever might allow us to investigate how such a claim, in a given context, might have been sustained. Again, any work of science or philosophy is more or less methodological, and we can certainly examine the actual methods the writers use, whether or not they pronounce on them themselves. However, I shall be concerned more especially here with the stricter senses, where the terms are used of the explicit statements of the writers themselves on such matters as the correct methods to be used, or the criteria that have to be met for a claim to knowledge to be justified. We have to examine how such explicit statements, when they are made, relate to the actual methods used or the knowledge claims made. How far do such statements tally with those methods? Or are there discrepancies between methodological theory and practice? On what types of occasions, and with what aims, are such statements made, and what role do they play in the economy of the arguments presented?

I. Mathematics: Greek

Having said that as students of Greek thought we are all familiar with the recurrent methodological statements that punctuate many of the classic texts we study, I begin with a Greek writer who never once, in the substantial body of complete treatises that we have, uses the term 'methodos': namely, Euclid. In the *Elements* he never reflects self-consciously on the procedures he adopts; nor does he explain what the object of the exercise is. Nevertheless, he proceeds with a self-confidence that certainly suggests that he knew exactly what he was doing, and there can be little doubt as to what that was. The Elements is the comprehensive systematization and proof of more or less the whole of the elementary mathematics of his time.

Of course, we can scarcely confirm that he indeed aimed at comprehensiveness. But such independent evidence as we have for contemporary mathematics (little enough, in all conscience), as well as the course of the development of Greek mathematics after Euclid, in Archimedes, Apollonius, and so on, points in that direction. Certainly Euclid sought systematicity, and, most important, rigorous axiomatic deductive proof. Book I sets out the definitions, common opinions, and postulates he needs, and further definitions are added in due course later. In principle, these are all the assumptions needed for the proofs he gives. In practice, for sure, there are terms that we might have expected him to define, but did not, especially the key term 'measure'. Conversely, some of the definitions included do not get to be used in the proofs. But such minor blemishes as these do not seriously call in question the overall strategy of the work.

The whole is a remarkably carefully articulated structure of demonstrations based on a small number of primary propositions and assumptions. The term 'elements' itself was used, as Aristotle tells us, of those propositions, the proofs of which are implied in the proofs of all or most of the others.

We are faced, then, with an interesting phenomenon, a highly methodical work, without any explicit methodology; but we can gain a perspective on the matter by considering first some later Greek mathematical texts, before turning back, later, to investigate the background to Euclid's *Elements*. One famous text illustrates very clearly one type of context in which Greek mathematicians sometimes thought it necessary or desirable to introduce explicit methodological remarks. This is Archimedes' short work called *ephodos*, conventionally translated *Method*. This opens by saying that he saw fit to write out and explain, for the benefit of Eratosthenes, his addressee, the peculiarity of a certain way or manner (*tropos*) that is useful for the investigation of certain problems in mathematics 'by means of mechanics'. Archimedes makes it clear that the method is heuristic, not demonstrative. The theorems discovered on its basis must thereafter be proved strictly: that is, by using the so-called method of exhaustion. Nevertheless, as he puts it, the procedure is 'no less useful even for the proofs of the theorems themselves. It is of course easier, when we have previously acquired, by the method, some knowledge of the question, to supply the proof, than it is to find it without any previous knowledge.'

As is well known, the 'mechanical method' depends on two assumptions: first, that a plane figure can be treated like a weight with a determinate centre of gravity (thus two plane figures can be imagined as balanced around a fulcrum and similarly for solid figures too); secondly, that a plane figure can be thought of as composed of the parallel line segments it contains (and similarly a solid as composed of the planes it contains). Now the method was, and remained, controversial, and both assumptions are indeed open to question. First, the idea of a geometrical figure having weight appeared to apply physical notions to mathematical objects, and thus was guilty of a category mistake. Secondly, the assumption that a geometrical magnitude is constituted by the indivisible line or plane segments it contains breached the principle of the continuum on which Greek geometry was based for Greek geometers normally assumed that geometrical magnitudes are *infinitely* divisible.

In practice, Archimedes' use of the method yielded true theorems, which he set about demonstrating independently. But it was easy to object that this was not guaranteed. It might, for example, have been objected that the application of a similar assumption to lines threatened to lead to the absurd conclusion that all lines are of equal length. In any pair of lines, any point on one could be held to stand in one-to-one correspondence with a point on the other. But in that case, if the lines were thought of as made up of their indivisible elements namely, their points they would all be of the same length. Whether Archimedes himself was perturbed just by the difficulty of applying mechanical assumptions, or just by those relating to the use of indivisibles, or rather by the combination of the two, is disputed. However, his cautious recommendation was, as we have seen, that all the theorems discovered on the basis of the method had thereafter to be demonstrated strictly.

This illustrates one type of context—a defensive one—in which explicit methodological remarks may be made: namely, as a response to the perceived controversiality of certain procedures. It is at least in part because the status of Archimedes' mechanical method might be called into question that he takes pains both to explain it and to give his view regarding its proper use.

In later Greek mathematics, the contexts in which explicit methodological discussions are introduced vary a great deal, but one recurrent motif is not just the description, but the justification or evaluation of a procedure. Thus both Hero (first century AD) and Pappus (in the fourth) frequently refer to the variety of methods that can be used to obtain the same result, and further add their own evaluative judgements about which, for example, is the more exact procedure (e.g. Hero, *Geometry IV* 290. 6f) or which can be deemed to be sound. Pappus is not just responsible for our fullest if still at points unperspicuous account of the general methods of analysis and synthesis in *Collection VII.* 1, but also several times lays down rules or sets out restrictions on the proper methods to be used in the investigations of certain problems.

One striking case is his discussion of the problem of finding two mean proportionals in *Collection III.* This opens with a lengthy account of a method of approximation used by an unnamed contemporary of his, which he criticizes as inexact, before going on to report some correct methods, including one for which he appears to claim some responsibility himself. Similarly, in both *III* and *IV* he criticizes those who ignore the methodological rule that each type of geometrical problem must be solved using the procedure appropriate to it: (1) plane problems by means of straight line and ruler constructions, (2) solid ones by means of conic sections, and (3) linear ones, where the solution required more complex curves, such as cochloids, cissoids, or quadratrices. At one point he even ventures criticisms of Archimedes and Apollonius themselves for breaching these category boundaries.

In the next century, too, Proclus comments extensively on mathematical methods, though less as a practising mathematician than for the philosophical lessons he wishes to draw. In his *Commentary on Euclid's Elements Book I,* he sets out the various component parts of a Euclidean proof, and discusses in particular the distinctions between the different types of indemonstrables. It was the great achievement of Euclid to have presented irrefutable (*anelegktos*) proofs.

A comparison with the *Commentaries on the Republic* and on the *Timaeus* reveals, however, that one of Proclus's strategic aims is to set up an analogy and a contrast between the methods of geometry and those of philosophy. Developing a line of argument for which there were good Platonic precedents in *Republic VI* and *VII*, Proclus praises mathematics as abstract and exact: yet he claims, nevertheless, that it is inferior to dialectic and to what he calls theology. But if geometry, as using hypotheses, is subordinate to theology, its great strength lies in the incontrovertibility of its proofs. For Proclus, as for so many other Greek writers, geometry provided the model or ideal for strict demonstration, a model that was then extended to all sorts of other fields. The title of Proclus's own metaphysical treatise, the *Elements of Theology*, echoes Euclid, and in other writers proof *more geometrico* was sought even in such unlikely areas as medicine. We shall come back to this.

Even this cursory glance at a selection of later Greek mathematical texts is enough to show that self-conscious reflection on methods is by no means rare. Yet Euclid himself, as I remarked, offers no such comments. The *Elements*, I said, gives every appearance of supreme self-confidence in the deployment of demonstrative procedures. But where did that confidence come from, and what gave him the ambition to attempt systematic demonstrations in the first place? It may seem absurd even to pose such questions, on two counts. Surely one needs no special motivation to attempt demonstrations: and given Euclid's notorious self-effacement, how could one set about trying to answer such questions, even if one thought it worthwhile asking them?

Now to the first objection we should remark that other mathematical traditions got along very well *without* attempting the type of strict axiomatic-deductive demonstration favoured by the Greeks. I shall have more to say on this later. As to the second, it certainly has to be acknowledged that there are bound to be large elements of conjecture in any attempted answers. In the nature of our evidence, it is not as if the long standing controversy over the extent of Euclid's debts, on the one hand to earlier mathematics, and on the other to philosophy, is ever likely to be resolved. The best we can do is to identify and evaluate *possible* influences and to broaden their scope in the light of the exceptional nature of Greekstyle demonstration.

First, so far as earlier Greek mathematics goes, let us consider those works of *Elements*, as Proclus calls them, that go back, he tells us, all the way to Hippocrates of Chios, active perhaps around 430 BC. First, it is not certain that that was their title. Secondly, so far as their contents and styles of argument go, we are reduced to guesswork in the main. In particular on one crucial point, for our concerns, we are in the dark. This relates to the question of whether, or how far, the notion of an *axiom* has been clarified and made explicit in the period before Aristotle. If we examine Hippocrates' own proofs on the quadratures of lunes, as reported by Simplicius, these are certainly rigorously deductive, but they are not based on *ultimate* primary premisses or axioms. Rather, they took as their starting-point (*archç*) the proposition that similar segments of circles have the same ratios as the squares on their bases. That proposition, so far from being primary, was one that Hippocrates *showed*, so we are told by showing that the squares on the diameters have the same ratios as the circles even though we are not told how he did that.

Of course, any systematizing of a body of mathematical knowledge will involve discriminating between primary and derivative theorems, and Proclus's history suggests that attempted syntheses became increasingly complete and well articulated in the period between Hippocrates and Euclid the work of such men as Archytas and Theaetetus. Yet when all is said and done, the very limited evidence we have for pre-Euclidean mathematics does not yield any indubitable examples of demonstrations based on ultimate primary premisses clearly recognised *as such*. For the concept of an axiom itself, we have to turn to philosophy. So far as our extant evidence goes, it was Aristotle, as is well known, who first clearly defined and classified the various types of indemonstrables: that is, in his view, definitions, axioms, and hypotheses. That demonstration must ultimately be based on primary propositions that are themselves indemonstrable is clinched.

But it is also well known that any claim that Euclid was simply following the *Posterior Analytics* will not do. First, the match between his triad of indemonstrables and Aristotle's is not exact, notably in that Euclid's postulates do not tally with Aristotelian hypotheses. But then, secondly and far more importantly, the *Posterior Analytics* insists that deductive reasoning should be cast in syllogistic form. Euclid not only shows no signs of presenting arguments syllogistically in the *Elements*; his deductions cannot even be recast in syllogistic form without gross artificiality.

Thus far the shape of my argument is familiar enough, though some of the details may, no doubt, be contested. But the point at which the comparativist will still legitimately be puzzled, and will press harder, but potentially more fruitful, questions, relates to the origins of the demand for the strictest style of demonstration, securing incontrovertibility. Here it is another part of the philosophical background that seems to me to be crucial, that relating to the definition of demonstration itself and to the analysis of what makes a demonstration.

We must bear in mind that the terms that both Plato and Aristotle use for strict demonstration, '*apodeixis*', '*apodeiknumi*', and cognates, had been, and continued to be, used extensively of a wide variety of more or less informal proofs and proving, showing, or exhibiting outside philosophy, in such fields as historical writing, political debate, and forensic oratory. Greek orators and politicians, for instance, readily and repeatedly claimed that they had proved their cases, using those very same terms, '*apodeixis*', '*apodeiknumi*', and again '*epideixis*', '*epideiknumi*', '*deiknumi*', as well as others such as '*dçloô*' and '*apophaiô*'. They spoke freely of proof when, for example, they had established, to their own satisfaction, what the facts of the matter were, or the guilt or innocence of the parties involved, or again when they had shown or at least declared that what they advocated was in the best interests of the state or of whoever it was they were addressing. Such informal notions—of proof beyond reasonable doubt were very common, though what counted as reasonable was itself always open to challenge.

But one point at which Plato, for one, objected, with some virulence, was that all that the arguments of the orators and politicians could achieve was the plausible, the likely, the persuasive: they could not legitimately claim to secure the truth. In the *Phaedo*, *Gorgias*, *Republic*, and *Theaetetus*, especially, a systematic contrast is developed between doxa (seeming, or opinion) and *alçtheia* (truth), and again between persuasion (*peithô*, *pistis*, *peithomai*) and proof (*apodeixis*), a contrast that draws, undoubtedly, on the previous use of many of these terms by the Eleatics and others, but goes well beyond that use. What the sophists, orators, and politicians trafficked in, in Plato's view, was just opinion and the plausible. What persuaded audiences might or might not be true. It is the claim to yield truth, and indeed certainty, and to be able to give an account, *logon didonai*, that marks out true philosophy: that is, *his* kind.

The conjecture, on this story, would be that it was the rivalry between competing claimants to intellectual leadership and prestige in Greece that stimulated the analysis of proving and of proof. The first main challenge came from Plato, though it was not until Aristotle that we find an explicit *definition* of strict demonstration. We should not imagine that those whose arguments and inquiries were thereby downgraded as being merely persuasive would have accepted the strictures of a Plato or an Aristotle. On the contrary, there is no sign in the fourth-century orators of any inhibitions about claiming to prove their points. But the effect of Plato's critique was certainly to *problematize* proof, and Aristotle's explorations of syllogistic and of causal explanation, combined with his classification of the indemonstrables, provided a comprehensive formal analysis of the axiomatic-deductive mode of demonstration, even though Aristotle himself was in some difficulty in implementing that ideal in practice in his own scientific treatises.

We must recognize that there is no evidence that Euclid or indeed any other Greek mathematician was directly concerned with the distinctions that Plato and Aristotle drew between the merely persuasive and the strictly demonstrative let alone with their categorizing of reasoners according to whether they delivered the one or the other. For all we know, Euclid may just have been following and developing earlier existing types of purely mathematical argument.

But we can certainly see, from those later writers we considered before, how, both for the mathematicians themselves and for others, geometry served as the model for demonstrations securing incontrovertibility Some might imagine—many have assumed—that the internal dynamic of the development of mathematics itself would, somehow inevitably, eventually lead to a demand for strict axiomatic-deductive demonstration, and that there is accordingly no need to postulate any external stimulus such as I have conjectured to come from the philosophical preoccupation with the contrast between the merely persuasive and the rigorously demonstrated. Yet the difficulty for that view is the one I have mentioned: reference to other, non-Greek, ancient mathematical traditions—Babylonian, Egyptian, Hindu, Chinese—shows that they all got along perfectly well *without* any notion corresponding to axioms, and accordingly without the particular notion of strict demonstration that went with it. It is time now to turn to the Chinese material in particular.

2. Mathematics: Chinese

When we consult our earliest complete extant Chinese mathematical texts, a series of contrasts with the Greek Euclidean tradition which we have been discussing present themselves. But the first point worth remarking is how common explicit references to methods and procedures are, the key terms being One passage in the *Zhoubi* makes large claims for what the Way (*Dao*) can achieve when someone follows it in mathematics, while it also brings out some striking features of the teacher-pupil relationship in this context. The pupil, Rong Fang, opens by asking Chenzi: 'Master, I have recently heard something about your Way. Is it really true that your Way is able to comprehend the height and size of the sun, the area illuminated by its radiance, the amount of its daily motion, the figures for its greatest and least distances, the extent of human vision, the limits of the four poles, the lodges into which the stars are ordered, and the length and breadth of Heaven and Earth?' Chenzi replies: 'It is true.' Rong Fang then proceeds: 'Although I am not intelligent, Master, I would like you to favour me with an explanation. Can someone like me be taught this Way?' Chenzi replies: 'Yes. All these things can be attained to by mathematics'.

Both procedures (I note in parenthesis) have analogues in ancient Greece, the latter with the technique which Archimedes used to get the upper and lower limits of the angular diameter of the sun, and the former with Eratosthenes' method of determining the circumference of the earth. The difference, there, however, is that Eratosthenes assumed the earth to be spherical, and the rays of light from the sun to be parallel, while in the *Zhoubi* it is assumed that the earth is flat, while the sun's distance can be obtained from the difference in the shadow lengths. Without some assumptions, on either side, the data relating to shadow differences would not, of course, yield anything.

The *Zhoubi* sets out certain methods and procedures, labelled as such, for use in astronomical investigations. The *Nine Chapters* deals with a variety of problems in arithmetic and geometry, to do with the addition, subtraction, multiplication, and division of fractions, for instance, and the determination of the areas and volumes of various rectilinear and curvilinear figures. The whole discussion is articulated in a highly formal style: first a question, then an answer, followed by the statement of the method to be used, this last section being introduced, standardly, by the expression.

The 'workings' in question generally give what we might call algorithms to be used for the solution of the original problems. As already remarked, there is nothing that corresponds to the notion of axiomatic-deductive demonstration, but anywhere in Chinese mathematics until after the arrival of Western influences with the Jesuits in the sixteenth century. However, the algorithms of the *Nine Chapters* are the subject of self-conscious reflection. This is where Liu Hui's commentary is so interesting, as a series of studies by Karine Chemla, following work by Don Wagner, has shown.

What Liu Hui does, in his commentary on several of the 'workings', is, in effect, to validate the algorithm, and indeed to do so, often, at a higher level of abstraction than the original. It is easiest to illustrate this with one of the simplest examples, to do with the procedure for the addition of fractions. He shows first that a fraction may be expressed in more, or less, simple terms: $a/b = ax/bx$. But then $a/b + c/d = (ad + bc)/bd$ is correct. Liu Hui attaches names to the two key procedures.

There are two cardinal points of interest in this and other texts where Liu Hui offers explicit comments on the mathematical procedures in question. First there is what can be learned from them about Liu Hui's own concerns. Here and elsewhere he investigates the formal patterns that underlie the mathematical reasoning; indeed, he looks for the *same* pattern in different contexts, thereby unifying the procedures used in those contexts. This may be compared with the aim stated in the *Zhoubi* itself: namely, to find methods that are 'concisely worded but of broad application'. The guiding principles or key general features in the mathematical reasoning. But secondly, if we confront Liu Hui's commentary with our comparative issues in mind, we can say this. What he does in the discussion of the addition of fractions and elsewhere is to *show* that the algorithms used are correct. Now that is as good a *proof* of the procedures as anyone could wish provided, of course, that we do not limit our notion of what will count as proof to axiomatic-deductive demonstration in the Euclidean style provided, that is, that we do not stipulate that for a proof to be a proof, it has to be cast in that style. For what more should we expect of the proof of a procedure than an explanation of how and why it works, however that explanation itself proceeds?

So, first, if we are considering Chinese styles of proof, here are some excellent examples; but, secondly, they are examples that occur in discussions that do not reflect any interest in axiomatic-deductive demonstration, but rather a concern to determine the patterns that underlie the mathematical procedures used.

The Greek preoccupation with proof *more geometrico* was certainly accompanied by notable efforts aiming to achieve, and often in fact achieving, clarity, exactness, and rigour in the logical articulation of sequences of arguments. But that was not the only way in which sophisticated mathematics could develop: the Chinese texts show this, for in China there was no such concern, and yet not just the securing of complex results, but also a considerable, self-conscious interest in the analysis and verification of procedures and in the search for the underlying principles uniting different areas of mathematical reasoning.

Moreover, the problem with proof in the Euclidean style was always that of securing a set of axioms that would meet the demands of being both indemonstrable and self-evidently true. It has often been conjectured that Euclid adopted the parallel postulate as a postulate because he realized that it could not be proved without circularity. But there is nothing to suggest that he did not also accept it as true. Yet with the development of non-Euclidean geometries, our understanding of its status has, of course, been transformed. From the point of view of other mathematical traditions that never sought axiomatic foundations, there is an evident irony in the fact that one of the bases of the claims made for Greek geometry, that it yields what is incontrovertibly true, turns out to be a proposition that is anything but.

3. Medicine: Chinese

I turn now, inevitably much more briefly, to my second main field, medicine, and for the sake of even-handedness will start this time with some of the Chinese evidence. Once again, some of the principal sections in the various recensions of the *Huangdi Neijing* take the form of dialogues. Often these are between the Yellow Emperor, who generally asks the questions, and his various respondents, such as Qi Bo and Shao Shi. The Yellow Emperor is no ordinary pupil; nor do the answers take the form of an instruction to go away and work it out for himself. However, there is much play here, as *in the Zhoubi, with the cardinal necessity to follow the Dao. The Way is the key, and not just as instrumental to an end, but as the end itself, at least in that the goal, sagehood, is its embodiment.*

'Among the men of high antiquity', says Qi Bo in Suwen 1, 'those who knew the Way took yin and yang as their model, harmonized themselves with the disciplines based on what is regular (ted them, passing on at the age of several hundred years. The men of today are totally different. . . .'

However, Qi Bo's answers do not always stay at the level of *obiter dicta*, for he also gives detailed explanations both with regard to the therapies to be adopted for particular complaints and on techniques of diagnosis and prognosis. Thus at one point, *Suwen 12*, he is questioned by the Yellow Emperor: 'When physicians treat illness, they differ in their therapy for the same disease, yet the patient recovers. Why is this?' Qi Bo's reply is rather along the lines of the Hippocratic *Airs Waters Places*: 'The disposition of the land makes this so.' In the five regions (East, West, North, South, and Centre), the varieties of illnesses reflect the climate and diet of the inhabitants, and different therapies have been developed to counter them (e.g. stone therapy, powerful drugs, moxa, needles, and exercise and massage respectively). Here, then, we have an account of the origins of certain treatments, an account that, moreover, legitimates the use of certain procedures partly by according them ancient authority. 'Their therapies differed but the illnesses got better. That was because they understood the real character of each disorder and knew the great principles of therapy'.

The analysis of the *Huangdi Neijing* recensions has suggested to specialists that the various points of view represented correspond to divergent literate medical traditions, and can therefore yield evidence for their interplay and development. If so, that interplay more often takes the form of the claim that new ideas go further than older ones, or spell out their message, than one of the rejection of earlier traditions. The past is built on, not demolished.

However, the existence of overt rivalry between medical practitioners and practices emerges more directly in the other text I proposed for examination, the *Canggongzhuan* of Chunyu Yi, in Sima Qian's *Shiji 105*. This material is exceptional in that it represents an explicit apologia by a doctor who had been subject to a denunciation, and it proceeds via the account of a series of individual case histories where Chunyu Yi's diagnoses and treatments are recorded. In the process he criticizes a number of other doctors, sometimes unnamed, but on occasion named.

Thus in case 20 his prediction that a particular patient will recover under treatment contradicts the view of a doctor Xin who claimed that he would die in nine days, and Chunyu Yi is vindicated by the outcome. Case 22 is even more remarkable, in that the patient whom Chunyu Yi treats is himself a doctor called Sui, who had actually set about treating himself in a way that Chunyu Yi says is inappropriate. However, Sui then cites the legendary doctor Bian Que as his authority, eliciting from Chunyu Yi the reply: 'how far your account is [from the truth!]'. Although Bian Que spoke as he did, there is a whole range of diagnostic questions that have to be evaluated. There are certainly rules (*fa*) for examination, but when the practitioners who try to apply them are ignorant, they are no use at all. Knowledge of learned texts by itself is evidently not enough to make one a doctor, for judgement and experience are also needed.

To justify his own prognoses and diagnoses—which all turn out to be correct Chunyu Yi refers repeatedly to what the Method of the Pulse says. In some cases it is not clear whether these remarks relate to texts or to a body of learning or to a combination of both: but in his own account of his early training he certainly refers to books on the pulse he received from his teacher Gongsheng Yangqing.

The way Chunyu Yi uses the Method can be seen, for example, in case 2. This is an illness of one of the grandsons of the King of Qi, which Chunyu Yi diagnoses as a *qi* diaphragm disorder. The reason he knew that this was the case was that when he took the pulse, 'it was the heart *qi*: it was muddy and agitated'. That allows the illness to be categorized as *yang*, or to do with the *yang* vessels. The text then continues: 'The Method of the Pulse says: if the pulse comes rapidly and it leaves with difficulty and is not united, the illness is settled in the heart.'

Here we have a typical justification of what a pulse of a particular type can tell one about a patient's condition. In each case this confirms what Chunyu Yi had determined. However, although the Method sets out detailed correlations between pulse types and internal conditions, the question that might be thought to arise is *how* to recognize those types. The Method evidently could take you directly from the quality of the pulse to the diagnosis or prognosis of the complaint: but everything depended, clearly, on your being able to *feel* the pulse correctly. This was a remarkably comprehensive and systematic diagnostic technique, but the practitioner had first to have a good deal of knowledge and skill, in recognizing the pulses he felt, in order to use the Method. Method was no substitute for knowledge, and indeed was useless in its absence: rather, it was a way both of systematizing that knowledge and of justifying the conclusions it led the practitioner to draw.

The evidence from the *Canggongzhuan* shows that it was perfectly possible, in classical Chinese medicine, for one doctor to criticize another openly, not just on a particular point to do with diagnosis or treatment, but more generally for their whole approach—for example, for an uncomprehending use of earlier authorities.

4. Medicine: Greek

When we turn to the evidence for classical Greek medicine, however, the range and intensity of explicit methodological disputes are far greater than can be exemplified from Chinese medicine or indeed than can be found in the Greek mathematical texts we reviewed earlier. The last main section of this study will attempt to explore the factors that may have contributed to this phenomenon. In particular, we shall see that on certain occasions methodology is not developed just to be applied in practice.

Rather, it is elaborated for the sake of the polemical points to be scored on its basis. A claim to superiority in Greek medicine is sometimes based on having the right *justifications* for practices—not on having different practices.

In our classical Hippocratic texts criticisms of others' methods range from the correction of faulty techniques of bandaging all the way to attacks in which the whole conception of the nature and status of the art of medicine is at issue, where indeed the epistemological issues of the basis of any claim for medicine to be a branch of knowledge at all are at stake. One of the best-known early examples where those general questions are debated is the work *On Ancient Medicine*, the principal aim of which is to expose the errors of what the author calls the new-fangled methods of his opponents, based on such 'hypotheses', or postulates, as the hot, the cold, the wet, and the dry.

Many points in the interpretation of this text are problematic, not least who precisely those opponents are. But the gist of one major complaint is that they 'narrowed down the causal principle of diseases. They appear to have attempted to base medicine on a very limited number of postulates from which the whole of medical practice could, somehow, be deduced. The author of On Ancient Medicine himself protests that this is completely to misconstrue the nature of medicine, which is an art (technic), with practitioners who vary in skill and judgement, which has a principle (archę) and a method (*hodos*) through which many discoveries have been made and by means of which the rest too will be discovered if the investigator is up to the task and proceeds on the basis of these principles. He does not himself deny that hot, cold, wet, and dry are among the factors at work in the body and in diseases, but they are, in his view, among the least important.

This is a dispute not between doctors of the literate élite, on the one hand, and radically different traditions of medicine, such as that of the itinerant purifiers, on the other, but *within* the groups of literate practitioners. The method of 'hypothesis' that the author of *On Ancient Medicine* attacks is one he associates with the investigation of meteorology and of 'things under the earth', and at one point he explicitly resists the intrusion of philosophical methods into medicine in particular. On other occasions, too, there are signs of philosophical influence on fifth and fourth century Hippocratic texts, not just where physical theories, but also where methodology, are concerned. There are echoes, close to verbatim quotations, of Heraclitus, Empedocles, and Anaxagoras in the treatise On Regimen I, for example. Where Diogenes of Apollonia had opened his work with a methodological statement to the effect that the starting-point (*archç*) should be indisputable, the Hippocratic treatise *On the Art* states that the starting-point of his *logos* is something that will be agreed by all.

This might suggest as a hypothesis that these methodological forays in Greek medicine reflect contemporary philosophical disputes, where, ever since Xenophanes in the sixth century BC, debate on substantive physical or cosmological questions had been punctuated by second-order epistemological controversies. Yet *just* to see here the effects of importations from philosophy would be too simple, even though the author of *On Ancient Medicine* writes of a tendency to 'veer towards philosophy' in his opponents. On his own view of the matter, at least, his own positive methodology owes nothing at all to philosophy, but is, precisely, the traditional method of 'ancient medicine'.

The methodological disputes that continue and intensify in Hellenistic medicine can be used to throw further light on the extent and degree of philosophical influences at work. The notion that there were, in the Hellenistic period, three clearly defined schools, Dogmatists, Empiricists, and Methodists, has been much exaggerated, by some ancient as well as by many modern commentators, not least because the Dogmatists never saw themselves as such. However, the disputes on questions such as whether underlying causes or hidden reality can be investigated, or whether, or under what circumstances, anatomical dissection is a valuable, or a justifiable, procedure these disputes, reported in such texts as the Proem of Celsus's On Medicine and Galen's On Sects for Beginners, are real enough. Evidently some of the issues in question are the same issues that were discussed in the Hellenistic philosophical schools, particularly those concerned with the various types of sceptical challenge to the existence of stable criteria for knowledge—though whether the influence was always from philosophy to medicine, or sometimes also in the reverse direction, is controversial. But just as evidently the issues to do with dissection are, at points, specific to medicine and to the life sciences.

Galen's polemic with the Methodists combines several of the features we have mentioned so far, and enables us to pick up themes from our earlier discussion of method in Greek mathematics. Galen is critical of all the chief medical groups he identifies, but the nature of his criticisms varies in a revealing manner. First he outlines the debate between the Empiricists and those he calls Dogmatists. He attacks the former chiefly on the grounds that while relying on experience, they have no theoretical underpinning to explain why they adopt the therapies they adopt. Accordingly, they are at a loss to deduce what should be done when they are confronted with a new disease. The Dogmatists are criticized for the reverse failing, not of relying on experience too much, but of not paying sufficient attention to it in the first place.

But this disagreement, as Galen reports it, was *just* about the account to be given of medical *method*. The Empiricists and Dogmatists did not, in general, according to Galen, differ in the *actual* therapeutic measures they used. It emerges here, then, that explicit methodology, in their hands, merely supplied a different justification for *agreed* practices. This was methodology for that polemical purpose, not to validate different medical procedures and therapies.

But in his attacks on the Methodists, Galen has opponents who diverged not just in methodology, but also in medical practice. Their techniques of diagnosis and treatment centred on the idea of the *koinotçtes*, common conditions, but these were not disease entities as normally understood in Greece, but, as their name implied, characterizations of the general state of the patient, whether 'lax' or 'restricted' or a mixture of the two. Therapy was, then, a matter of countering the lax with the restricted, or vice versa.

The general background to the disputes in Hellenistic medicine on the relative importance of reason and experience as criteria of knowledge, is, to be sure, philosophical, though the debate had ramifications throughout the inquiry into nature, including in the mathematical branches of physics, as we can see from Ptolemy's *Harmonics*, for instance. But the applications to medicine were distinctive, as was the Methodists' version of an alternative. For Galen, what they considered the proper method was a travesty, and, as he never tires of saying, they are the most unmethodical of medical practitioners: in his view, after all, they rejected the whole of what he considered to be the essential theoretical basis for medicine.

By contrast, Galen's own idea of method included the ambition to give, wherever possible, demonstrations in the geometrical manner. Here we come back full circle to Greek mathematics, for the existence of that goal, in that field, had a catalytic effect in other domains of inquiry. While the sceptical doctors resisted even limited knowledge claims, the most aggressive anti-sceptics, such as Galen, claimed to be able to deliver certainty, via the deployment of proof *more geometrico*. Galen's onslaught exhibits at its most vituperative a debate in which rival practitioners sought to undermine one another not just in terms of their therapies or diagnoses, but in terms of the underlying conception of the nature of the medical art itself.

Summary

The various types play in China and in Greece. Even such a selective survey as this serves to show one negative point rather clearly: namely, that no straightforward generalization contrasting the Chinese data as a whole with the Greek will do, any more than one attempting to set up a simple opposition between mathematics (in both cultures) and medicine (in both). We have, rather, a spectrum of uses, and differences of degree rather than of kind.

Thus both in China and in Greece, and in both mathematics and medicine, methodological statements have certain pragmatic and defensive roles. They are used to introduce and describe particular techniques in particular contexts (algorithms, or formulae of other types, or statements of the method to be used in medical diagnosis or treatment), and the introduction and description of a procedure easily shade into the validation and justification of its use (as in Liu Hui with the rewriting of algorithms) or the explanation of its status (Archimedes on his method).

However, explicit methodological statements may also have a further, more overtly polemical function. True, self-conscious methodology and epistemology often *present themselves* as the neutral analysis of secondorder questions, of how to conduct an inquiry and on the status of the inquiry itself. Focusing on such questions may, and did, bring to light important features to do with observation, experience, hypothesis, definition, proof, explanation, understanding, and much else besides. More attention is paid to epistemology as such in our Greek sources than in our Chinese ones; but we should bear in mind that some of the classical Chinese philosophers who were most interested in such issues are particularly badly served in our extant sources: that is true especially of the Mohists. Besides, such topics as the need for experience in understanding are referred to commonly enough for example, in Chinese medicine (as we have seen in Chunyu Yi).

But what we also find, not just in Greece, but especially there, and not just in medicine, but again particularly there, is that methodology can be invoked as the basis of an argument to undermine opponents, whose study or practice (the claim was) must be wrong, since their methods were. We can understand the frequency of that move in medicine, where the effects of treatment are so often in doubt. If patients got better, why they did so can be argued about indefinitely, and so too if they did not, but died. But in mathematics too we occasionally find in Greece evidence of rivalry relating not just to results, but to methods, as we saw in Pappus.

Methodological disputes can thus throw light not just on the dialectic of the development of epistemology, but also on the dynamics of the relationships between rival practitioners, whether individuals or groups. It often seems that those group dynamics tend to maximize disagreement in Greece, but to minimize it in China. But in both cases we must beware. Evaluating the common ground, or lack of it, between individuals and groups, is, in any event, no simple matter. We have, for instance, to make allowances for a shared vocabulary masking underlying deep differences of view. One striking case, on the Greek side, that I have discussed elsewhere, is the use of the term *katharsis* (purging) *both* by those who believed that ritual purification is the secret of healing *and* by those who held that the purging needed in medicine was a matter of emetics or evacuants of other types. Again we have seen that the same term 'apodeixis' was used by orators and philosophers of proving of rather different kinds. Similarly on the Chinese side, the eventual deployment of *yin* and *yang* owed something, though not a great deal, to the original uses of those terms for the shady and sunny sides of a hill. Clearly, here too a common vocabulary could conceal very divergent understandings of how it should be applied.

Conversely, there may be shared practices, but disagreement about the account to be given to justify them. As we noted, Galen thought that both those he called Dogmatists and the Empiricists shared the same basic therapies, but gave different rationales for them. In the former respect, that is more like China, where learned doctors generally employed the same types of remedies. But there is still this difference, that Chinese learned doctors did not group themselves, and were not grouped by others, into sects, *haireseis*, that were locked in methodological disputes about the foundations of medicine.

The Greek sects, by contrast, whether in philosophy or in medicine, were often sustained by their polemic with their opponents. Their aim was not just to hand on a body of learning associated with a founder or leader, but to win debates with their rivals. In that highly competitive situation, each group needed, in a sense, their rivals, the better to define their own position. What was at stake was not just prestige victory in argument in what were often public confrontations but even survival, for those debates were one of the principal means of recruiting pupils or new members to the group. Whereas Chinese pupils generally owed unswerving allegiance to their teachers, it was common enough for aspiring Greek intellectuals not just to pick and choose between lecturers, but even openly to criticize some of those who had taught them directly.

To be sure, Greek methodological disputes are not confined to indeed, they antedate the formation of more or less clearly demarcated philosophical or medical sects. But those groupings often saw themselves, or were seen by others, as defined by their methodologies, and it was often on methodological points that they focused in their controversies with their competitors.

In that respect one may say that Greek methodological self-consciousness came to be reflected in, and itself to reflect, the institutional frameworks within which much Greek intellectual exchange took place. Certainly, in so far as there are differences between China and Greece, and as between mathematics and medicine, they relate not just to the sophistication of individuals, not just to the internal dialectic of epistemological analysis, but also to those institutional frameworks. Methodology was not purely an abstract intellectual concern. It provided some of the chief argumentative weaponry used by individuals and groups competing for acclaim and influence. The bitterest methodological disputes in Greece are a sign not just of a general insecurity one that Galen tried to remove by way of the demand for certainty in at least parts of medicine but also of a sense of vulnerability to rivals, an awareness that the very existence and credibility of the groups with which individuals identified were at risk. The further investigation of the character and influence of those institutional frameworks must, however, be left for another study.

Bibliography

Alexander, Peter. Ideas, Qualities, and Corpuscles: Locke and Boyle on the External World. Cambridge University Press, 1985.

Allison, Henry E. Benedict de Spinoza: An Introduction. Yale University Press, 1987.

Ariew, Roger and Marjorie Grene. Descartes and His Contemporaries. University of Chicago Press, 1995.

Ashcraft, Richard. Locke's Two Treatises of Government. Allen and Unwin, 1987.

Balz, Albert G. Descartes and the Modern Mind. Shoe String Press, 1967.

Baumgold, Deborah. Hobbes's Political Theory. Cambridge University Press, 1988.

Becker, C. L. The Heavenly City of the Eighteenth Century Philosophers. Yale University Press, 1932.

Boonin-Vail, David. Thomas Hobbes and the Science of Moral Virtue. Cambridge University Press, 1994.

Botwinick, Aryeh. Hobbes and Modernity: Five Exercises in Political Philosophical Exegesis. University Press of America, 1983.

Bowle, John. Hobbes and His Critics: A Study in Seventeenth Century Constitutionalism. Oxford University Press, 1952.

Burtt, E. A. The Metaphysical Foundations of Modern Physical Theory. Humanities Press, 1967.

Cambridge University Press, 1980. Vaughn, Karen Iverse. John Locke, Economist and Social Scientist. University of Chicago Press, 1980.

Carter, Richard. Descartes' Medical Philosophy: The Organic Solution to the Mind-Body Problem. Johns Hopkins Press, 1983.

Caruth, Cathy. Empirical Truths and Critical Fictions: Locke, Wordsworth, Kant. Johns Hopkins, 1991.

Cassirer, Ernst. The Philosophy of the Enlightenment. Princeton University Press, 1951.

Clarke, Desmond. Descartes' Philosophy of Science. Pennsylvania State University Press, 1982.

Copleston, Frederick. A History of Western Philosophy, Vols. 4-6. Image Press, 1946 sqq.

Curley, E. M. Descartes Against the Skeptics. Harvard University Press, 1978.

Davis, Philip J. and Reuben Hersh. Descartes' Dream: The World According to Mathematics. Harcourt, Brace, Javanovich, 1986.

Deely, John. New Beginnings: Early Modern Philosophy and Postmodern Thought. Toronto, 1994.

Della Rocca, Michael. Representation and the Mind-Body Problem in Spinoza. Oxford, 1996.

Diaz-Mas, Paloma. Sephardim: The Jews from Spain. University of Chicago Press, 1992.

Doney, W. Descartes. Notre Dame University Press, 1968.

Duff, R. A. Spinoza's Political and Ethical Philosophy. Kelley Press, 1975.

Edwards, Paul, ed. The Encyclopedia of Philosophy in 8 vols. Macmillan, 1967.

Ferguson, Margaret W., et al., eds. Rewriting the Renaissance: the Discourses of Sexual Difference in Early Modern Europe. University of Chicago, 1986.

Foster, John. The Immaterial Self: A Defense of the Cartesian Dualist Concept. Routledge, 1991.

Foucault, Michel. The Order of Things: An Archaeology of the Human Sciences. Vintage Books, 1973.

Galtier, Jules de. From Kant to Nietzsche. Books for Libraries, 1971.

Garrett, Don, ed. The Cambridge Companion to Spinoza. Cambridge, 1996.

Gaukroger, Stephen, ed. The Soft Underbelly of Reason: The Passions in the Seventeenth Century. Routledge, 1998.

Gaukroger, Stephen. Cartesian Logic: An Essay on Descartes's Conception of Inference. Oxford at Clarendon, 1989.

Gibson, James. Locke's Theory of Knowledge. Cambridge University Press, 1917.

Goldsmith, M. M. Hobbes's Science of Politics. Columbia University Press, 1966.

Graeme, H. Spinoza: The Enduring Questions. University Press of America, 1994.

Grant, Ruth. John Locke's Liberalism. University of Chicago Press, 1987.

Groshoiz, Emily. Cartesian Method and the Problem of Reduction. Oxford University Press, 1991.

Hallyn, Fernand. The Poetic Structure of the World; Copernicus and Kepler. Zone Books, 1990.

Hankins, Thomas L. Science and the Enlightenment. Cambridge University Press, 1985.

Herbert, Gary B. Thomas Hobbes, The Unity of Scientific and Moral Wisdom. University of British Columbia Press, 1989.

Hooker, Michael, ed. Descartes: Critical and Interpretive Essays. Johns Hopkins Press, 1978.

Jeffreys, Montagu. John Locke: Prophet of Common Sense. Methuen, 1967.

Jolley, Nicholas. Leibniz and Locke: A Study of the New Essays and Human Understanding. Oxford University Press, 1984.

Jones, W.T. A History of Western Philosophy, Vols. 3 & 4. Harcourt, Brace, Javanovich, 1969, 1975.

Kavka, Gregory S. Hobbesian Moral and Political Theory. Princeton University Press, 1987.

Kendall, Willmoore. John Locke and the Doctrine of Majority Rule. Urbana, 1959.

Kenny, Anthony. Descartes, A Study of His Philosophy. Random House, 1968.

Konecsni, Johnemery. Scotus to Kant: A Survey of Modern Philosophy. University Press of America, 1977.

Kraus, John L. John Locke: Empiricist, Atomist, Conceptualist, and Agnostic. Philosophical Library, 1969.

Kuhn, Thomas. The Copernican Revolution. Harvard University Press, 1957.

Lamprecht, Sterling. The Moral and Political Philosophy of John Locke. Russell and Russell, 1962.

Lloyd, Genevieve. Spinoza and THE ETHICS. Routledge, 1996.

Mackie, J. L. Problems from Locke. Oxford University Press, 1976.

Mandelbaum, Maurice, and Eugene Freeman, eds. Spinoza: Essays in Interpretation. Open Court, 1975.

Marshall, John. John Locke: Resistance, Religion & Responsibility. Cambridge University Press, 1994.

Montag, Warren, and Ted Stolze, eds. The New Spinoza (Theory Out of Bounds, Vol. 11). University of Minnesotat Press, 1997.

Nadler, Steven M. Arnauld and the Cartesian Philosophy of Ideas. Princeton University Press, 1989.

Nadler, Steven, ed. Causation in Early Modern Philosophy: Cartesianism, Occasionalism, and Preestablished Harmony. Pennsylvania State University Press, 1993.

Norris, Christopher. Spinoza and the Origins of Modern Critical Theory. Basil Blackwell, 1991.

O'Connor, D. J. A Critical History of Western Philosophy. Free Press, 1964.

O'Neil, Brian E. Epistemological Direct Realism in Descartes' Philosophy. University of New Mexico Press, 1974.

Pickering, Samuel F. John Locke and Children's Books in Eighteenth Century England. University of Tennessee Press, 1981.

Quintana, Ricardo. Two Augustans: John Locke and Jonathan Swift. Oxford University Press, 1978.

Rapaczynski, Andrzej. Nature and Politics: Liberalism in the Philosophies of Hobbes, Locke, and Rousseau. Cornell University Press, 1987.

Russell, Bertrand. History of Western Philosophy. Touchstone Books, 1984.

Saw, Ruth. The Vindication of Metaphysics. Russell and Russell, 1972.

Schipper, Lewis. Spinoza's Ethics: The View from Within. Peter Lang, 1993.

Shahan, Robert W. and J. I. Biro. Spinoza: New Perspectives.

Shapin, Steven. A Social History of Truth. University of Chicago Press, 1997.

Shelton, George. Morality and Sovereignty in the Philosophy of Hobbes. St. Martin's Press, 1997.

Sorell, Tom. The Rise of Modern Philosophy: The Tension between the New and Traditional Philosophies from Machiavelli to Leibniz. Oxford at Clarendon, 1993.

Spinoza, Benedictus de. The Principles of Descartes' Philosophy. Open Court, 1974.

Spragens, Thomas A. The Politics of Motion: The World of Thomas Hobbes. University Press of Kentucky, 1973.

Tipton, I. C., ed. Locke on Human Understanding. Oxford University Press, 1977.

Tully, James. A Discourse on Property: John Locke and His Adversaries.

Wawrytko, Sandra A. The Undercurrent of Feminine Philosophy in Eastern and Western Thought. University Press of America, 1981.

Wienpahl, Paul. The Radical Spinoza. New York University Press, 1979.

Willey, Basil. Seventeenth Century Background. Columbia University Press, 1965.

Wilson, Catherine. The Invisible World: Early Modern Philosophy and the Invention of the Microscope. Princeton University Press, 1995.

Wilson, Margaret D. Ideas and Mechanism: Essays on Early Modern Philosophy. Princeton University Press, 1999.

Yolton, John W. Locke and the Compass of Human Understanding. Cambridge University Press, 1970.

Index

A

A Diverse Range of Schools, 76
  Kantian Argument, 223
  Pseudolibertarian Argument, 142
  Vindication of the Rights of Women, 188
Abigail Adams, 198
Abolition of Distance, 235
Affirmative Action, 193
All Men Are Created Equal & Independent, 29
American and French Revolutions, 190
  Civil War, 210
Anarchism, 103
Ancient Medicine, 246
  Philosophy and Philosophy Today, 80
  Theories and the Modern World, 64
Anticipatory Resoluteness, 237
Arghiri Emmanuel, 212
Aristotle and Authority, 65
  on Nature, 55
  'Four Causes', 58
  Teleological Approach, 60

B

Being Free for Death, 237
  Naturally Free, 16
Book of the Courtier (1528), 36
British Moralists, 35

C

Capitalism and Freedom, 87
Cartesian Meditations, 228, 230
  Revolution in Philosophy, 117
Central Intelligence Agency (CIA), 216
Christian Socialism, 105
Classical Colonialism, 210
  Liberalism, 84
Clear and Distinct Perception, 120
Commentary on Euclid's Elements Book I, 251
Concept of Substance, 5
Consolation of Philosophy, 2

D

Dante's Divine Comedy, 2
Deeper Sense of Politics and Philosophy, 185
Dialogues on Metaphysics, 123
Differing Views on the Greeks' Originality, 67
Divine Comedy, 2

E

Each Man His Own Moralist, 35
Elements a High Point, 54
  of theology, 252
Emancipatory Consciousness, 200
Ephodos, 249
Ethics of a Lifeboat, 213
Eusebius, Bishop of Caesarea (AD C.260-339), 68
Everything is Water, 66
Existence Precedes Essence, 239

F

Far East Philosophy, 226
Form of Inner Sense, 233
Formal and Fair Equality of Opportunity, 192
Free Will and Human Nature, 10
From Freedom to Bondage, 87

G

Geisteswissenschaften, 233
Geometrical Method, 122
Good Life for Man, 11
Groundwork of the Metaphysic of Morals, 224

H

Human Sciences, 233

I

Ideas for a Pure Phenomenology, 228
Ideology of Socialism, 111
Imperialism, 208
Inalienable Rights, 26
Inner Canon of the Yellow Emperor, 246
Inquiry Concerning Moral Good and Evil, 38
  Virtue or Merit, 35
International Monetary Fund, 211

J

Jim Crow, 193
Jiuzhang Suanshu, 246
John Burnet, 1892, 69
Jürgen Habermas, 201

K

Knight's Tale, 2

L

Laws of Nature, 13
Liberalism and Liberty, 84
Libertarian Challenge for Modern Philosophy, 83
  Philosophy, 96
  Property Rights: A Critical Assessment, 133
  Theory of Justice, 97
Lifeboat Ethics, 213
Lived Environment, 232
Locke Second Treatise, 18
Logic, 50
  and Critical Thinking in Philosophy, 49
Logical Investigations, 228, 230

M

Mathematics: Chinese, 256
 Greek, 248
Means of Mechanics, 249
Medicine: Chinese, 259
 Greek, 262
Modern Philosophy, 1
 Science and Philosophy, 33
Moral Evil, 39
 Science, 35
 Sense theory, 42

N

Natural Equality, 25
 Law, 21
 Philosophy, 2
 Rights and Human Nature, 188
 Rights and Property Rights, 101
 Rights in Modern Philosophy, 15
 Rights, 19
 Constitutional and Chartered Rights, 17
Nature and Science, 53
 of Universals, 6
Neo-Platonic Tradition, 1
New Way of Thinking, 69
Nicomachean Ethics, 11
Nothing More Evident, 29
Novum Organum, 13

O

Ontological Argument, 8

P

Patterned" theory of Justice, 83
Perceivable Property, 39
Phenomenological Reduction, 229
Phenomenology and Existentialism in Philosophy, 227
 of Spirit, 243
Philosophy as a Subject, 72
Physics and Metaphysics, 54
Planet Earth as a Public Good, 220
Plato's 'Theory of Forms', 55
 Theory of Ideas, 8
Political Philosophy, 225
 and Its Global Trends, 207
 of Patriarchy, 186
Pragmata, 235
Present to Consciousness, 227
Principles of Philosophy, 118
Progress for the Better, 47
Property as an Adventitious Right, 141
 Rights, 100
Public Goods and Collective Action, 216
 Markets, and Externalities, 218
 Problems, 219
Pure Phenomenology, 228

R

Radical Implications of Libertarian theory, 92
Reason and Understanding, 71
Revealed Law, 22
Reverse Discrimination, 195
Rights, 18
 Based theories, 89
Roman Catholic Church, 65

S

Self-Evident Rights, 28

Social Despotism, 87
Socialism and Communism, 112
Spenser's Faerie Queene, 2
Spirit of Plato, 1
Structure of Global Capitalism, 210
Structures, 205
Summa theologica, 4

T

Teacher-Pupil Relationship, 257
Techniques and Dialectic Method in Philosophy, 245
Teleology with Design, 60
Teleology without Design, 58
The Anarchist Critique of Private Property, 103
- Brothers Karamazov, 88
- Final Break, 78
- Freedom of Her Ways, 188
- Globalization thesis, 221
- Meaning of Being, 234
- Metaphysics of Rights, 128
- Origin of Species, 47
- Personal and the Political, 197
- Phenomenology of Internal Time Consciousness, 233
- Phenomenology of Perception, 244
- Problem of Original Acquisition, 133
- Psychology of the Imagination (1940), 239
- Rejection of Scholasticism, 11
- Ricardian Socialists, 104
- Road To Serfdom, 87
- Role of Free Markets, 144
- Runaways, 81
- Socialism of Marx and Engels, 106
- Tragedy of the Commons, 214
- Wretched of the Earth, 200

Theory of Forms, 55
Through the Looking Glass, 240
Timaeus, 61
Tradition of Reasoning, 68
Tragedy of the Commons, 216
Treatise on the Passions (1649), 35
Triumph of Thomism, 11

U

Universal Rights, 30

W

Western Philosophy, 187, 225
- Rationalism, 81

Workers' Rights, 143

Z

Zhoubi Suanjing, 246